HULL

THROUGH TIME

Philip C. Miles

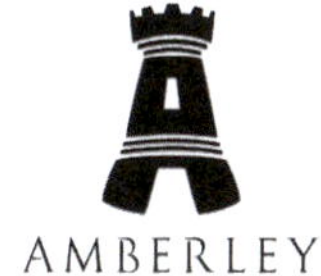

AMBERLEY

First published 2011

Amberley Publishing
The Hill, Stroud
Gloucestershire, GL5 4EP

www.amberley-books.com

Copyright © Philip C. Miles, 2011

The right of Philip C. Miles to be identified as the Author of this work has been asserted in accordance with the Copyrights, Designs and Patents Act 1988.

ISBN 978 1 84868 280 1

All rights reserved. No part of this book may be reprinted or reproduced or utilised in any form or by any electronic, mechanical or other means, now known or hereafter invented, including photocopying and recording, or in any information storage or retrieval system, without the permission in writing from the Publishers.

British Library Cataloguing in Publication Data.
A catalogue record for this book is available from the British Library.

Typeset in 9.5pt on 12pt Celeste.
Typesetting by Amberley Publishing.
Printed in the UK.

Appointed GPSR EU Representative: Easy Access System Europe Oü, 16879218
Address: Mustamäe tee 50, 10621, Tallinn, Estonia
Contact Details: gpsr.requests@easproject.com, +358 40 500 3575

Introduction

Kingston upon Hull was founded by King Edward I in 1293, when the two districts, then known as Wyke and Myton, were purchased by the King. The name of the city was originally called Kingstown upon Hull.

Hull, or to give it its full and proper name of Kingston upon Hull, is a medium sized city situated on the north bank of the River Humber. It is divided into two by the River Hull, hence where it gets its name from. The area on the west side of the river is known as West Hull and on the eastern side of the river as East Hull. The old City of Hull was encircled by the town walls (nothing today remains of these). The town grew and grew outside of the walls, spreading in all directions except the south, which was not possible because of the River Humber.

In the very early part of the 1900s, much of the old city centre was demolished, which consisted of slum housing to create new wide streets, now known as King Edward Street and Jameson Street. Queen Victoria Square was built on the site once covered by Waterworks Street, St John's Street, Engine Street and Junction Street. Further pre-Victorian slum houses were demolished in the early 1930s. This was from an area from the corner of Beverley Road/Spring Bank to Anlaby Road and is now Ferensway (named after the local city benefactor, T. R. Ferens). Many of the people who lived in the slums were moved into the new housing estate to the north of the city, which became known as North Hull Estate.

Hull was severely bombed during the Second World War, with severe loss of life and much of the city centre was turned to ruins. But after the war the city centre was rebuilt to its present modern style.

As early as 1316 a ferry service was operating between Hull and Barton, while the ferries across the River Humber to New Holland began in 1826 and carried on until 1981. A new ferry service between Hull and Rotterdam (Europoort), operated by North Sea Ferries, began in 1965. As early as the fourteenth century, Hull handled much of England's wool trade and by the eighteenth century the importation of timber.

Whaling was also very important to Hull. Fishing has always been important to Hull, with several hundred trawlers operating out of Hull in any one year. Several docks were purposely built for the fishing industry. Hull was once the third largest port in England and at one time boasted no fewer than eleven docks; the earliest, Old Dock (later renamed Queen's Dock), opened in August 1778. Sadly now only four docks remain in use with the others converted to gardens, a marina, shopping centre, or new housing.

Because Hull expanded outside the town walls, road transport was required to transport people into the town; first, horse-drawn buses operated, which were followed in 1875 by horse-drawn trams operated by the Hull Street Tramways Co. This in turn gave way to the electric tramway which first operated on 5 July 1899 on two routes from St John Street, one down Anlaby Road,

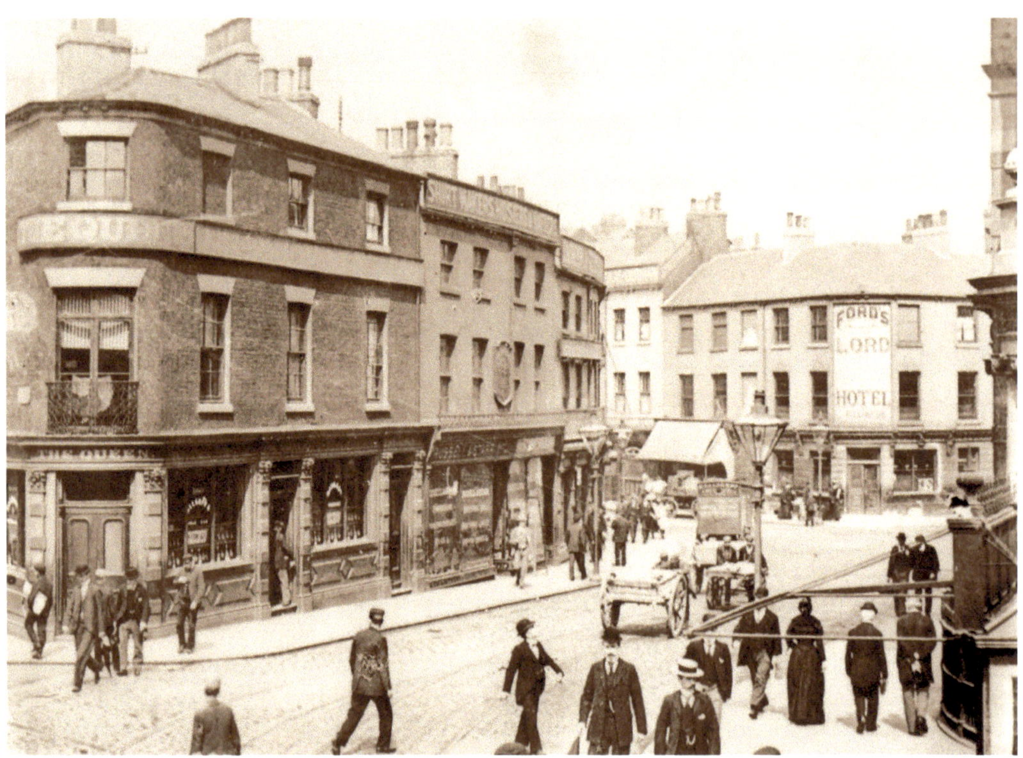

The Old City Centre

Much of the old city centre was demolished at the end of the 1890s in preparation for the building of King Edward Street. In this rare photograph taken before the demolition commenced, in the foreground can be seen The Queen public house, while in the background can be seen the Lord Londesborough Hotel. The street just visible going off on the right is Savile Street.

while the other was down Hessle Road. Further electric tram routes soon commenced along Beverley Road, Spring Bank, Holderness Road and to the Pier. The electric trams remained part of Hull's scene for over forty years. The electric trams were replaced by trolleybuses and eventually the trolleybuses were replaced by the motorbus. The first motorbuses to be operated in Hull were on 31 July 1909, operated by the City of Hull Tramways.

Kingston upon Hull has had many famous and important people born in the city. Perhaps the most famous of all was William Wilberforce, born on 24 August 1759 in High Street (his house is now the William Wilberforce Museum, and well worth a visit), and baptised at Holy Trinity church. He was a politician and a leader of the movement to abolish the slave trade.

Amy Johnson was born in Hull on 1 July 1903 and lived in Hull until 1923. She was the first female pilot to fly from England to Australia on 5 May 1930.

Other important people born in the city include Stevie Smith, born 1902, poet and novelist. Joe Longthorne, born on 31 May 1955 into a show business family, became a well known singer. Later well known people have included the pop group The House Martins, and later the Beautiful South.

Philip C. Miles
Kingston upon Hull

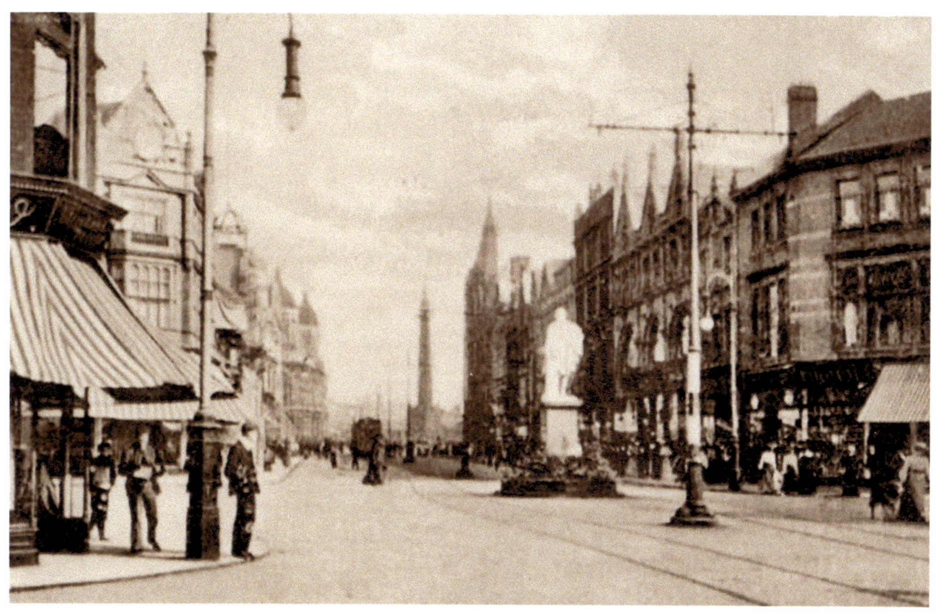

King Edward Street Looking South

This is King Edward Street, looking down the full length of the street. This photograph was taken before the Second World War from the top of Prospect Street and Jameson Street. Visible is the statue of William de la Pole, seen in the centre of the road. The impressive buildings can be seen on both sides of the street. This area was constructed at the very beginning of the 1900s and formed part of the new modern city centre improvement scheme. Much of the old slums were demolished to make way for this. Looking down King Edward Street, William Wilberforce's Monument is clearly visible, while on the far left are the Dock offices. In today's view, nothing remains in the photograph apart from the Dock offices. All the new buildings which now form King Edward Street were built after the Second World War.

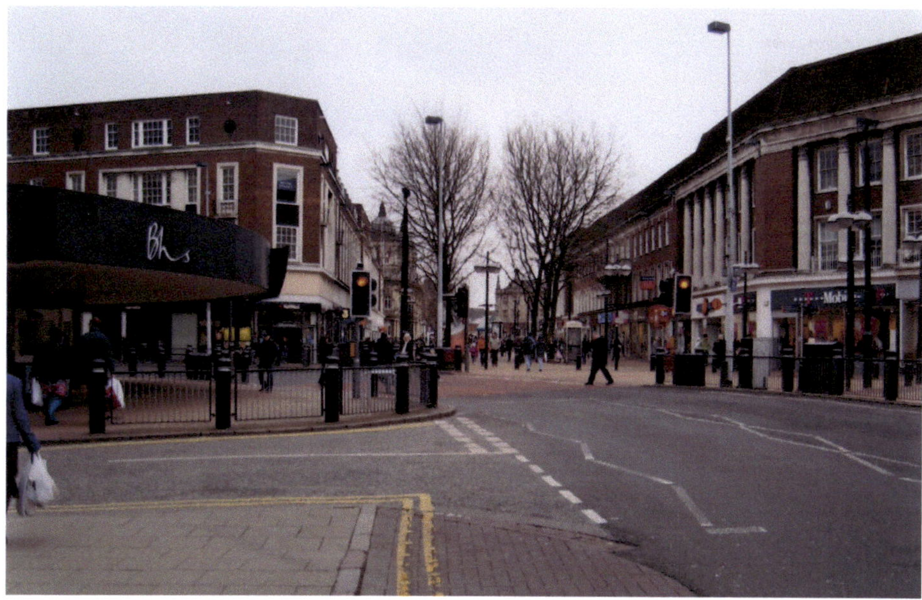

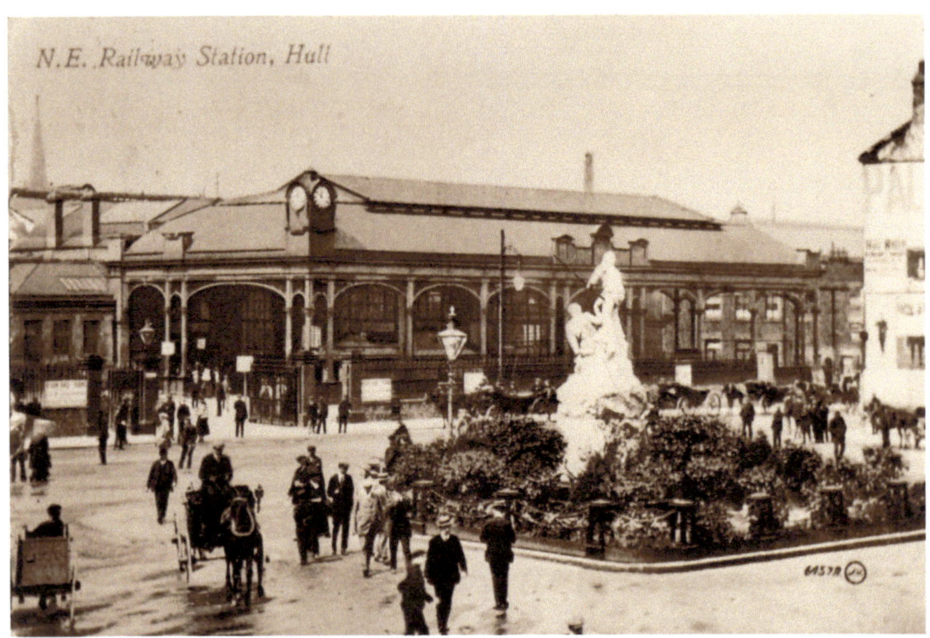

Hull Paragon Railway Station

Opened on 8 May 1848, Hull Paragon Railway Station replaced an early railway station situated at Railway Street. In this early photograph, *c.* 1916, Ferensway is yet to be built. The war memorial is in the foreground. The front of the exterior of the railway station was altered with the building of a new office block for British Rail which opened in 1962. After over forty years the office block was demolished and, as can be seen in the present day photograph, the front of the exterior has returned back to its former glory days. The Royal Hotel is on the left, while the new St Stephens Shopping Centre can be seen on the right.

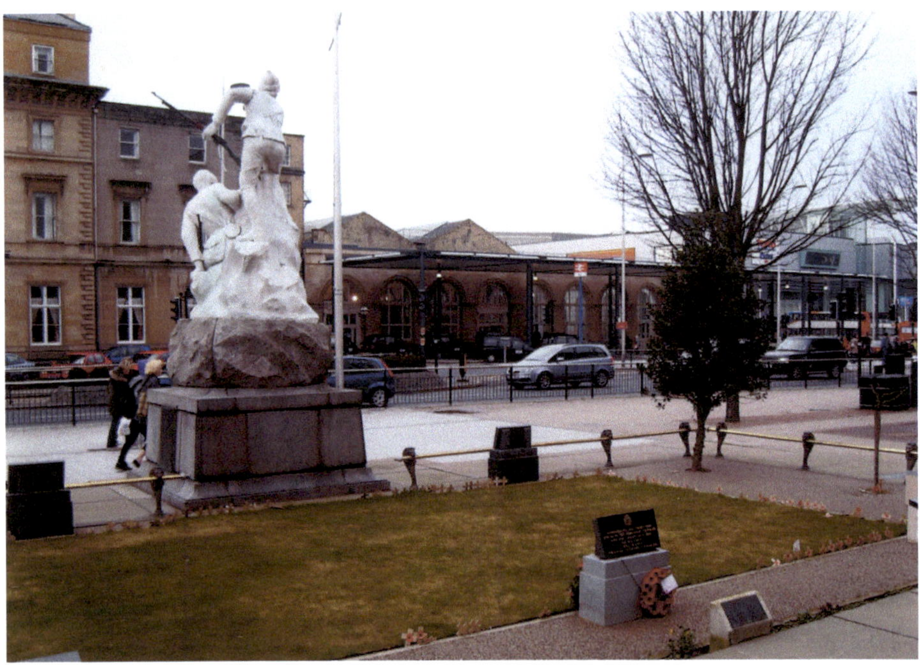

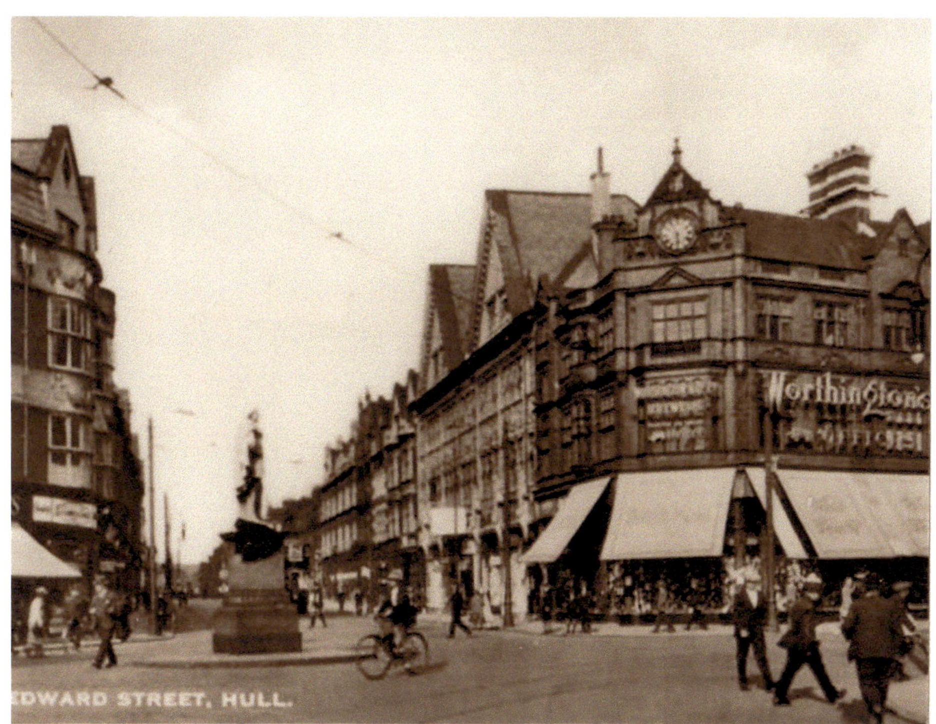

Jameson Street

Time stands still. This is a pre-Second World War photograph looking down Jameson Street from the junction of King Edward Street. The statue in the centre of the road is of William de la Pole, which at one time was situated here. The building on the right was once the offices of Worthington & Co. Ltd Brewers. This area would change beyond recognition in only a few years after this photograph was taken. The large modern building, now on the left in the modern day photograph, was once the Co-operative store; it is now part of the huge store which is British Home Stores.

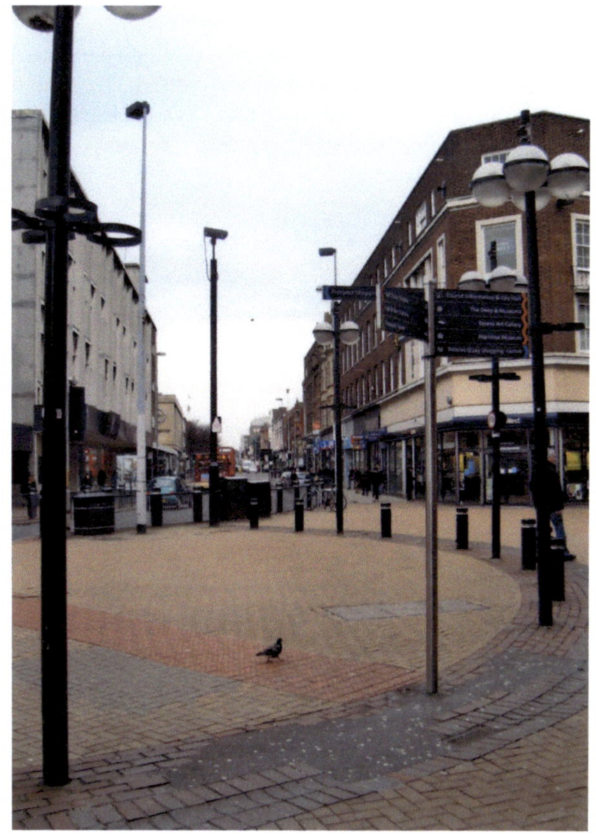

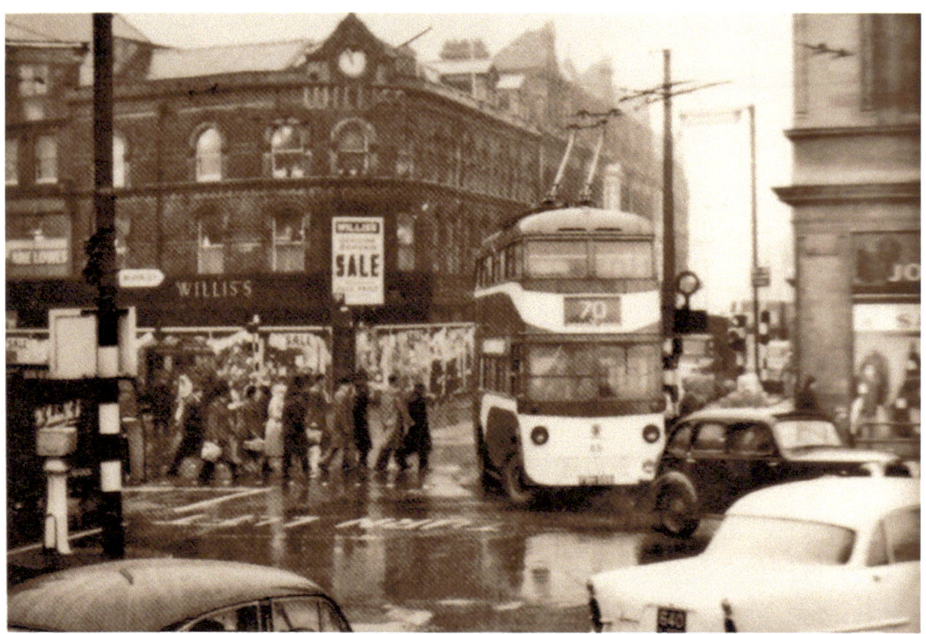

Willis's Store

One of the main large, important department stores in Hull was Willis's store which was on Carr Lane. In this view, the departmental store is having a sale. A Hull Corporation Transport trolleybus on the 70 service from Hessle Road is seen turning from Carr Lane into Queen Victoria Square, passing the Johnston men's shop, which was located under the City Hall. Today's view shows the modern departmental store which replaced the old Willis's store and is now Primark and adjoins the Princes Quay shopping centre. Johnston men's shop is now the Hull City Hall booking offices. Note the lack of transport in the present day photograph. The Punch Hotel is on the left.

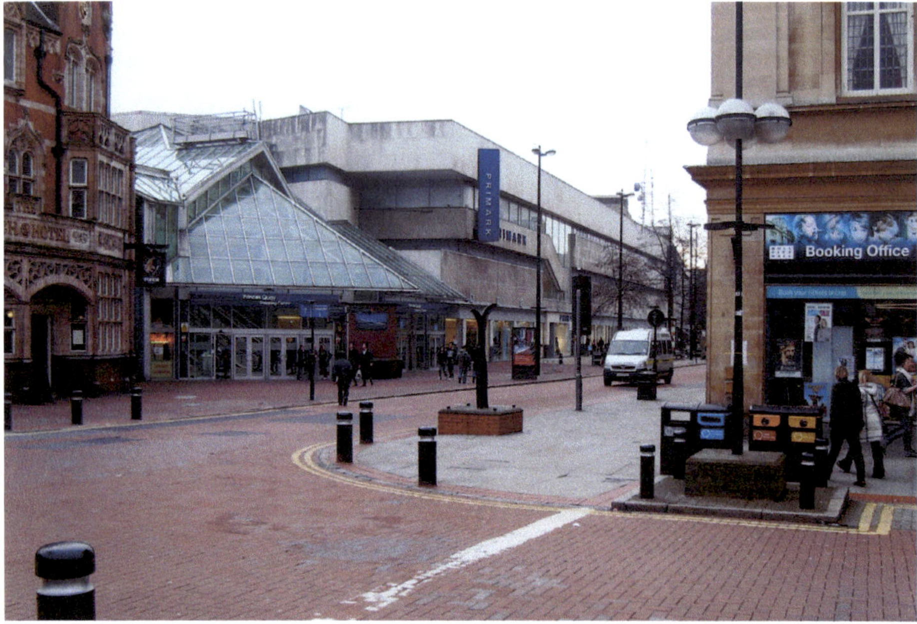

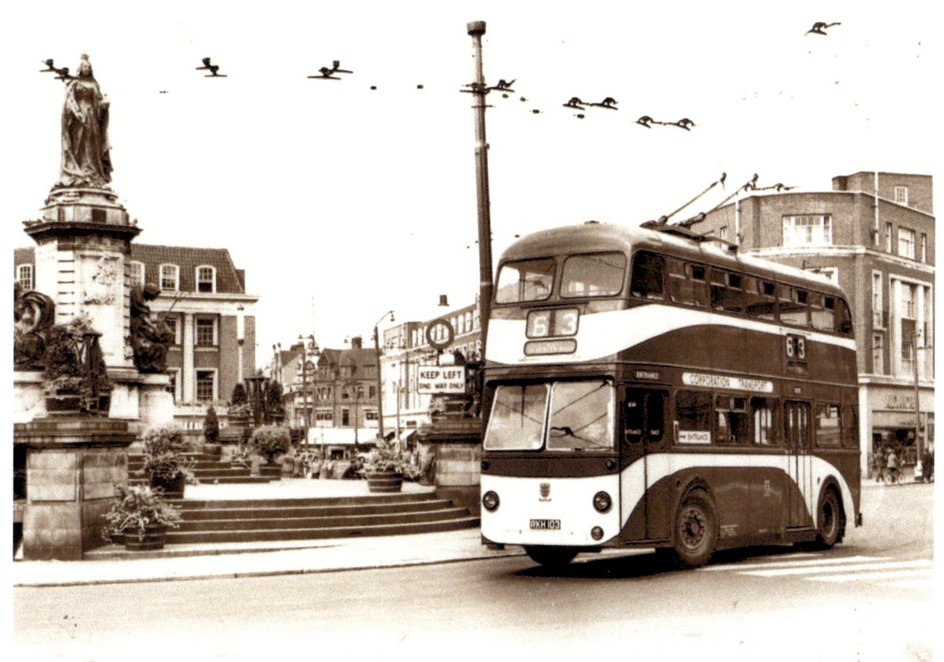

Queen Victoria Square

A late 1950s or early 1960s photograph showing the rebuilt King Edward Street and Paragon Street. This was totally demolished during the Second World War. A Hull Corporation dual-door, dual-staircase trolleybus is seen passing the staue of Queen Victoria while on the 63 service to Beverley Road. Saville Street is on the extreme right. King Edward Street is seen in the centre of the photograph, with Paragon Street seen behind the statue.

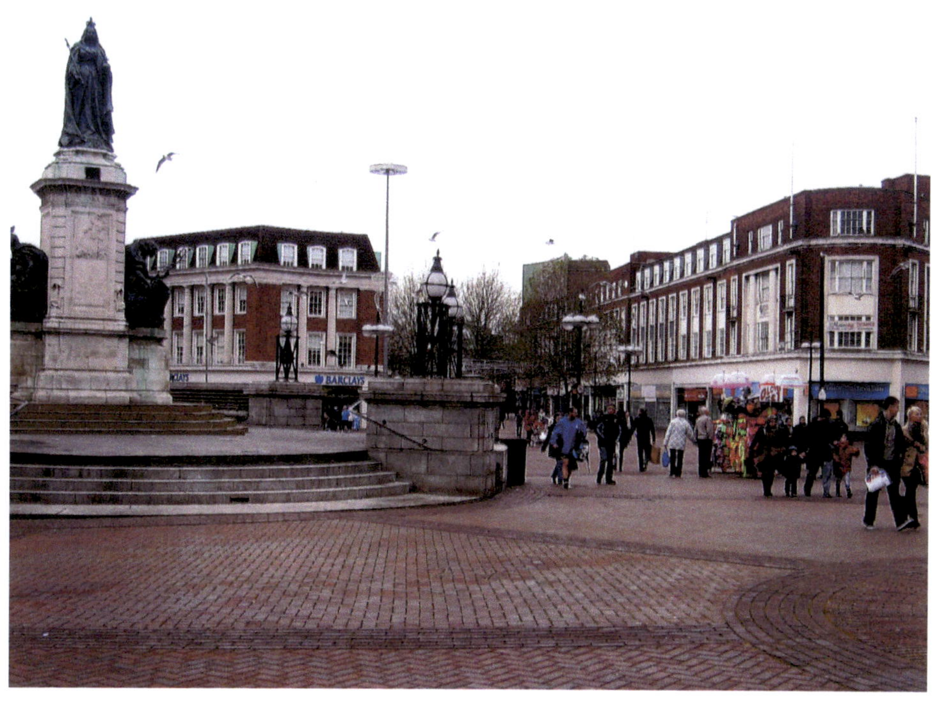

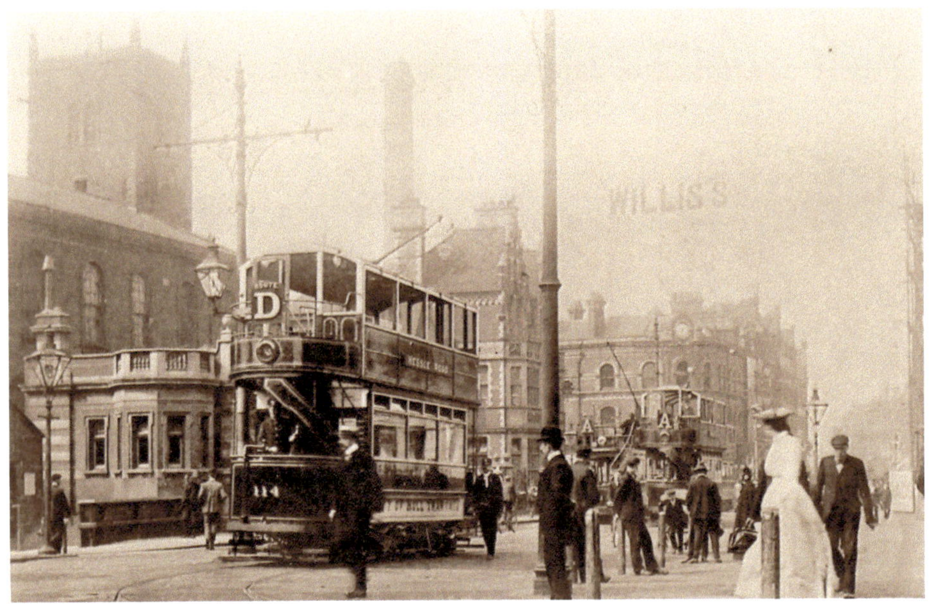

St John Street

One lady, obviously quite well off in her long dress, is seen in an otherwise male picture. This is St John Street, *c.* 1905, the terminus for electric trams 'D' (Dairycoates) and 'A' (Anlaby Road). On the left is St John's church, built in 1791 and not demolished until around 1924. The Punch Hotel is visible just behind the tram, while in the background can be seen Willis's store. Behind the tram on the left can be seen the tall chimney of Hull electric tram's electricity generating station in Osbourne Street. In today's photograph, the Ferens art gallery now stands on the site where St John's church stood. The Punch Hotel remains a pub, but the old Willis's store was demolished and a new ultra modern building built on the site. Its name was changed to Willis Ludlow. The store is now Primark and now forms part of the Princes Quay shopping centre which was opened in 1991.

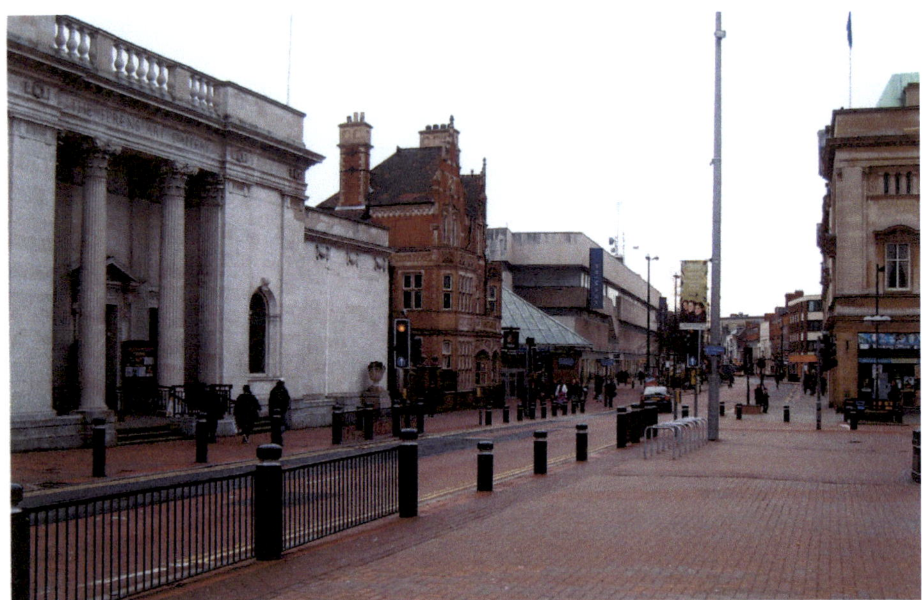

C&A and Hammond's Stores

A Hull Corporation Transport
AEC Regent double-decker bus is
photographed entering the bus station
from Ferensway passing a Bedford
lorry. Behind the lorry is C&A stores,
while Hammond's store is on the right.
The street in between the two stores
is West Street. In today's photograph,
T. J. Hughes replaced the C&A store,
while Hammond's is now called House
of Fraser. Much of West Street was
demolished, including The Star of the
West public house and Thearne's pet
shop, to make way for the Prospect
Shopping Centre.

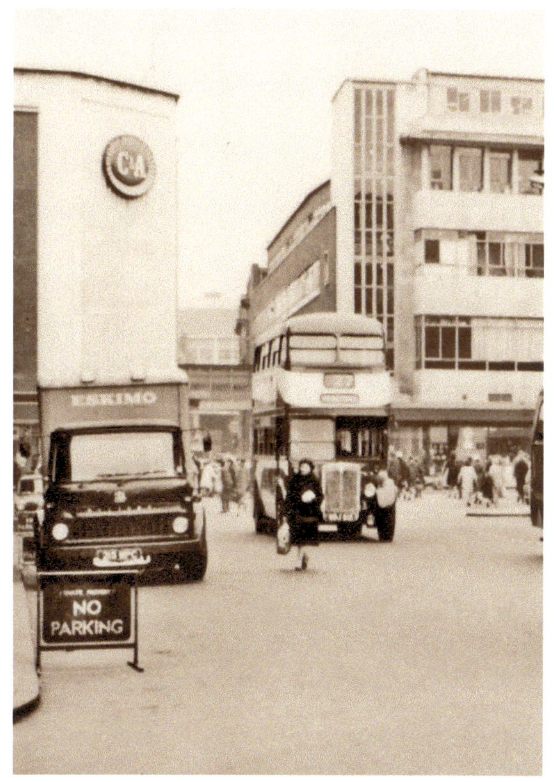

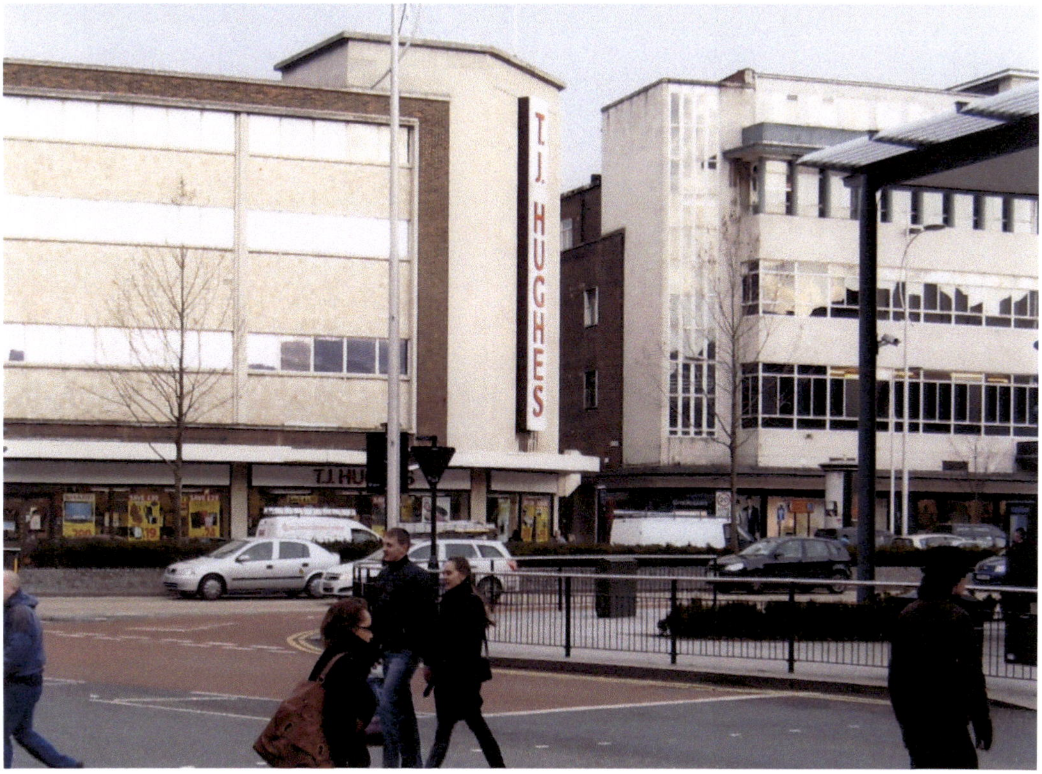

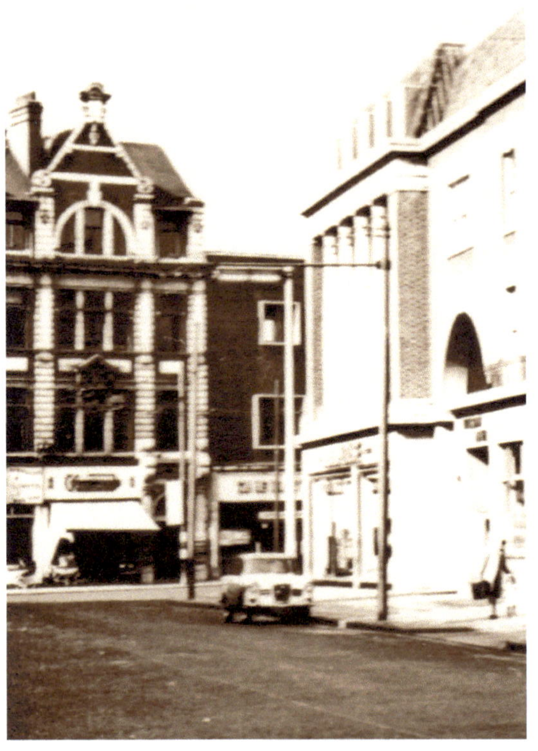

Chapel Street

One of the short streets in between Paragon Street and Jameson Street is Chapel Street. The buildings in the background in Jameson Street include Greenwood's men's shop and Zerney's the dry cleaners. The modern buildings seen on the right were built after the Second World War to replace the bomb damaged buildings. The Bass House public house is visible on the right. One of the older buildings is visible in the background, now demolished in the present day photograph to make way for a new building. Zerney's is now Greggs, while the Bass House public bar is now Sgt Peppers, which is now closed.

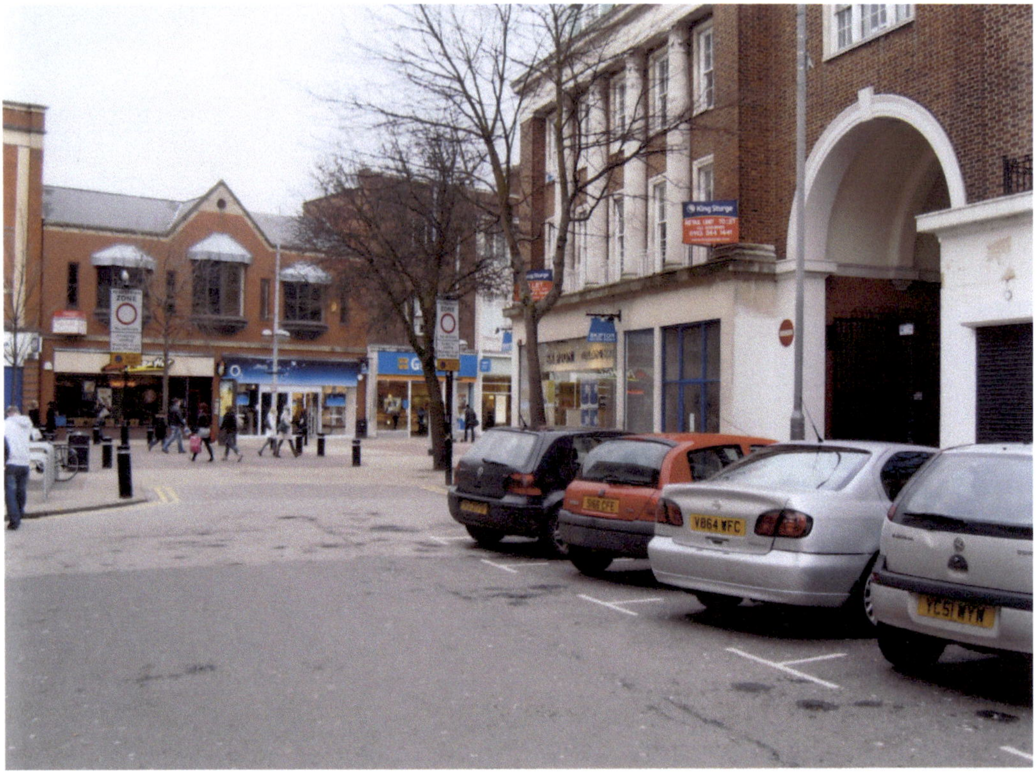

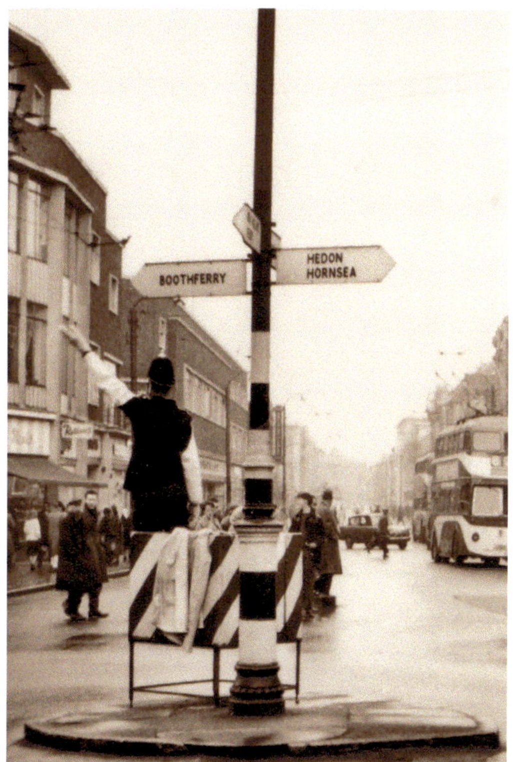

Prospect Street

Once a familiar sight on many of the busy road junctions in Hull was the policeman on traffic control duty; the policeman here is looking up Prospect Street at the junction of Jameson Street. The modern building on the left behind the policeman was, for many years, a Woolworths store. A trolleybus on the 63 service can be seen in this early 1960s photograph. Today, this busy junction is controlled by traffic lights. Woolworths store is now just another memory, as is the trolleybus.

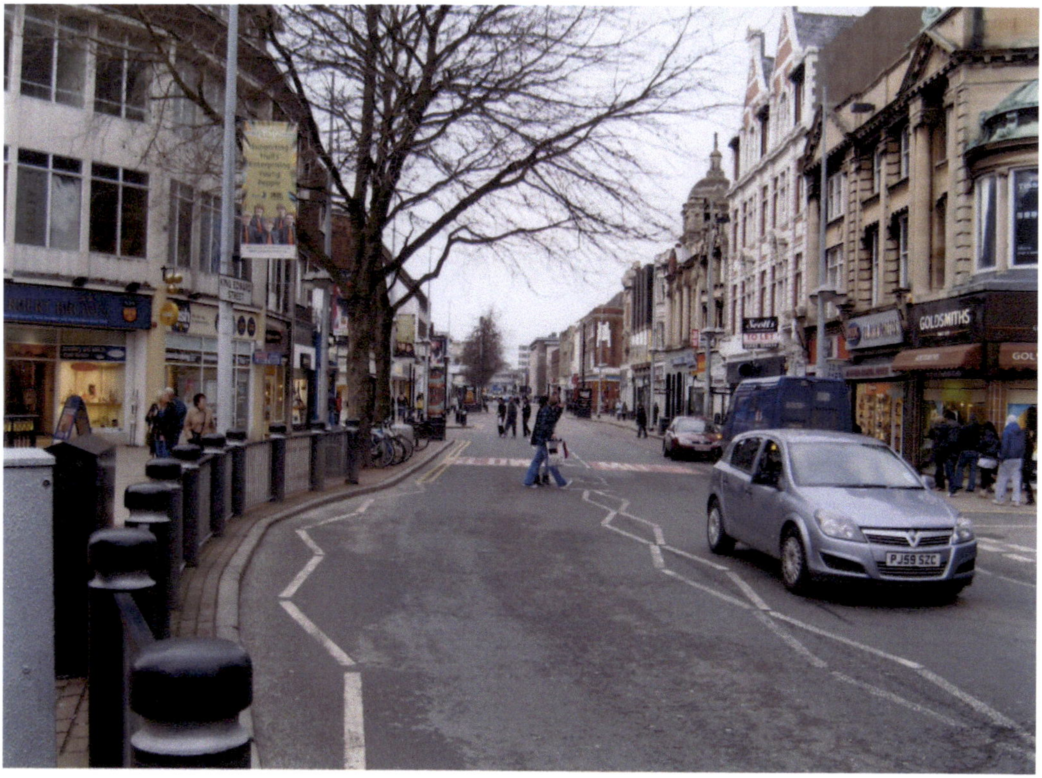

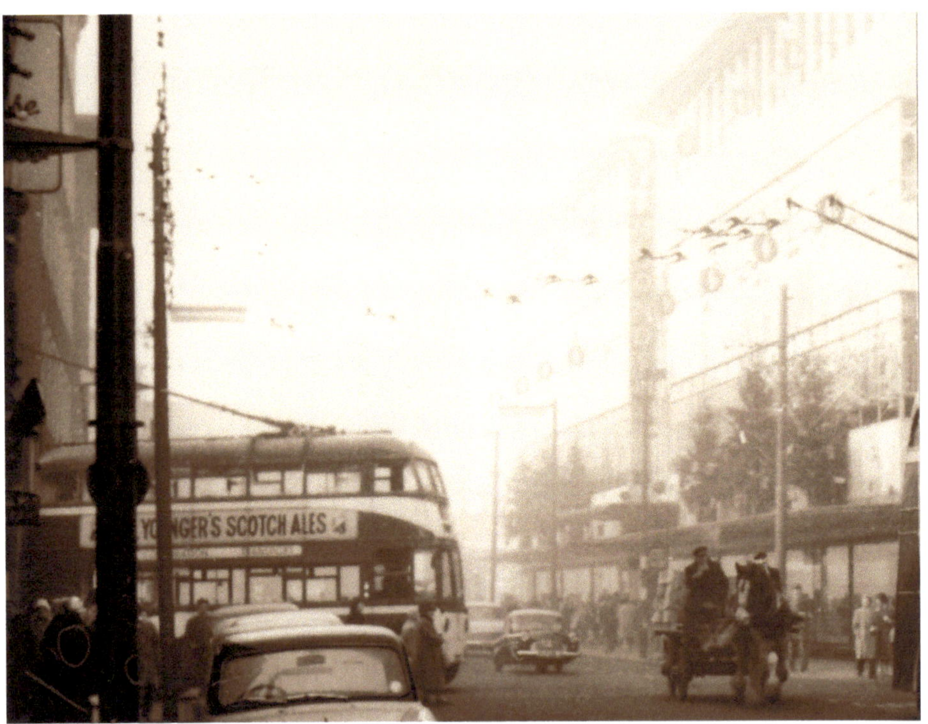

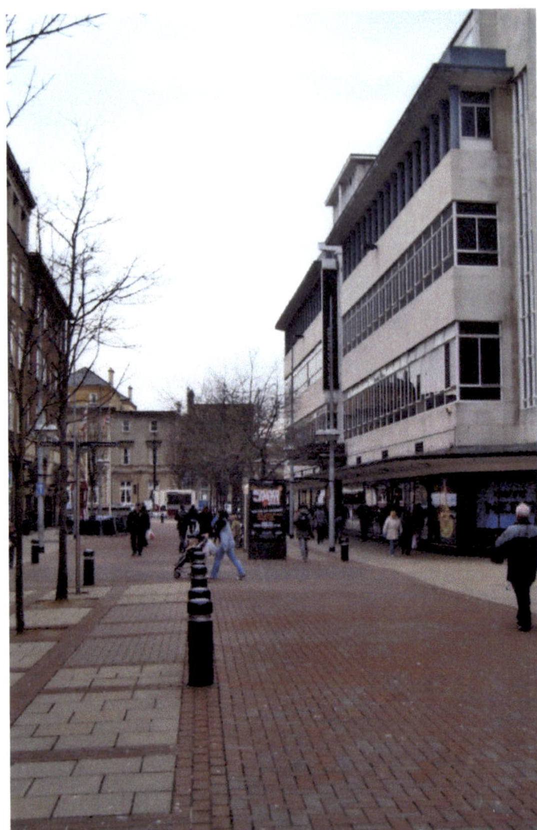

Jameson Street Looking West

The rebuilt Hammonds store can be seen on the right complete with Christmas trees, while a horse-drawn vehicle is seen heading up Jameson Street. A Hull Corporation transport trolleybus is seen turning into Jameson Street from South Street. Note the three-wheeled car to the right of the trolleybus. Today, Hammonds is House of Fraser and this area is now a car free zone. Pedestrians are able to walk in comfort down this once busy street.

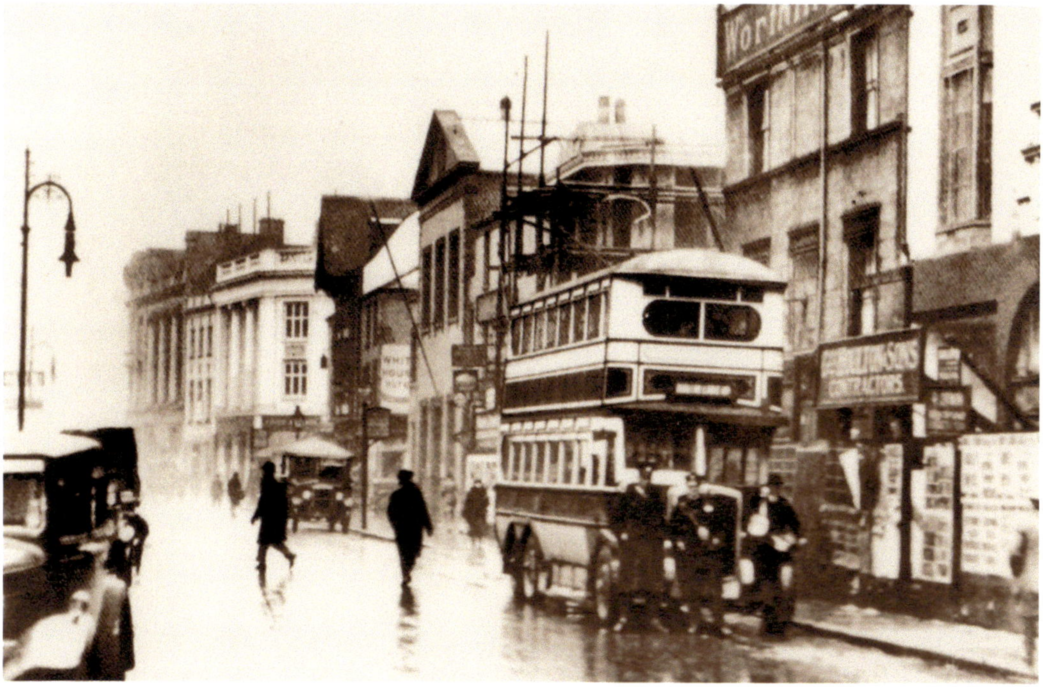

Paragon Square

The driver and conductor pose proudly in front of a Hull Corporation Transport six-wheeled double-decker bus in Paragon Square. The buildings on the right are due to be demolished, while visible in the background is the Theatre Royal, which was built in 1871; it later became the Tivoli Palace. The new photograph shows Paragon Square today.

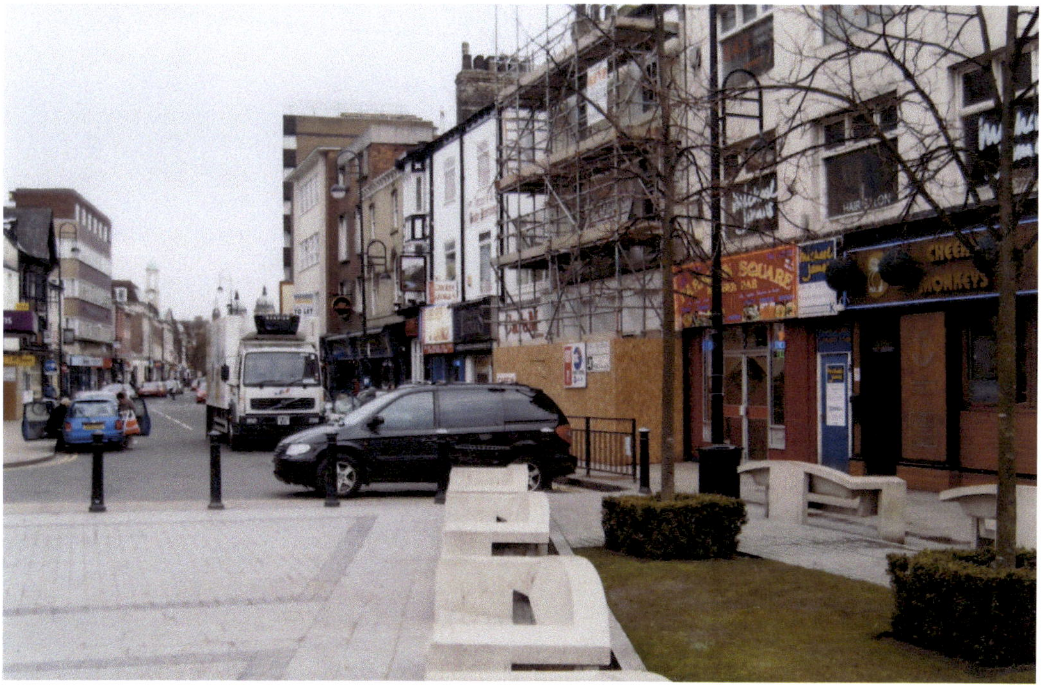

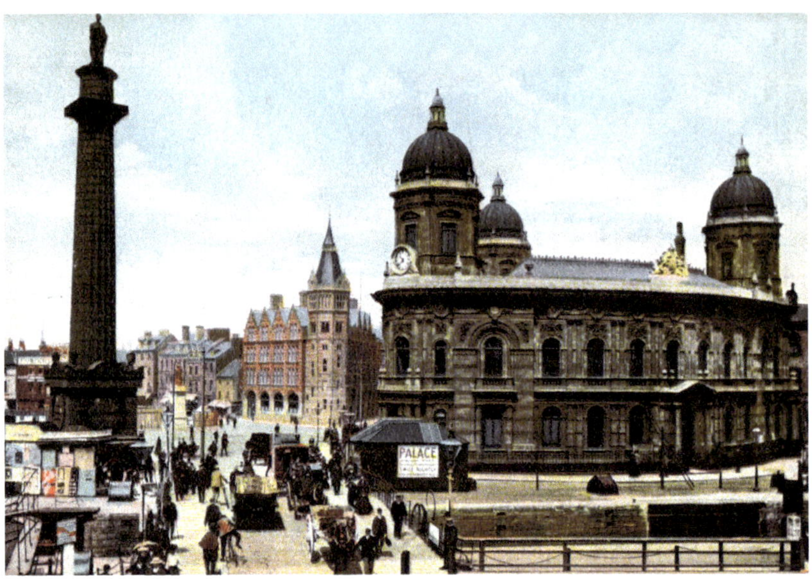

Town Dock Offices and Monument Bridge

The large building with its three domes is the Dock offices. It was built between the years 1867-1871 and built on land alongside Queen's Dock. In the foreground can be seen the entrance to Queen's Dock and the original Monument Bridge. On the left of the Dock offices is the Prudential building, built around 1903. The road running along the Prudential building is Waterworks Street. The City Hall is yet to be built, as this was completed in 1909/10. Other streets demolished, as can be seen in this photograph from St John's Street, included Engine Street, Junction Street and Waterworks Street; these were demolished to create Queen Victoria Square. William Wilberforce's Monument is also clearly visible in this view.

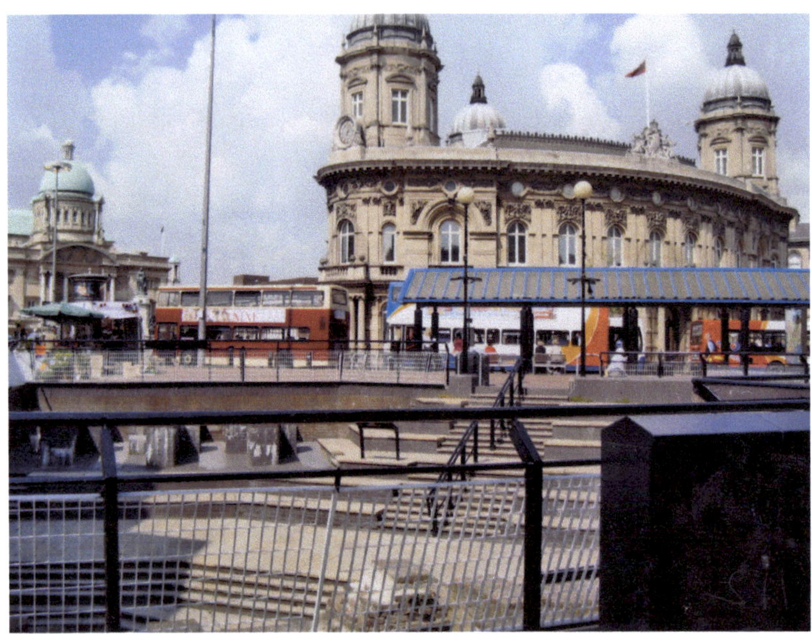

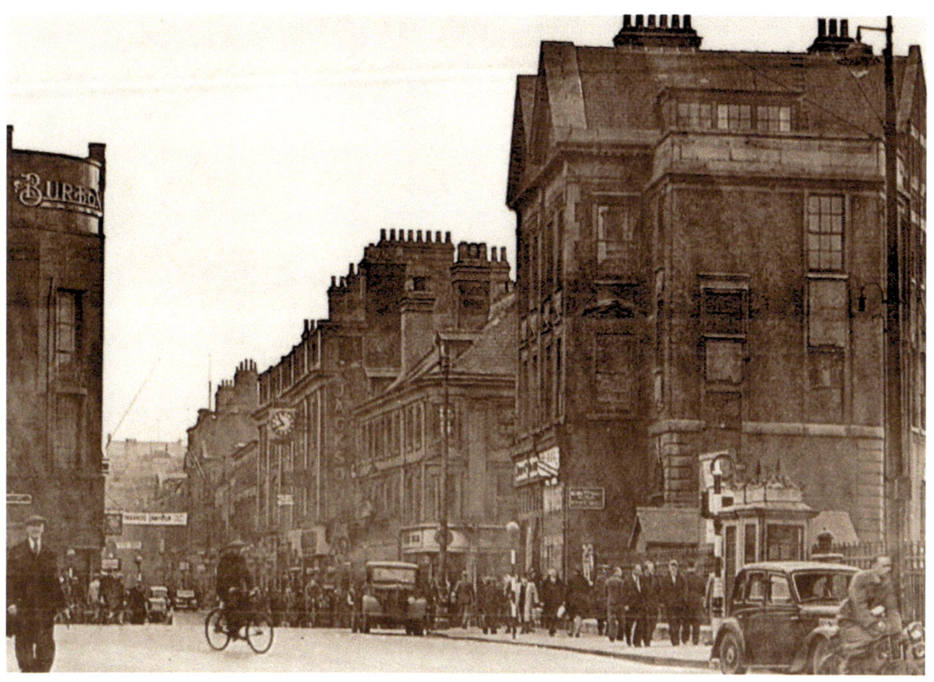

Burton's Store Whitefriargate

A photograph looking across Monument Bridge, which was originally called Junction Bridge. (The dock is just visible on the right.) It was later changed to Monument Bridge. On the left of the photograph can be seen the new Burton's men's shop. On the right of the photograph are Monument buildings, built in 1908, and Bridge Chambers, built in 1914. The street just visible on the right is Prince's Dock Street. Note the old-style telephone boxes behind the car. Today's photograph shows the excavations of the old Beverley Gate and the some of the remains of the fourteenth-century brick town walls, which once surrounded the old City of Hull. Junction Dock, later Prince's Dock, is not used any more.

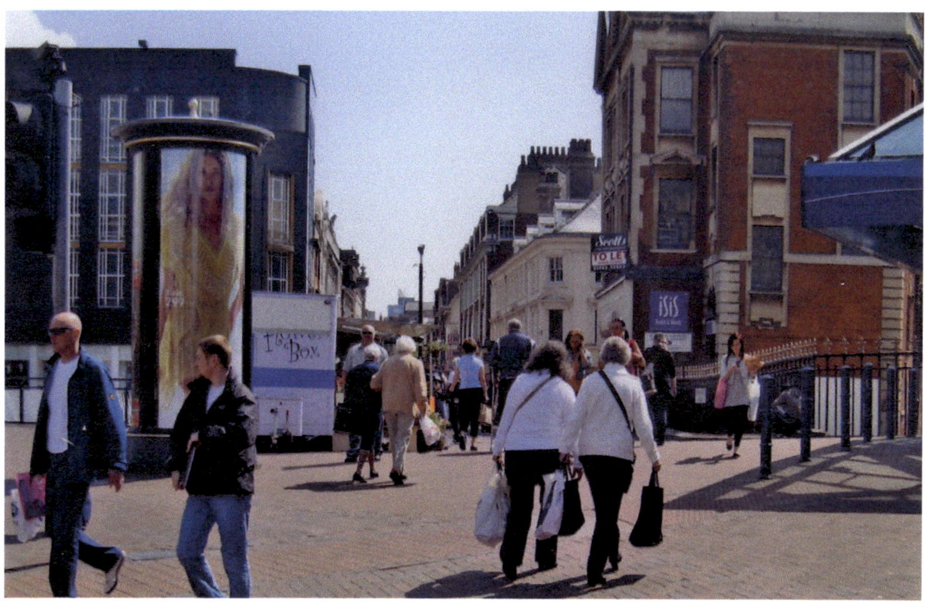

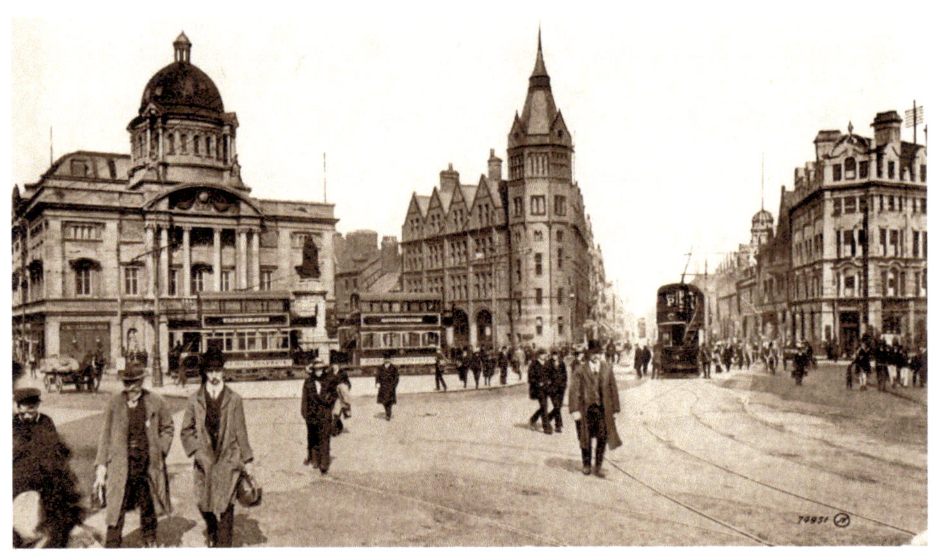

Queen Victoria Square and King Edward Street

This photograph, taken before the Second World War, shows what the city centre looked like before it was bombed. On the left is the City Hall, an imposing Edwardian building. The building was completed in 1909/10 and stood intact during the war. To the right of the City Hall is Waterworks Street. Queen Victoria's statue stands directly in front of the City Hall along with two electric trams. In the centre of the photograph can be seen the Prudential building. This was totally destroyed, along with much of King Edward Street and the surrounding area on the night of 7 May 1941. To the right of the Prudential building is King Edward Street with a tram on the 'P' service to the Pier. Savile Street is on the far right. In today's photograph the modern buildings can be seen, which were built to replace the buildings destroyed during the war. Waterworks Lane is now called Paragon Street.

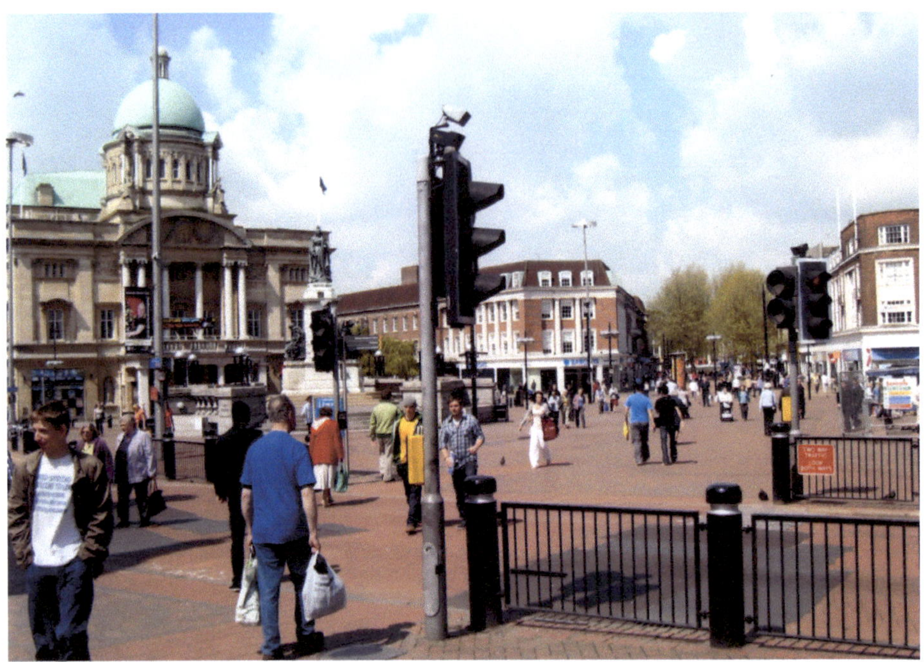

High Street

High Street in the old town dates back many hundreds of years. Many of the original buildings dated from the fourteenth century. Some of the buildings were timber framed, as can be seen on the building on the right. On the left can be seen the George and Dragon coaching inn. William Wilberforce was born down High Street and his house today is a museum dedicated to him and is well worth a visit. All the buildings in the old photograph have now been demolished.

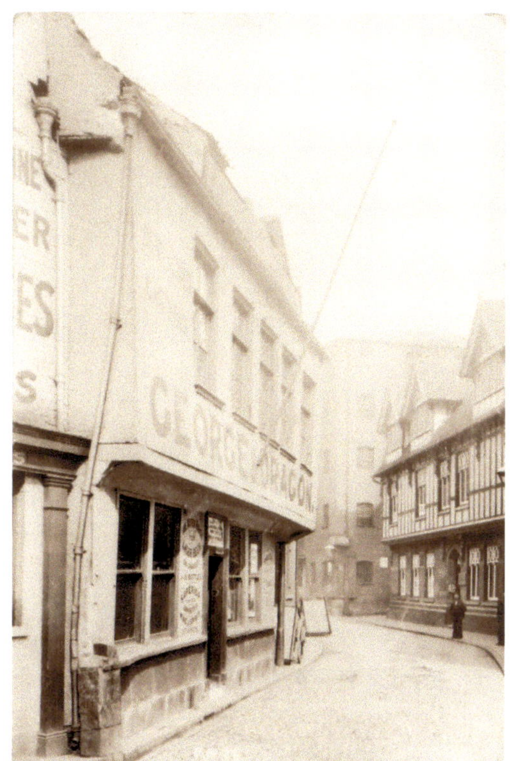

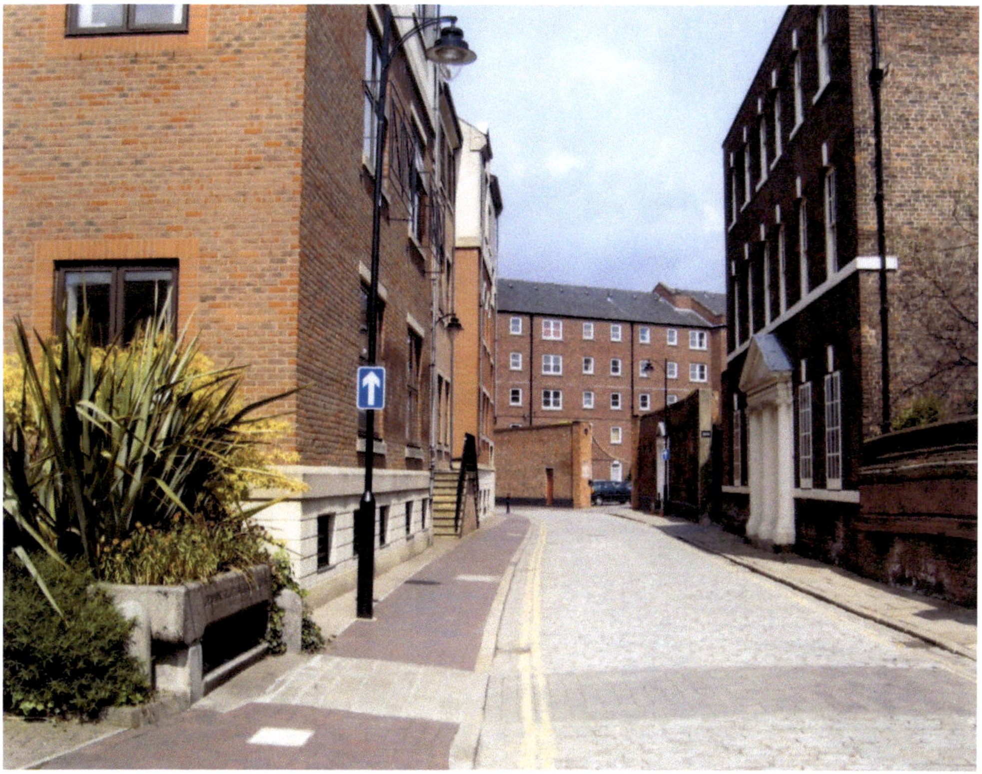

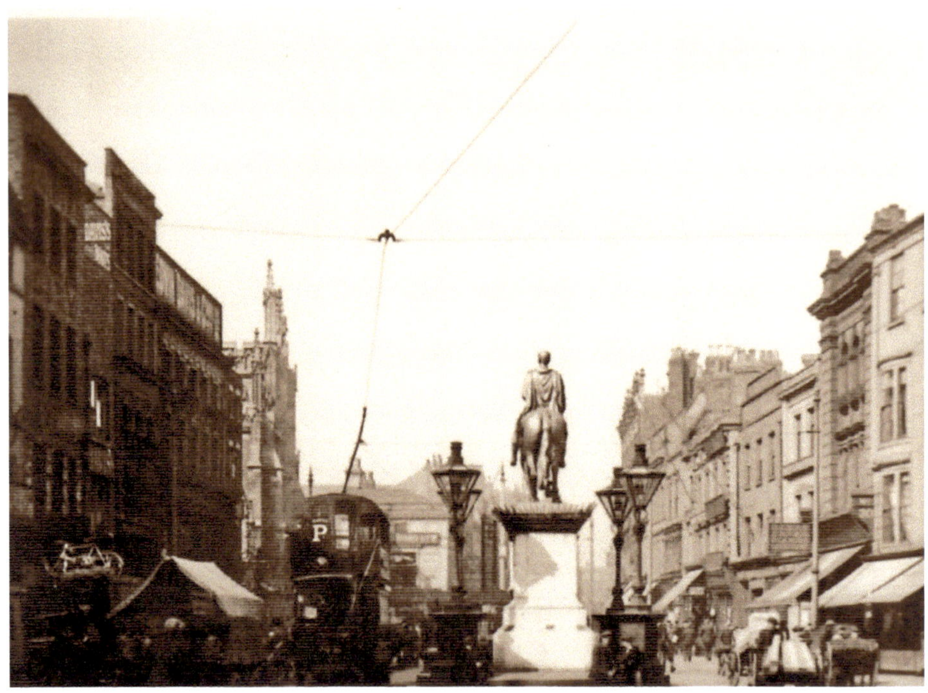

Market Place

A Hull tram on the 'P' service to the Pier is seen passing the statue of King William III, which was erected in 1734. On the right of the photograph is the old Cross Keys Hotel, which closed in 1922. This area was demolished some years later. In today's photograph, the King William House and multi-storey car park now stand where the hotel once stood.

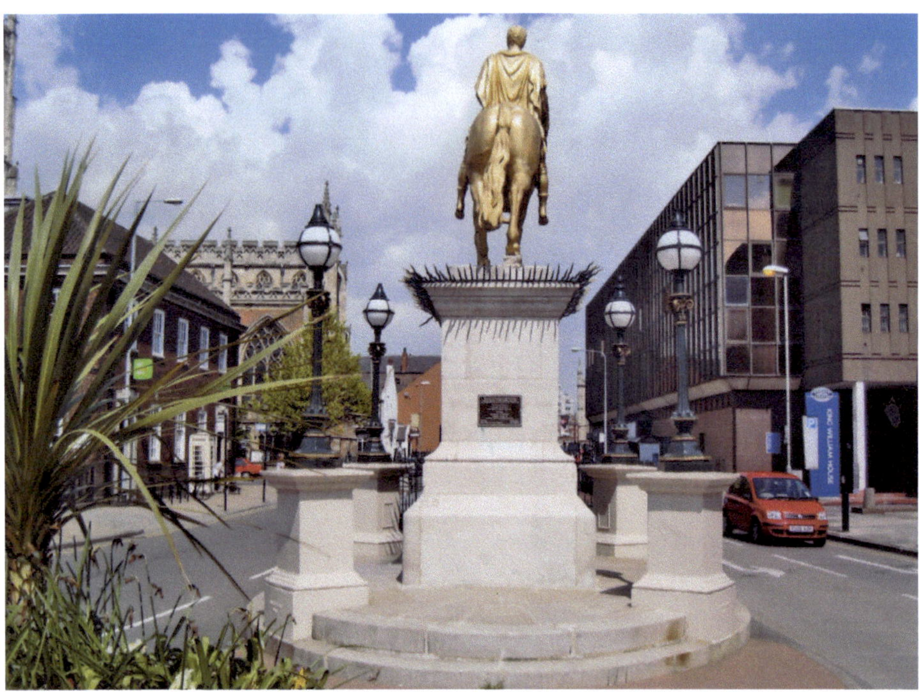

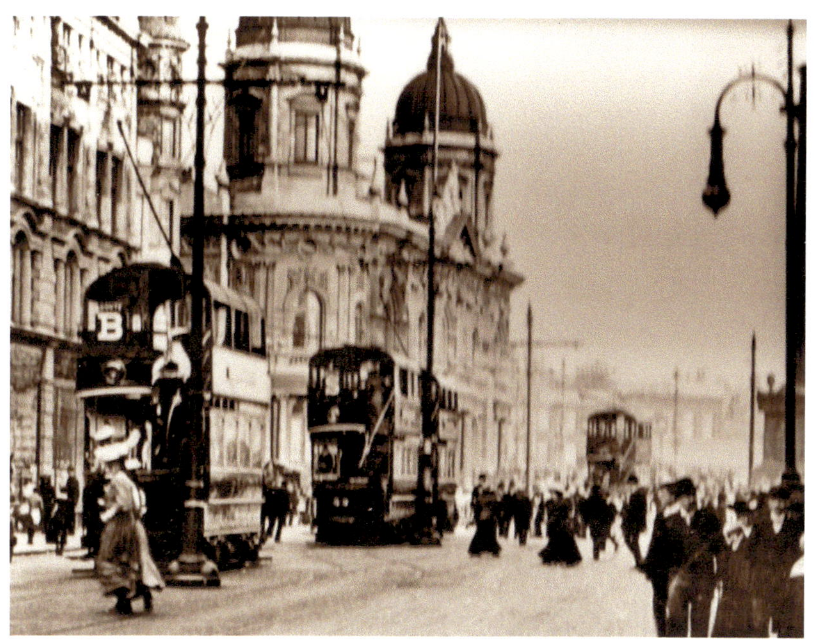

King Edward Street

Electric trams on the 'B' (Beverley Road) route and the 'S' (Spring Bank) route are seen in this photograph, along with another two trams in King Edward Street. Trams were once a prominent feature in many old photographs of Hull. The Dock offices are clearly visible to the left of the photograph. King Edward Street is now pedestrianised. The buildings on the left were built in the 1960s to replace buildings destroyed during the blitz on Hull during the Second World War. In the background can be seen the new Princes Quay shopping centre.

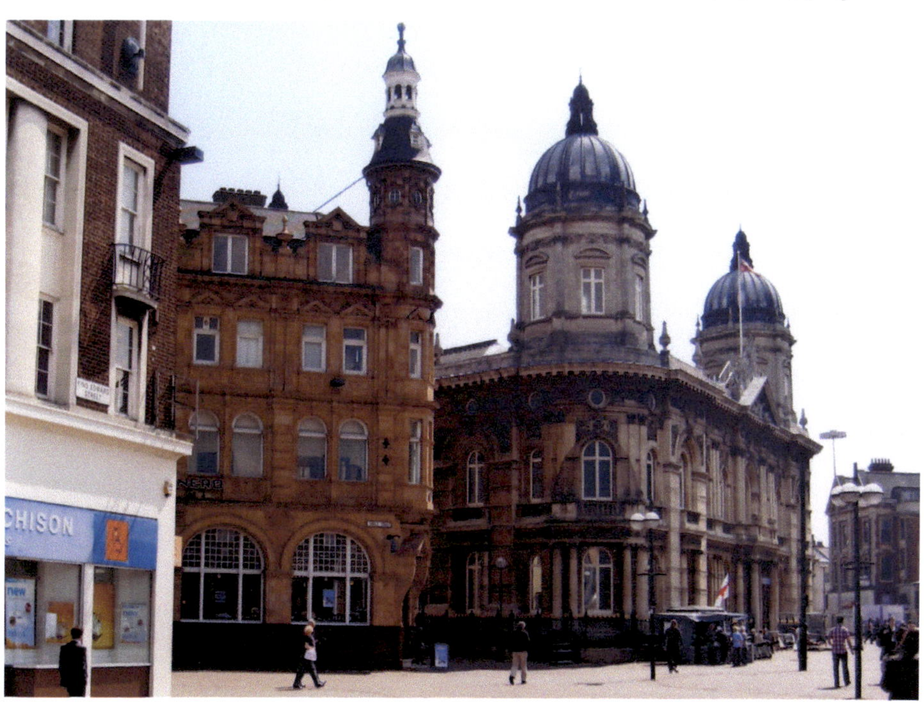

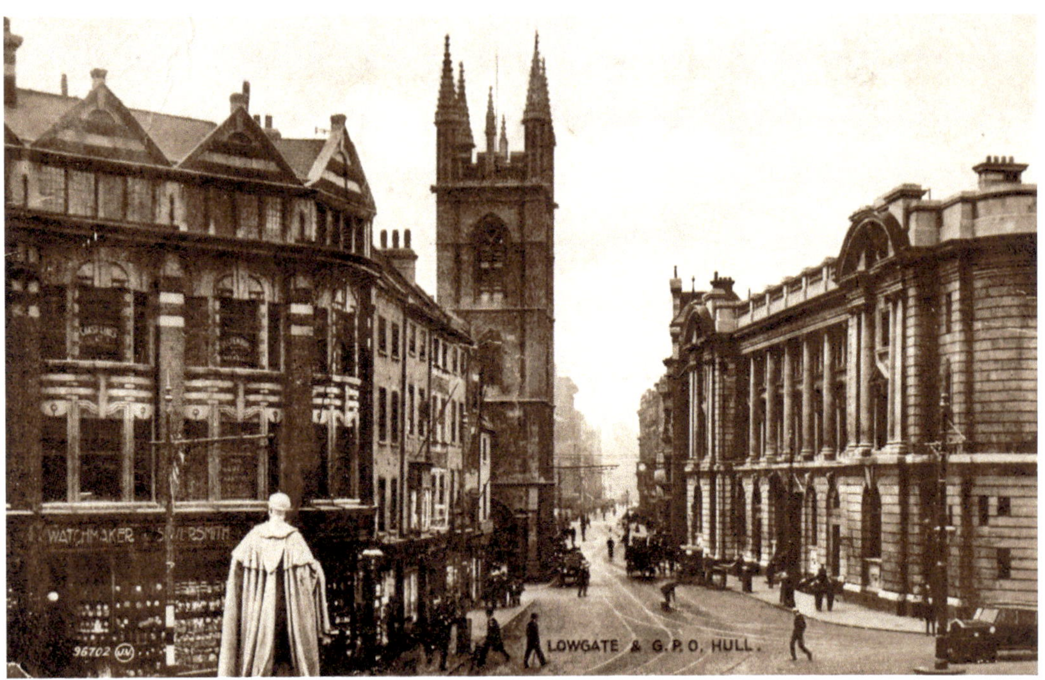

Lowgate

The main General Post Office is seen on the right of this photograph. This site was occupied by the Manor house of Sir William de la Pole, who was the first Mayor of Hull in 1331. This site later became Suffolk Palace and after it was seized by the Crown in 1504 it was called 'The Kings' Manor'. Looking down Lowgate towards Market Place can be seen the impressive St Mary's church. In today's view, the General Post Office is now apartments and a Weatherspoon's public house, while the buildings on the left were demolished and the modern Crown Courts now stand on this site.

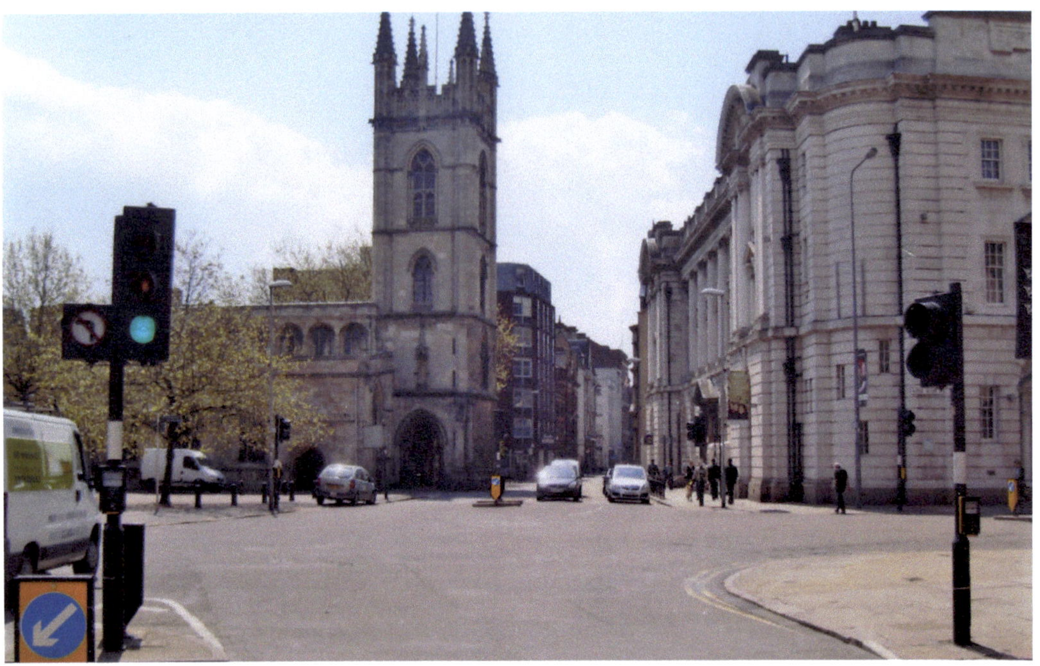

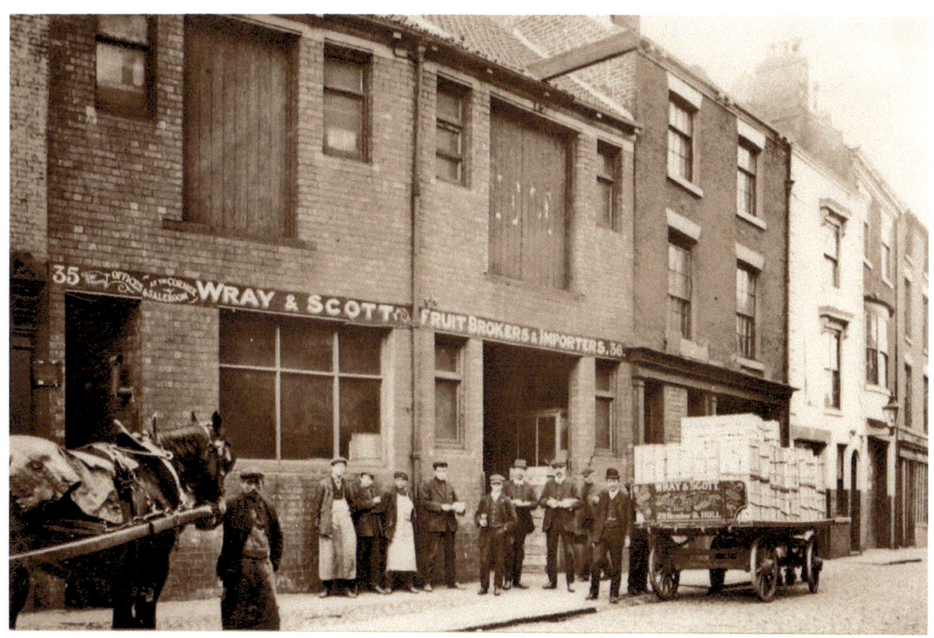

Humber Street

Humber Street in the old town was where all the fruit traders and importers were based. This street boasted many such companies, including Thomas Bulman & Co. Ltd, fruit merchants of 12-13 Humber Street and, as can be seen in this photograph, Wray & Scott, fruit importers of 29 Humber Street. A horse-drawn wagon belonging to them is seen here fully laden with fruit. This area mainly lies empty and nothing now remains of the fruit wholesalers.

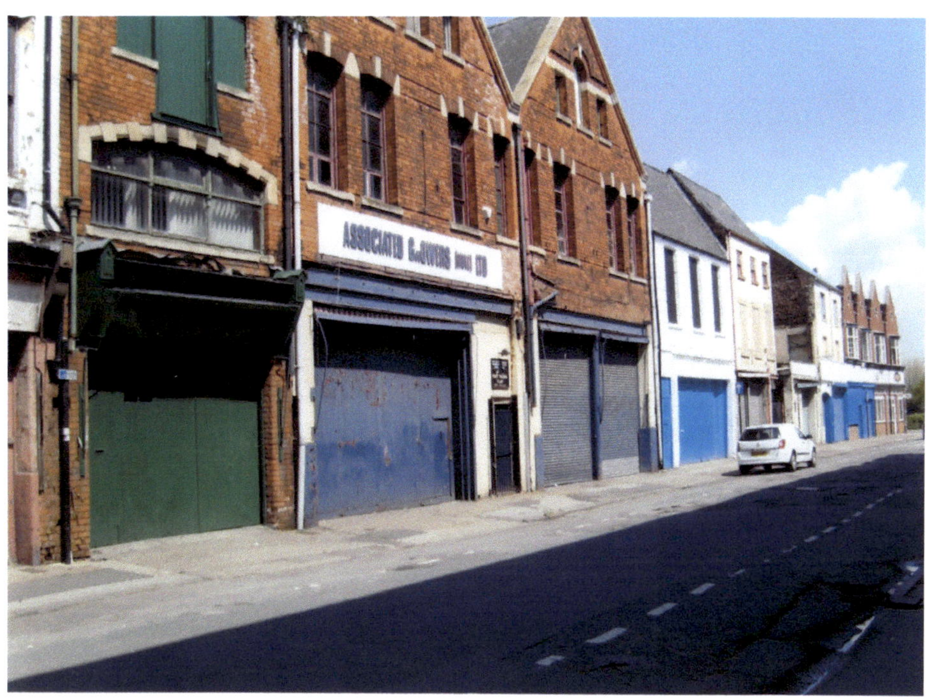

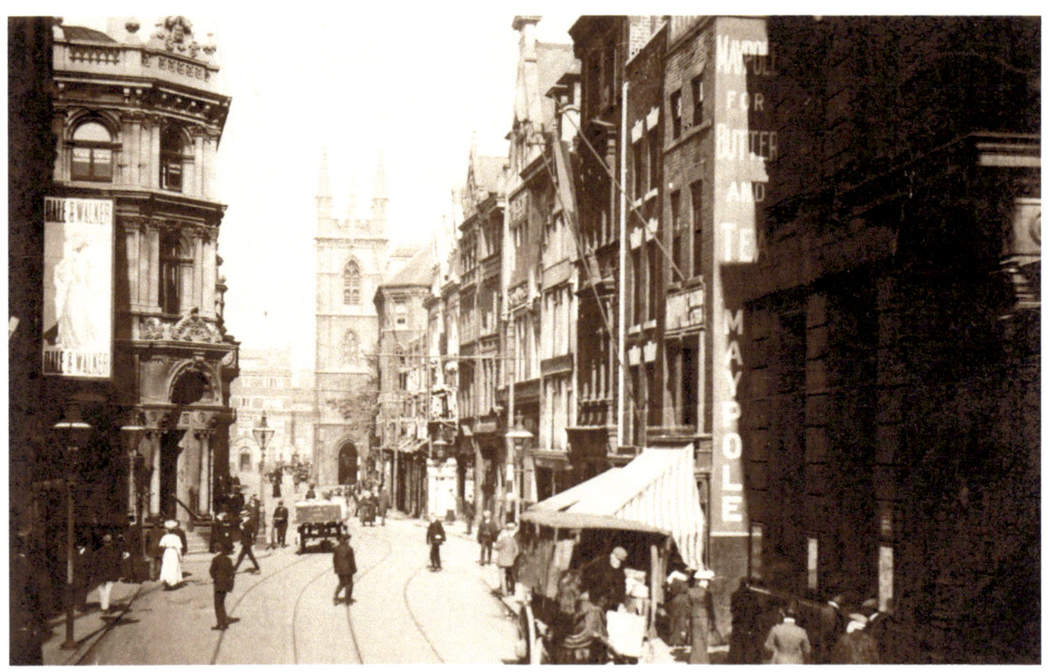

Lowgate

St Mary's church is clearly visible in the background in this photograph of Lowgate. The archway under the tower of the church was put in during the restoration of 1863. The bank can be seen on the left of the photograph. This area has seen many changes over the last hundred years with many of the old buildings having been demolished. The bank is now the Mint public house; Silver Street can be seen on the left.

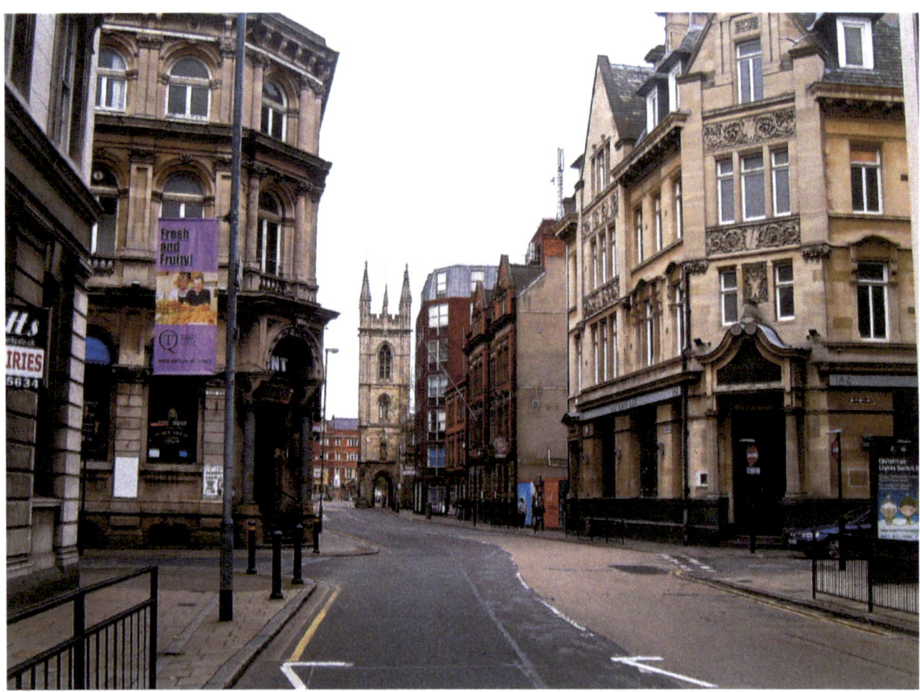

Carr Lane

The City Hall can be seen in the distance on the left, while on the right telephone house is yet to be built. Just visible is the new Cecil Cinema on the right of the picture and also visible is Darley's public house; today this is a Weatherspoon's, The Admiral of the Humber. This very busy junction is now controlled by traffic lights. Telephone house now stands where the derelict land in the upper photograph used to be. The Cecil Cinema is now a bingo hall.

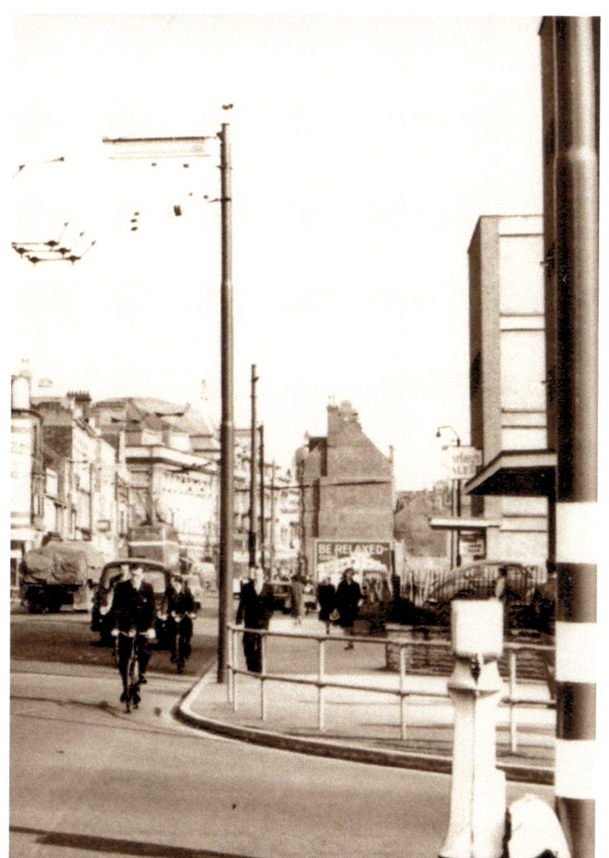

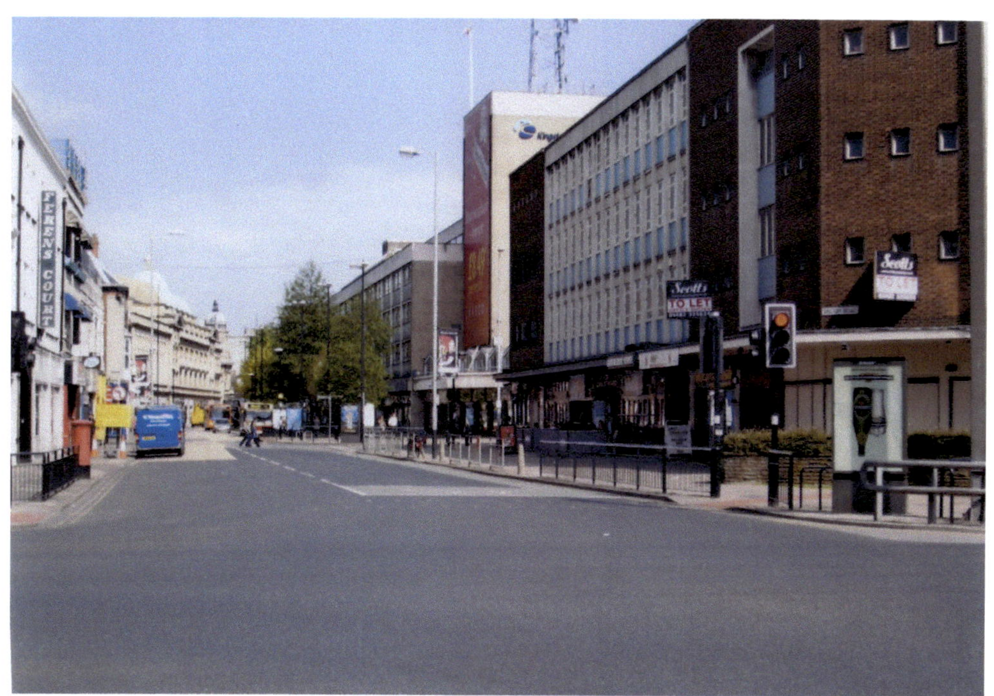

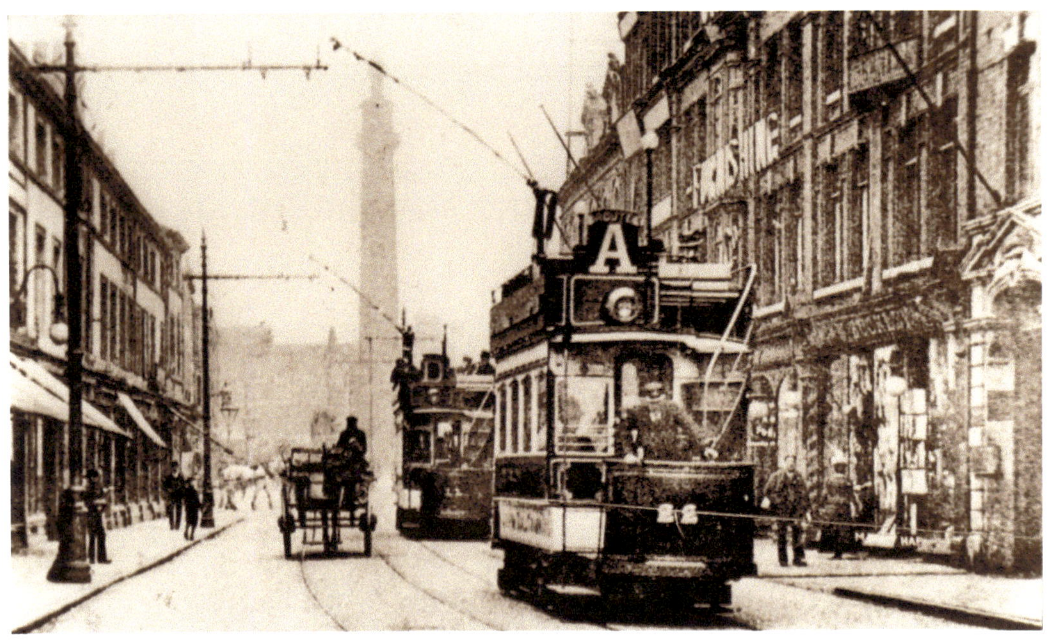

St John Street

Looking towards William Wilberforce's monument, this road was called St John's Street. Two open-top trams are visible; the nearest one is on the Anlaby Road route, while the tram behind is on the Dairycoates route. The area on the left of the photograph was demolished to make way for the city hall. Today this road is called Carr Lane and all the buildings in the upper photograph have long gone, replaced by a modern shopping centre.

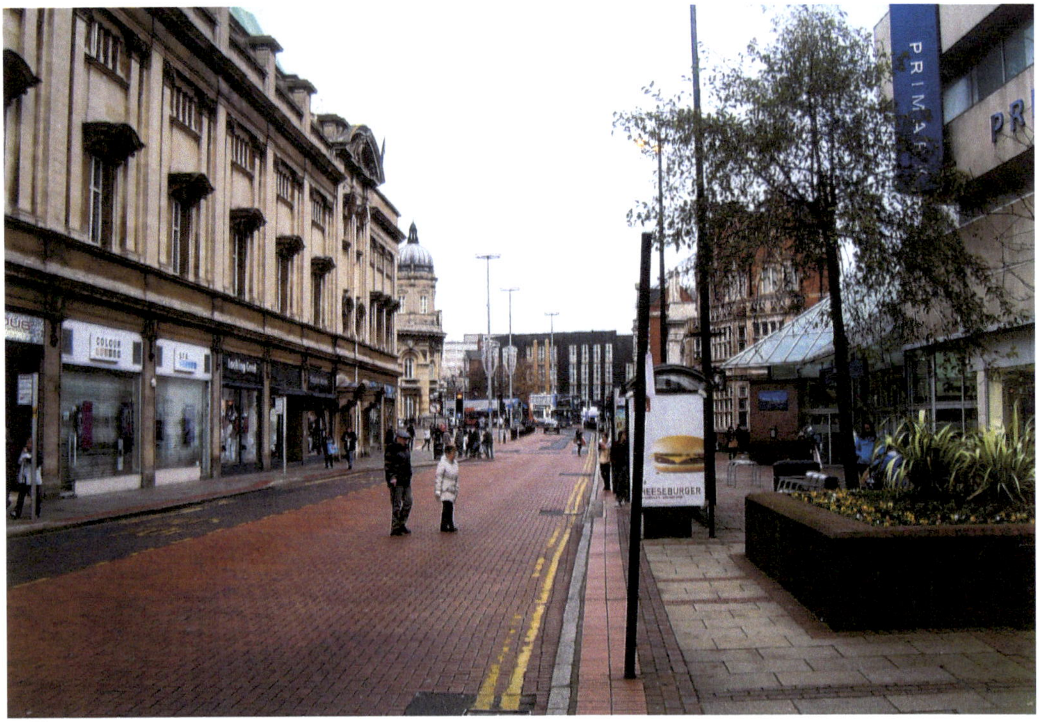

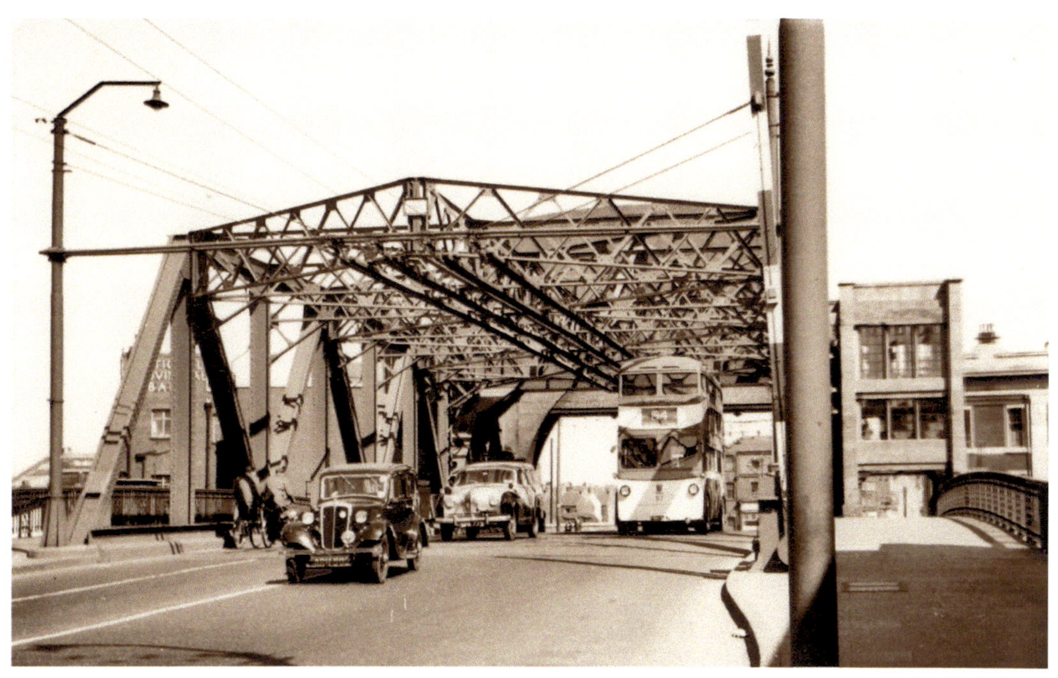

North Bridge

North Bridge was opened in 1931, replacing an early bridge which was built in 1870. Modern cars of the day and a Hull Corporation Transport trolleybus on service 64 are seen crossing the bridge back to the city centre. This is an important bridge linking the city centre with Holderness Road, East Hull and the eastern suburbs and villages. North Bridge looks as impressive today as it did when it was first built and is even busier these days than it was in the 1930s.

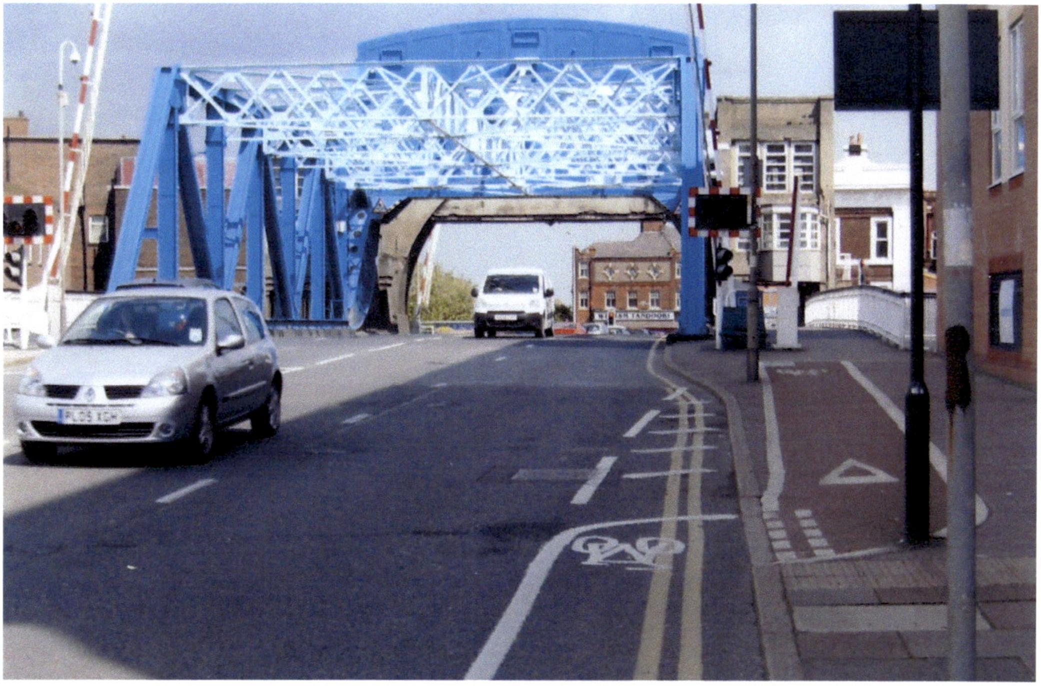

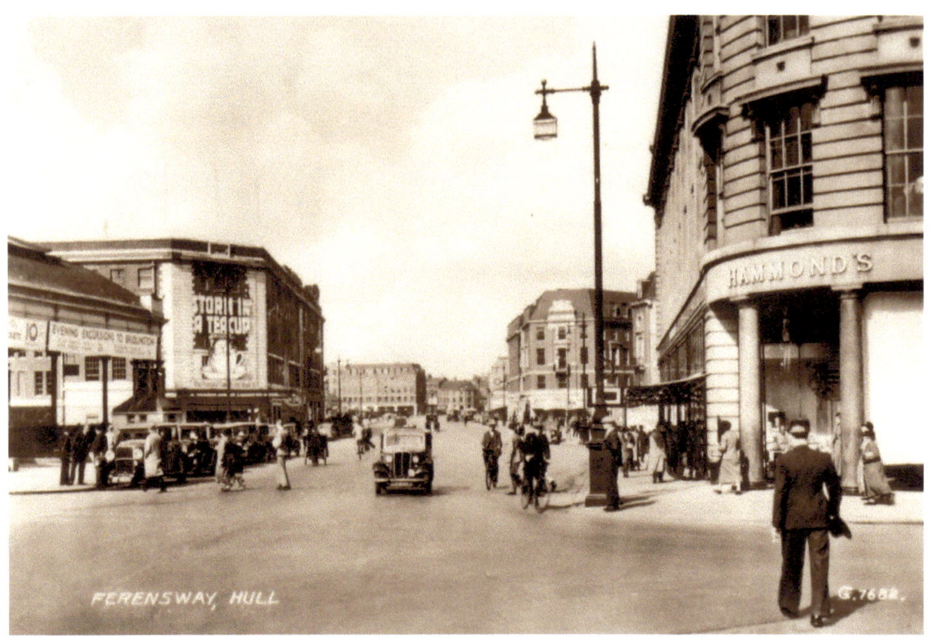

Ferensway

The construction of Ferensway was built on land once occupied by slum houses and was built in the 1930s. On the right is Hammond's store while on the left is Hull Paragon railway station. Note the advertisements for unlimited travel holiday season tickets at 10/- (50p) and also special excursions every Wednesday evening to Bridlington for 2/6p (12 and half pence). Past the railway station is the ABC Cinema, showing a comedy film, *Storm in a Teacup*. To the right is Brook Street and Trippets store. The new St Stephen's shopping complex now stands on the old ABC Cinema site.

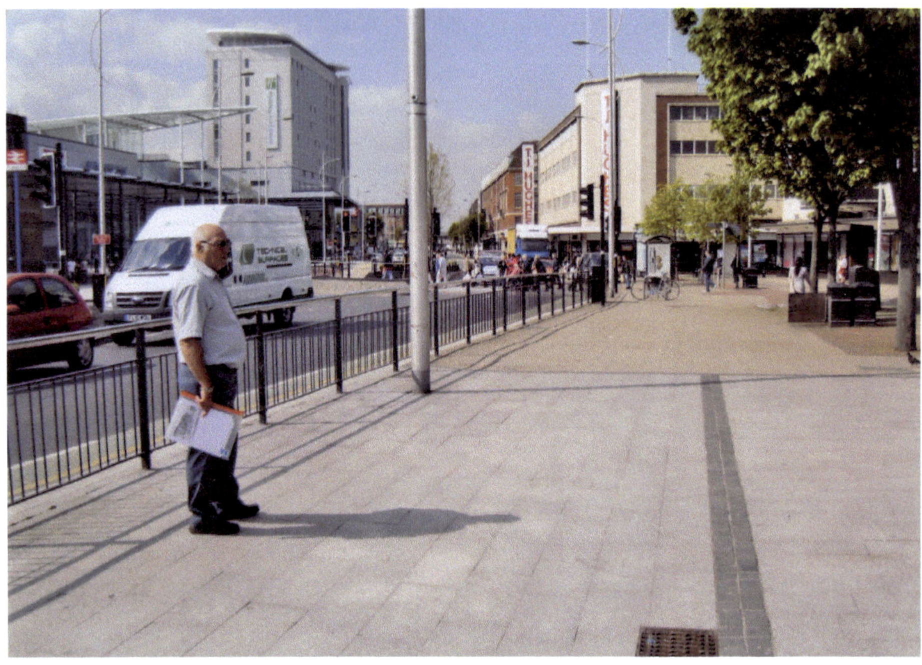

This photograph looks up Ferensway from the corner of Trippett Street, and shows the very wide road of Ferensway. This area was once a much built up area with slum houses; these were demolished in the early 1930s for the new Ferensway and bus station (now demolished). The shop on the corner of Pearson Street on the left of the picture is Electric O Appliances Ltd. Behind the modern buildings is Spring Bank and Blundell's Corner. In the present day photograph, Electric O Appliances is now Job Centre Plus and One Step. The buildings down Spring Bank were demolished some years ago and now the *Hull Daily Mail* offices stand on this site.

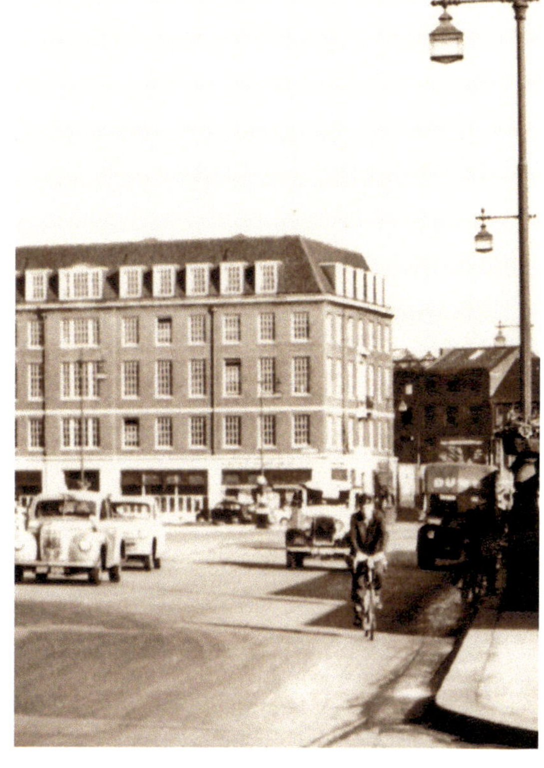

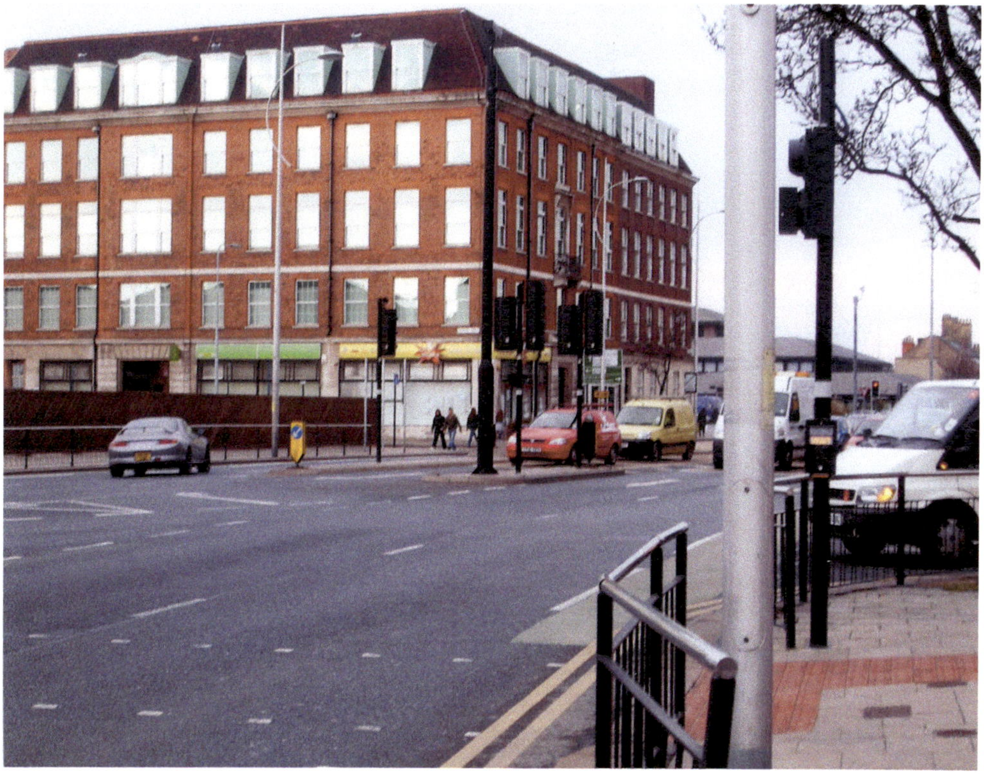

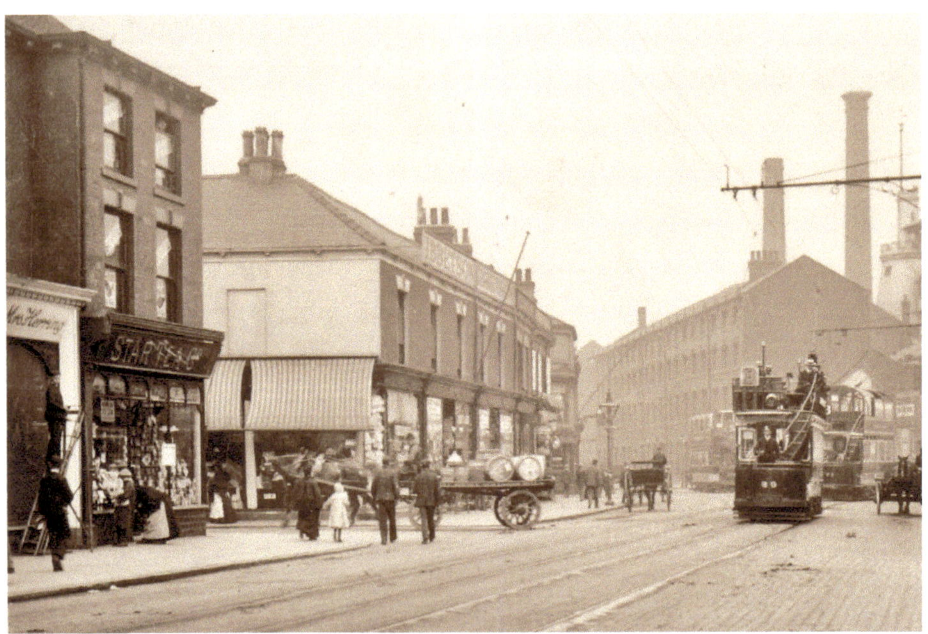

Prospect Street

In this early 1900s photograph, one has a good idea what the city centre looked like; this is Prospect Street looking towards Beverley Road and Spring Bank. A number of horse-drawn wagons are visible, along with three electric trams; the nearest tram is No. 30, an open top tram, while behind are two semi enclosed trams. These trams are on the Beverley Road and Spring Bank routes. On the left of the photograph is Miss Batty and Mrs Herring's store of 54 Prospect Street. In the background can be seen the Blundell, Spence & Co., paint and varnish manufacturers. Everything in the upper photograph has long gone and been replaced with modern buildings.

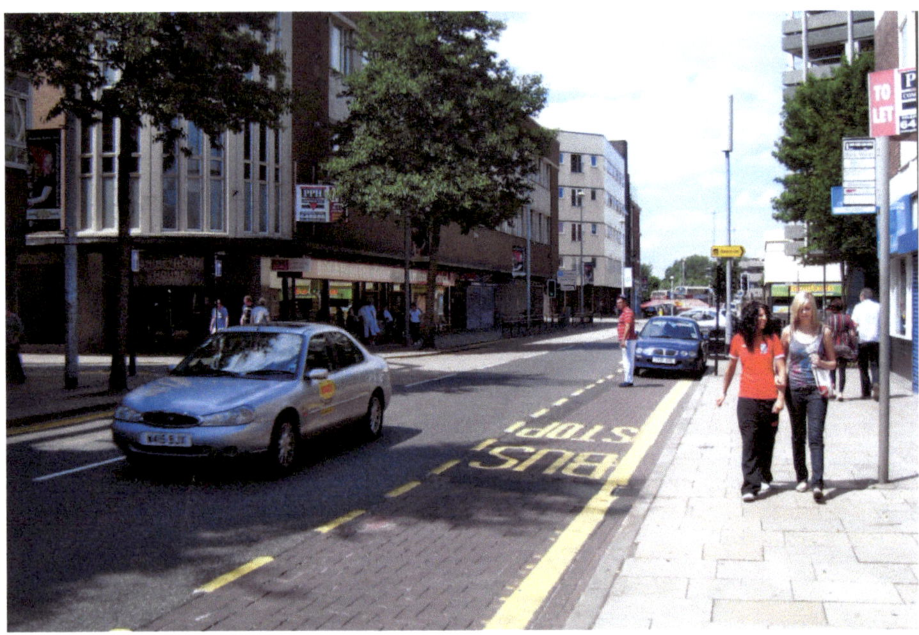

Old City Centre

This fine photograph, taken from the old Monument Bridge in the late 1800s, shows the old city centre as it was.

All the buildings in this view, except Wilberforce's Monument and the Dock offices, were demolished to make way for the construction of King Edward Street and Queen Victoria Square. The roads included John Street, Junction Street, Waterworks Street and Engine Street. The centre building was the Queen's Hotel. Queen Victoria Square and King Edward Street were built in the early 1900s. From this photograph, one can see how high William Wilberforce's Monument is. Only the Dock offices now remain.

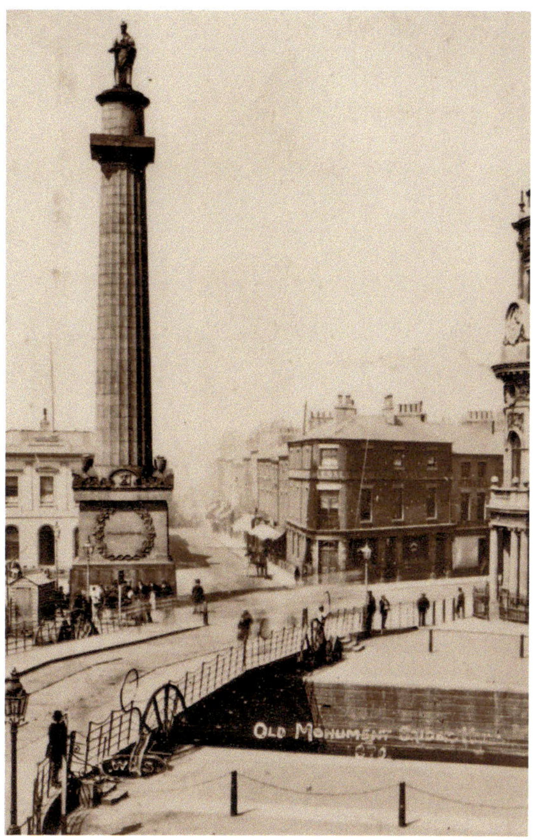

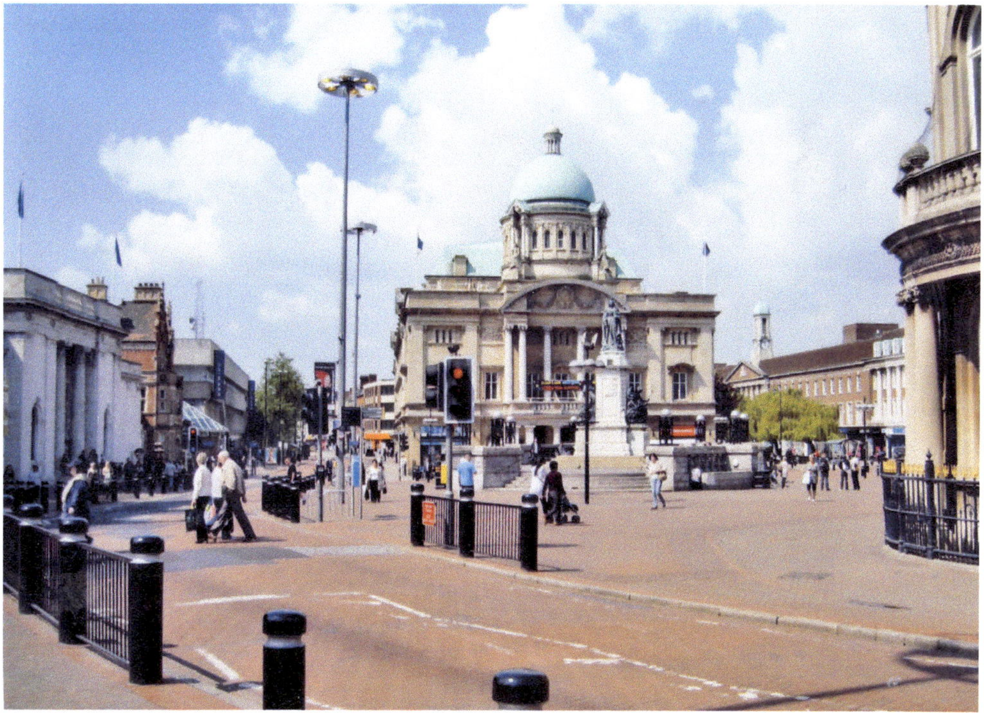

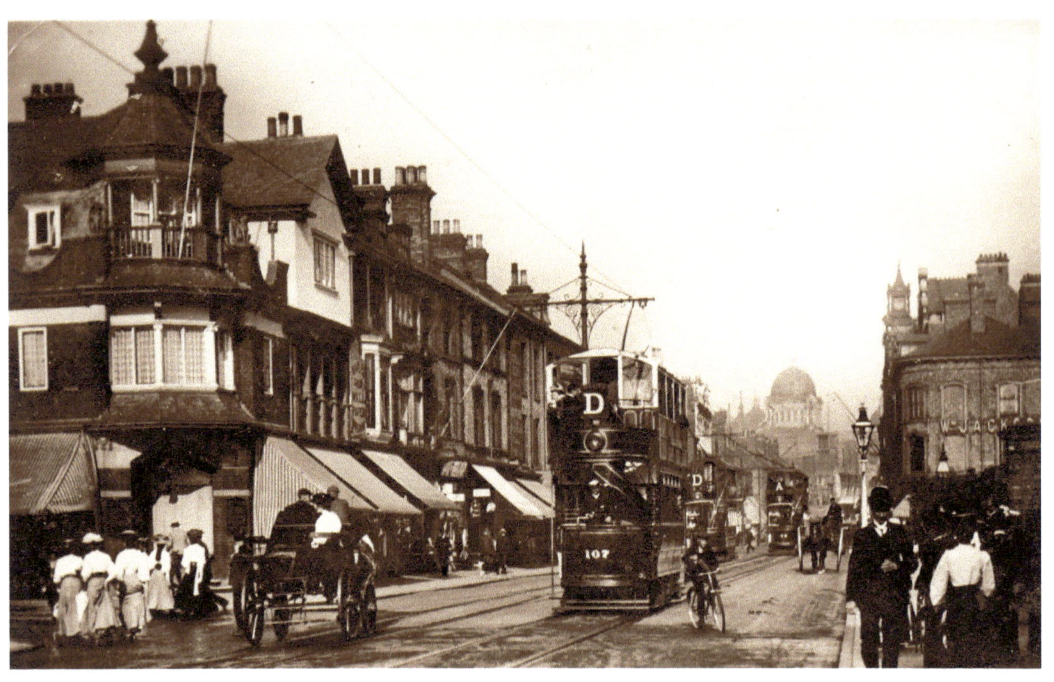

Brook Street and Anlaby Road

In later years the electric trams were enclosed, although the motorman and the stairs were still in the open as seen by this tram on the 'D' service to Dairycoates, with a similar tram in the background on the 'A' service to Anlaby Road, *c.* 1910. This photograph was taken before the new Ferensway was built looking down Anlaby Road and Carr Lane. In the background can be seen the City Hall. In today's photograph very little now remains; the only remaining building is the corner building. Ferensway runs immediately in front of this photograph.

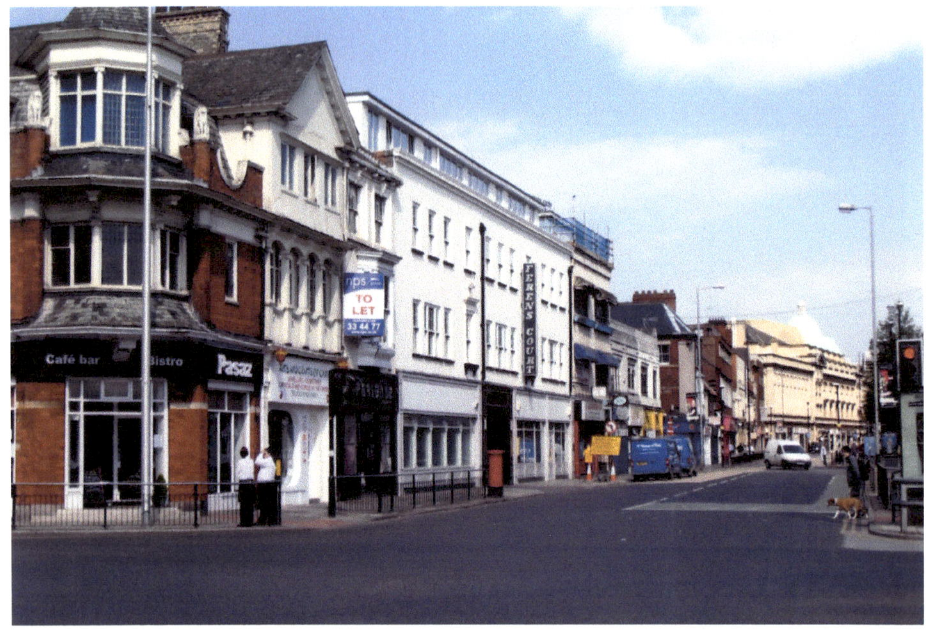

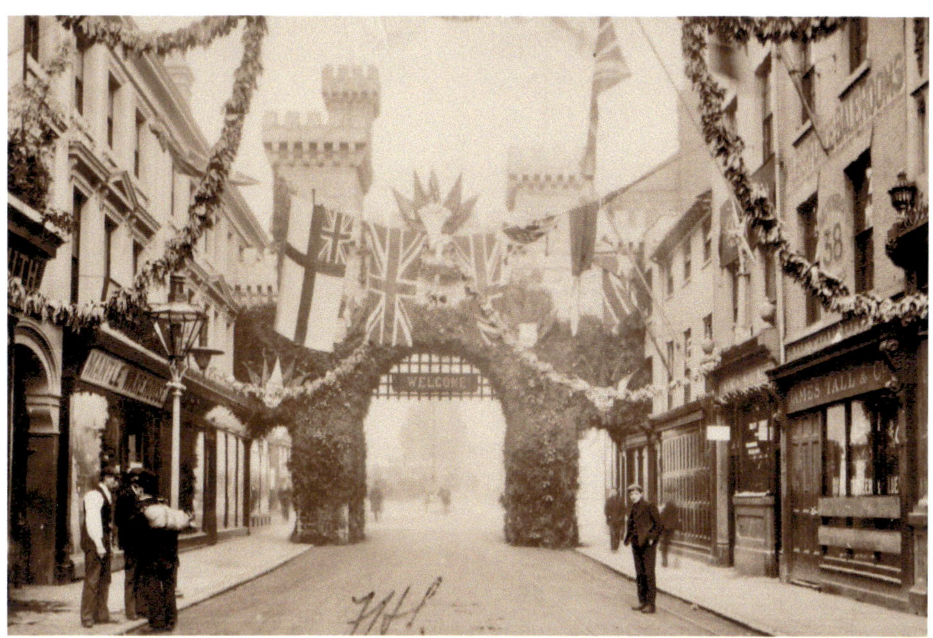

Whitefriargate

On 12 May 1903, the Prince of Wales, later King George V, unveiled the statue of Queen Victoria in Queen Victoria Square. This was followed by the laying for the City Hall of the foundation stone by the Princess of Wales, later Queen Mary. This rather magnificent archway at the entrance to Whitefriargate was built in their honour. The arch was built as near as possible to the original Beverley Gate. The archway is seen with bunting and Union Jack flags flying. William Wilberforce's Monument is just visible through the centre arch. On the right is No. 38 Whitefriargate, which was the business of James Tall & Co., auctioneer; on the left the Mantle Warehouse is just visible.

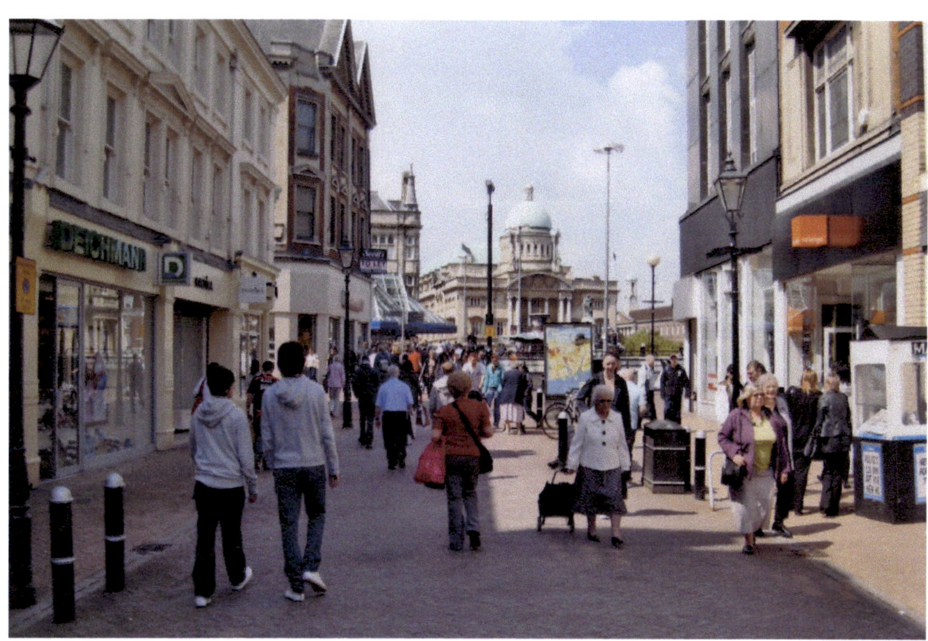

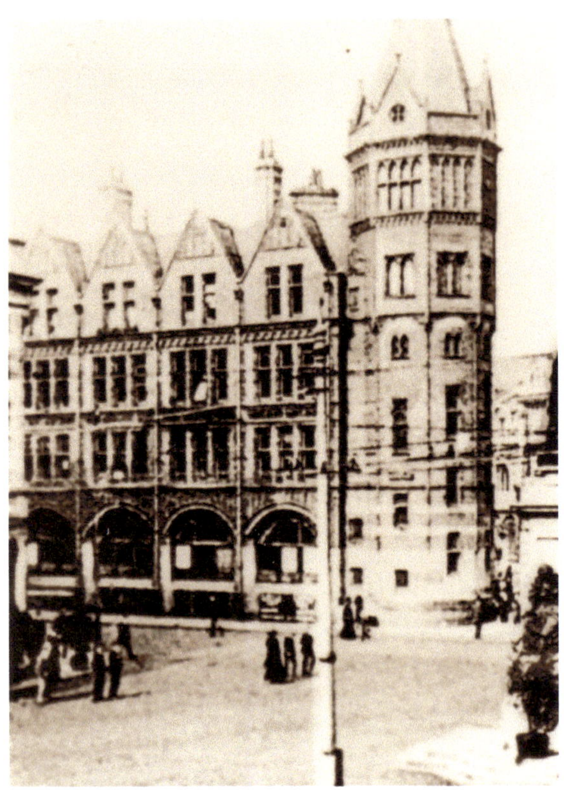

Prudential Building

This large impressive building, which stood on the corner of King Edward Street and Waterworks Street (now called Paragon Street), was the Prudential building, built in 1903. The building took a direct hit during the bombing of Hull on the night of 7 May 1941. Fifteen people lost their lives while sheltering in the basement of the building. In today's photograph, modern shops now stand on this location. Note the plaque in front of the circular pavement, stating that this was the location of the Prudential building.

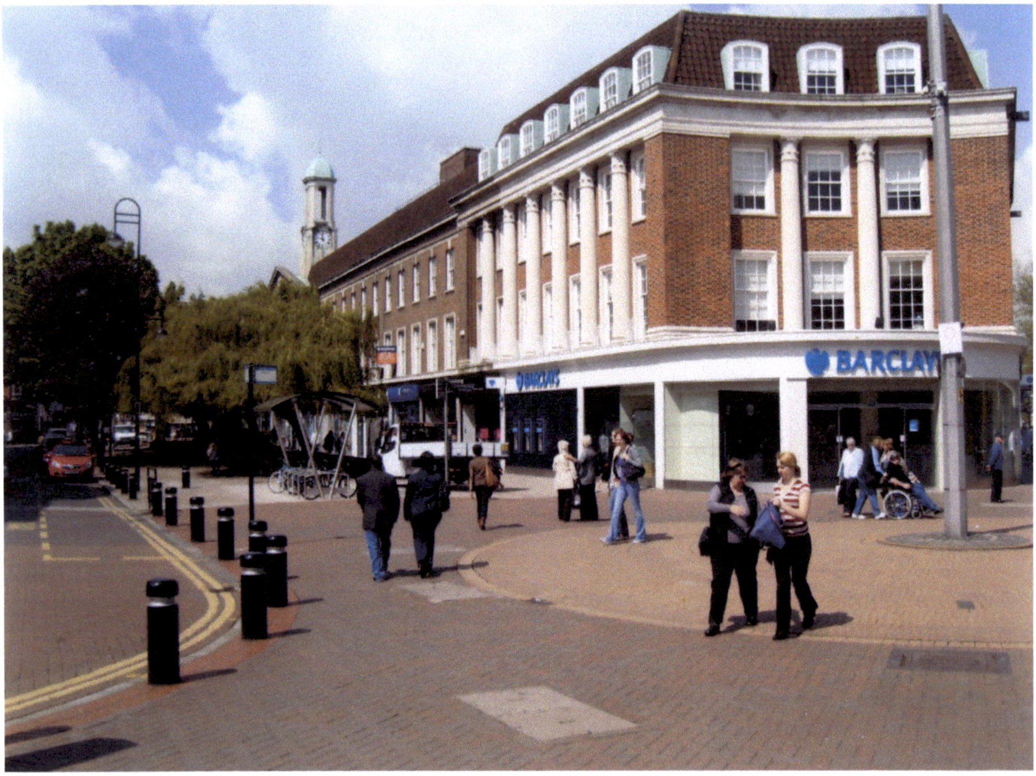

Queen Victoria Statue

Hull is one of the few places to
have a statue of Queen Victoria in
her youth and newly-crowned. The
monument to her is aptly placed in
Queen Victoria Square. She is seen
looking across the square towards
Whitefriargate. In the background
can be seen the Monument buildings,
built in 1908, with W. H. Smith
newsagent's on the left.

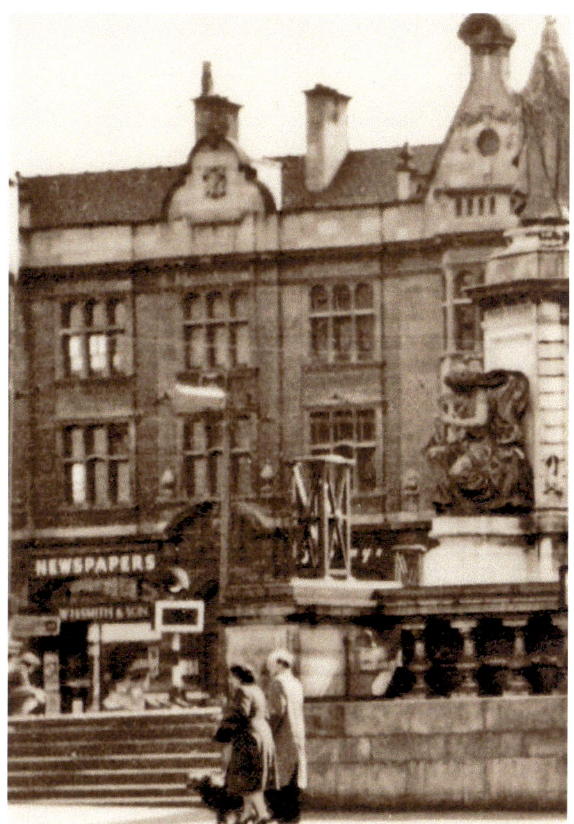

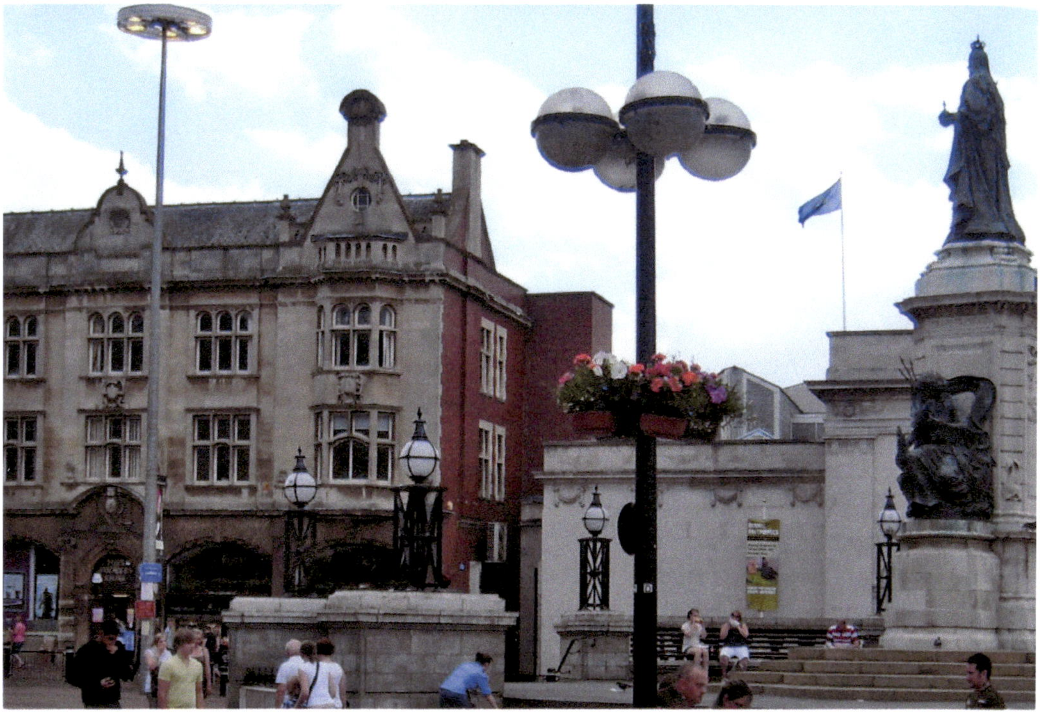

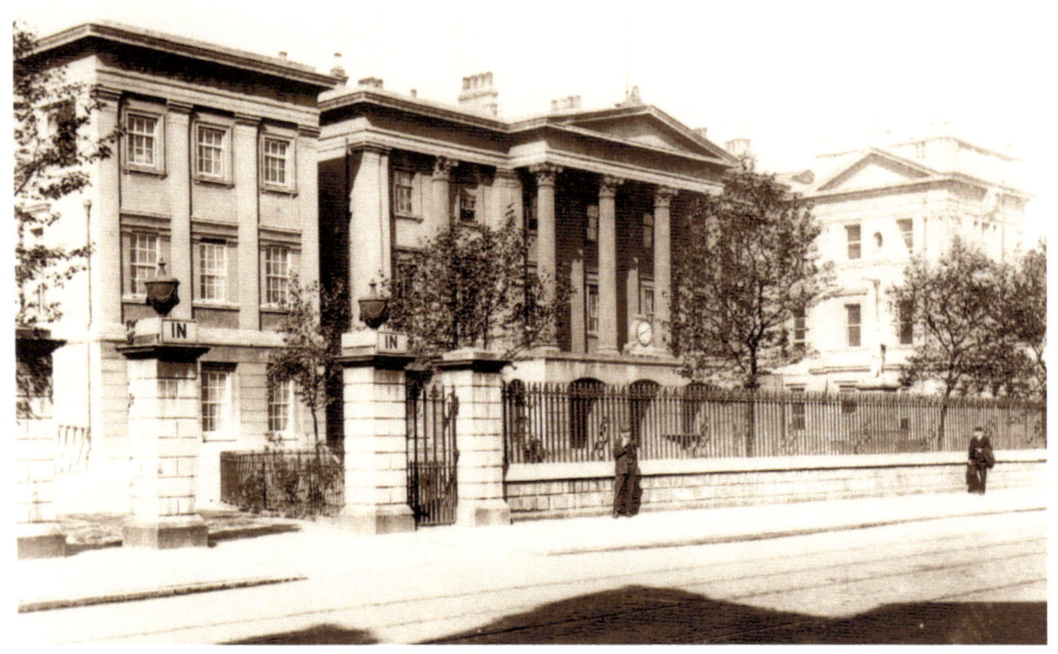

Old Infirmary

The Infirmary was built in 1784, built on what was then called Beverley Road (today this is called Prospect Street), away from the old town in the open, and the Infirmary was surrounded by fields. Further extensions to the Infirmary were added between the 1850s and the 1880s. The name was changed in 1884 when it became the Royal Infirmary. It was demolished in 1972 and replaced by the modern Prospect shopping centre, as evident in today's photograph.

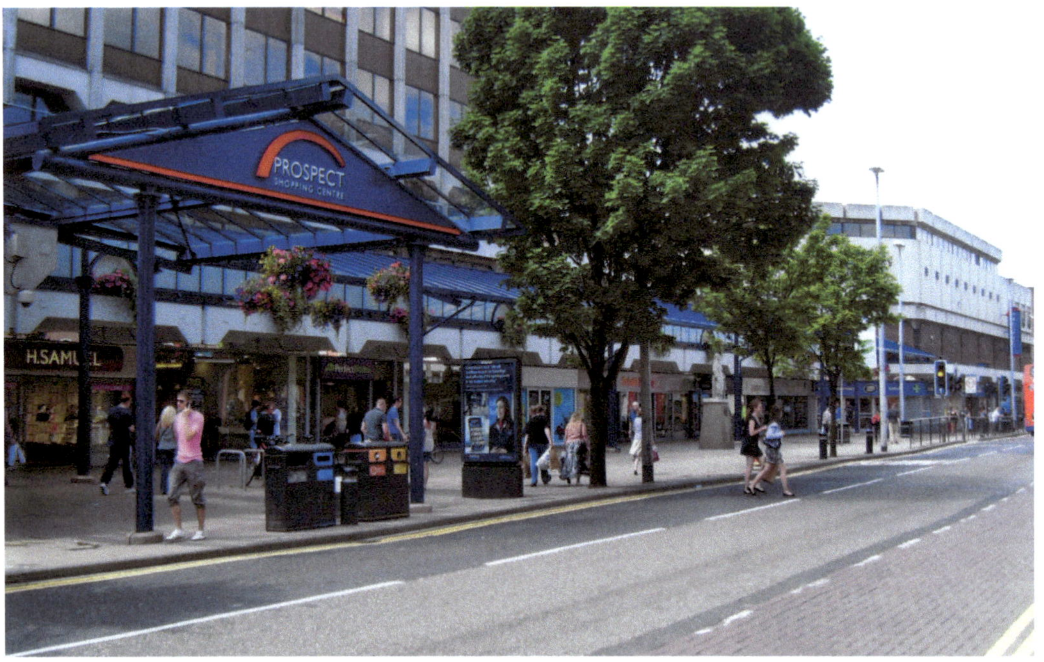

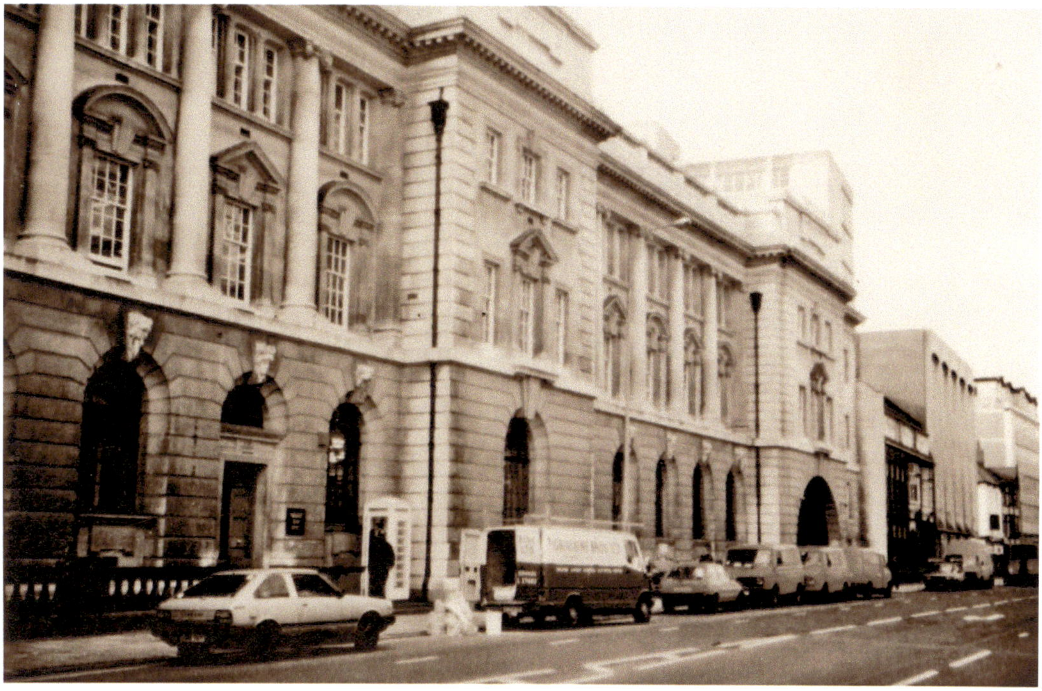

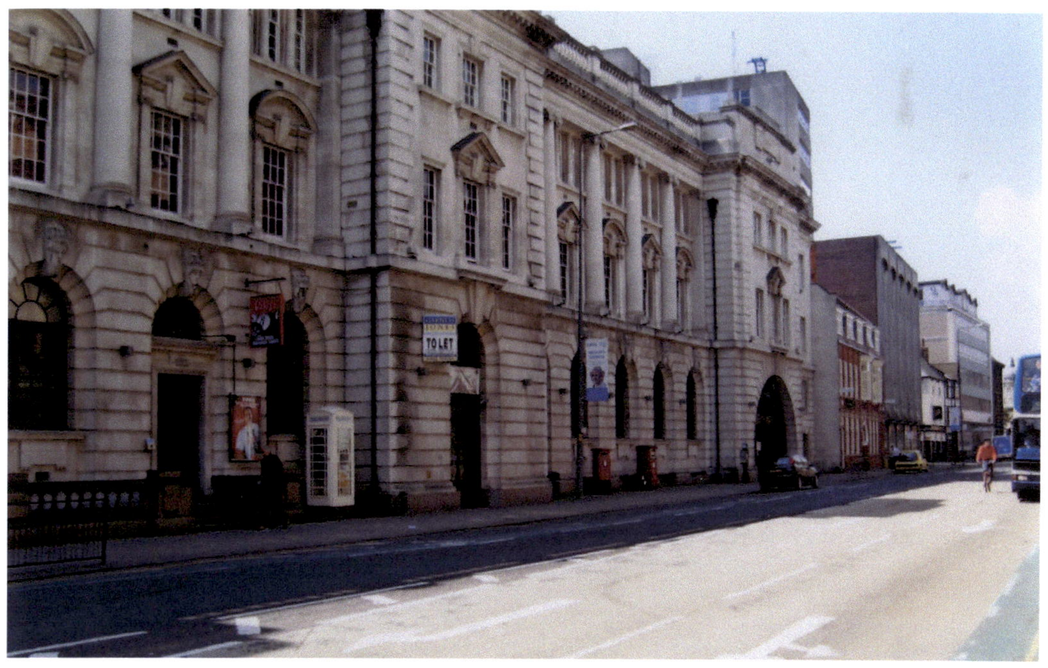

General Post Office, Lowgate

This elaborate building was once the General Post Office. It was opened in 1877 and is located at the corner of Lowgate and Alfred Gelder Street. Leyland Royal Mail vans are seen parked outside the building, along with a van belonging to Graybine Bros. Ltd, builder, plasterer and electrical works. The General Post Office stands on the former site of Suffolk Palace. Today the General Post Office is apartments and a pub.

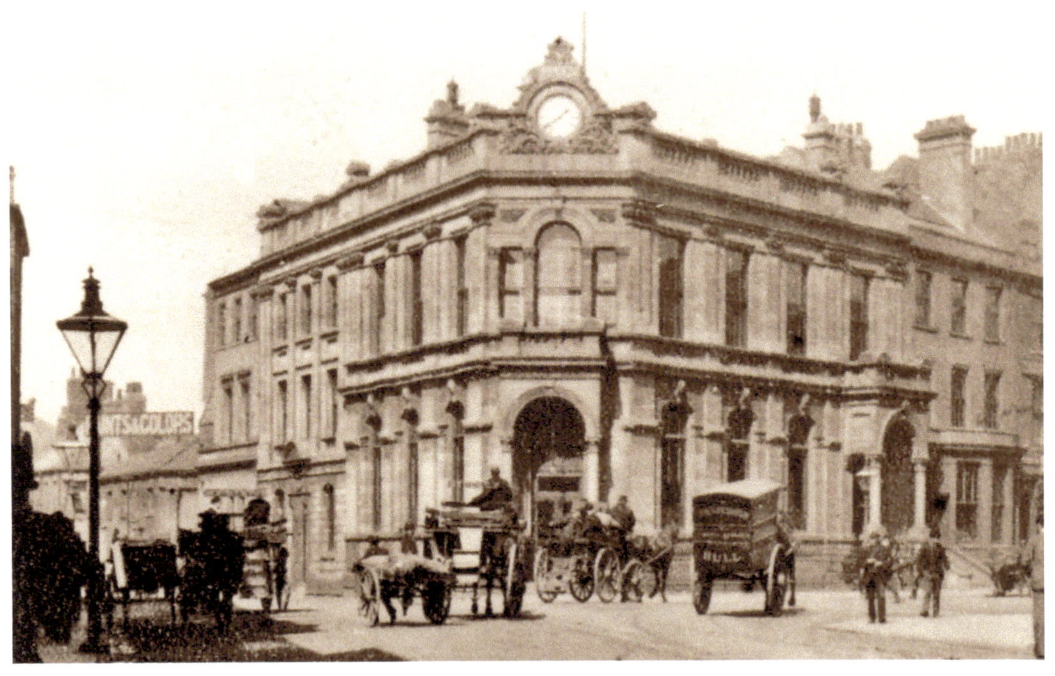

Hull Savings Bank

Smeaton Street ran parallel with Bond Street starting at Silvester Street to George Street. On the corner of Smeaton Street and George Street was the Hull Savings Bank as seen in the top photograph. Several horse-drawn wagons are clearly visible. Smeaton Street was later demolished and Bond Street was made much wider. Today the old Hull Savings Bank building has been replaced by a new building and is now the Lloyds TSB Bank.

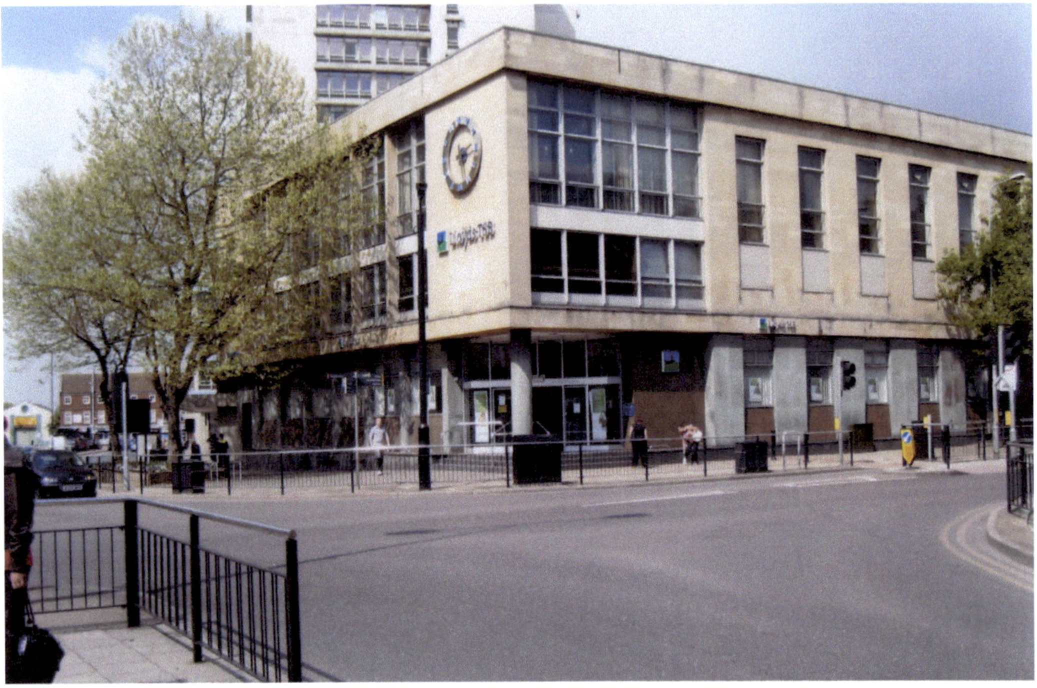

Guinness Clock

For many years the Guinness clock was a popular landmark in the city centre above the shops in Paragon Street. The wording on the left of the clock reads, 'Guinness is good for you'. Lockings and The Wholesale Bargain Store are seen underneath the clock. The same photograph shows the buildings without the Guinness clock. Lockings is now Star Nails, while the Wholesale Discount store is now Stanley's Brasserie. Ferensway is a very busy road and is the main road from Hull city centre for the motorway (M62), the docks and the Humber Bridge.

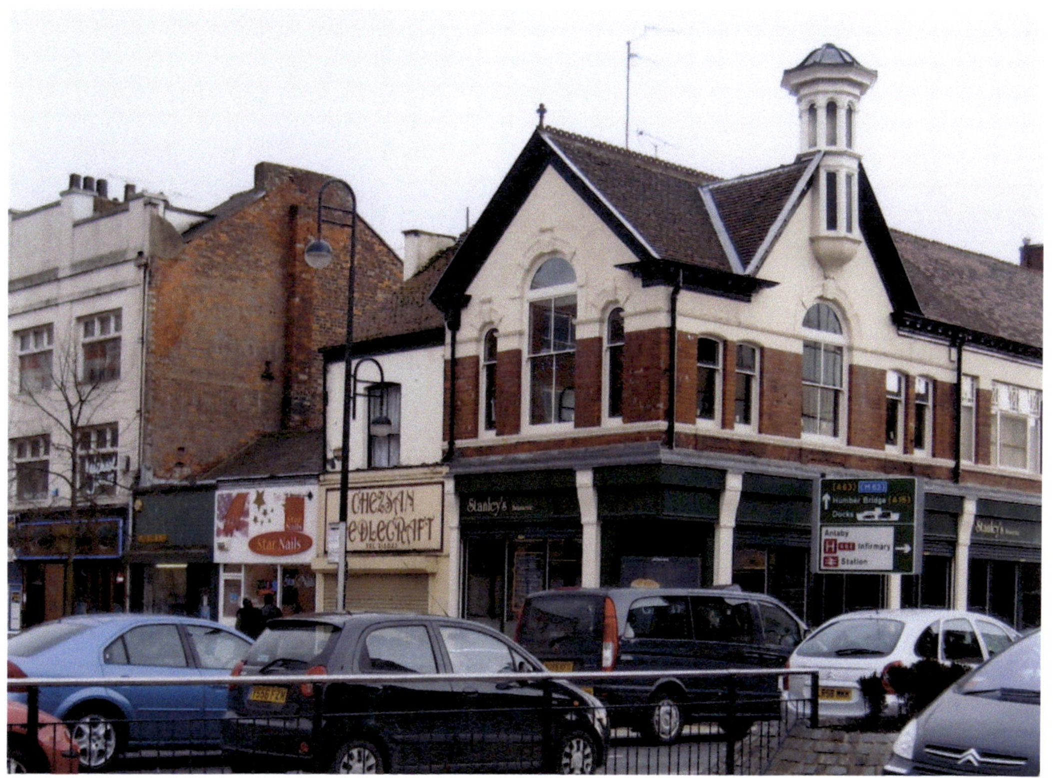

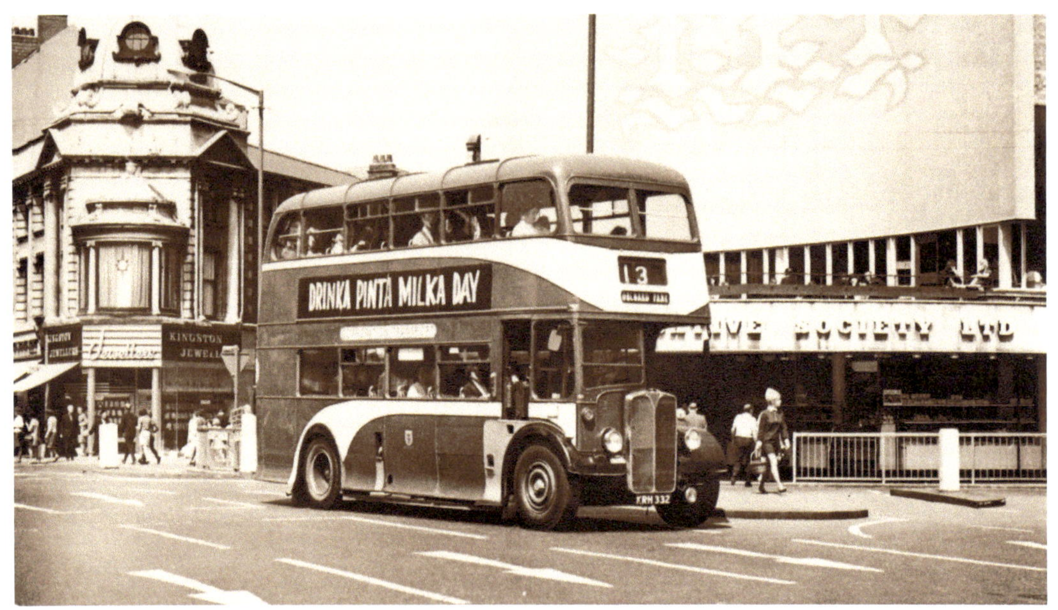

Hull Co-operative Store

A Hull Corporation Transport double-deck rear entrance bus on the 13 service from Orchard Park is seen passing the Hull & East Riding Co-operative departmental store at the corner of Prospect Street and Jameson Street. Note the people sat outside on the veranda of the restaurant of the Co-operative store. One of few buildings to remain intact after the Second World War can be seen behind the bus, which was Kingston Jewellers shop. Today the Co-operative store is British Home Stores and Kingston Jewellers is Goldsmiths.

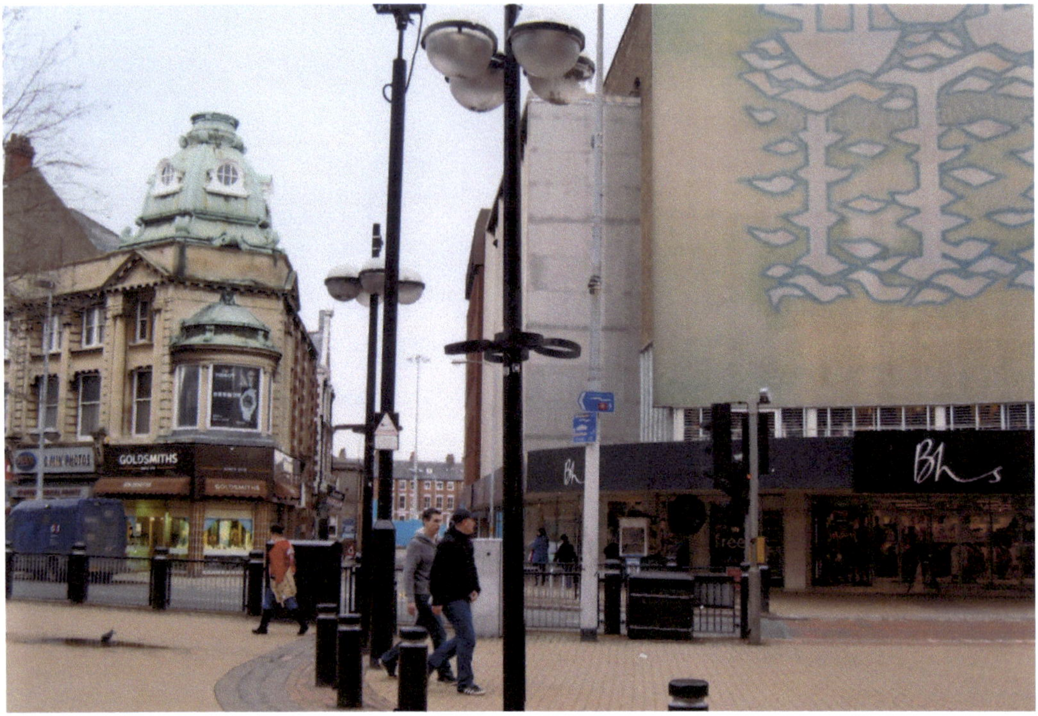

Prospect Street Shops

The new and old buildings are visible in this photograph of Prospect Street. On the left of the photograph in the new building is Fine Fare supermarket. The beautiful architecture of the old building can be seen. Central Carpet Warehouse is next to Fine Fare, while Brooks the pram shop is seen on the right. In today's photograph, all but one of the shops in the previous image has gone and that shop is renamed. Fine Fare supermarket is now Home Bargains; Central Carpet Warehouse is now Richer Sounds and Dove House hospice shop, while Brooks is now called Silver Cross babyshop.

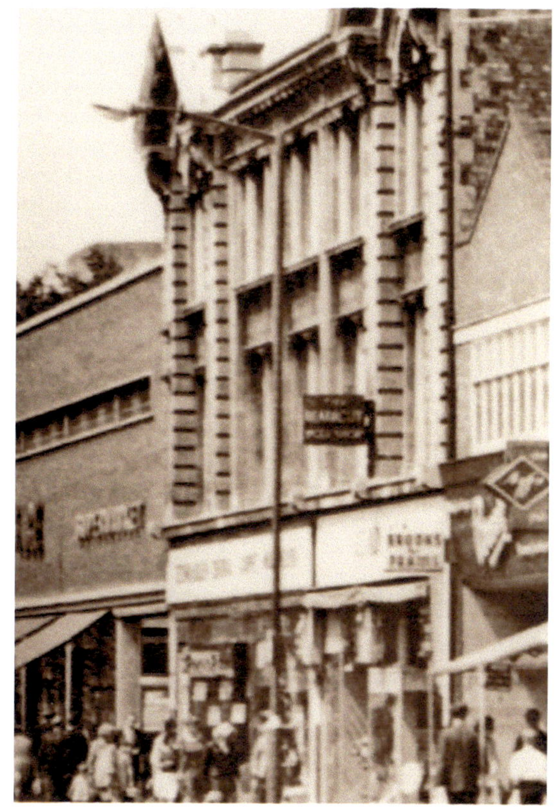

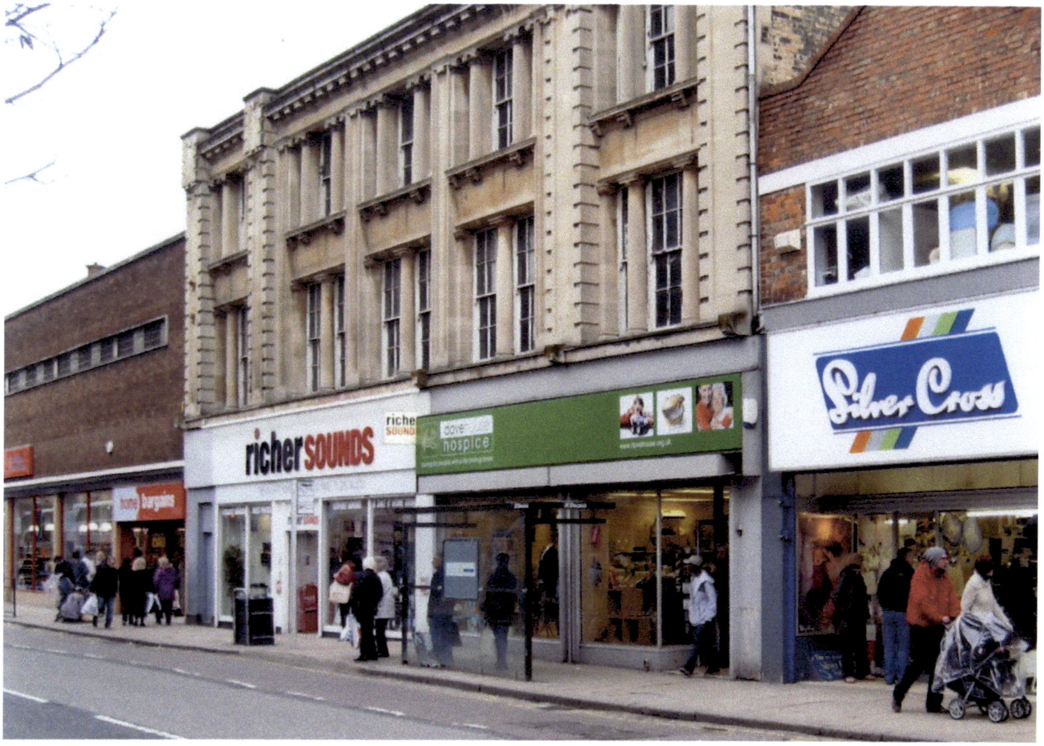

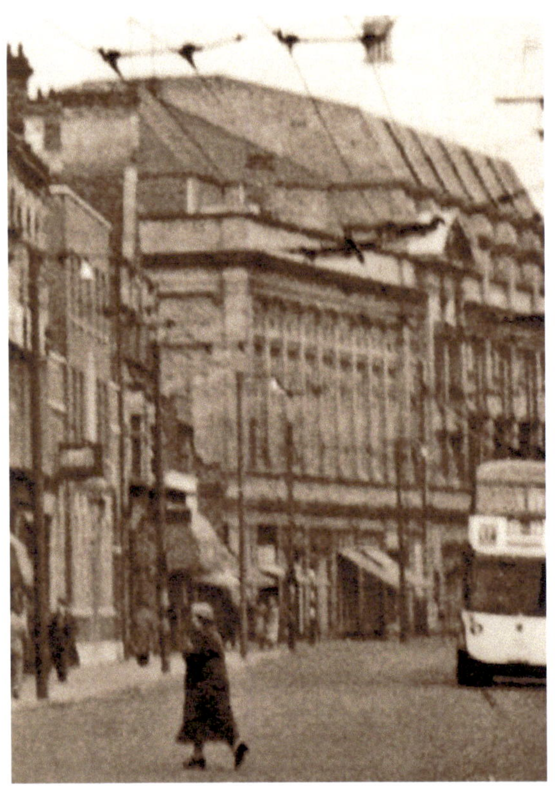

City Hall

A view of the trolleybus wires is clearly visible in this view of Carr Lane. A Hull Corporation Transport trolleybus is seen heading towards the cameraman. In the background can be seen the City Hall, which was completed in 1909/10, while the White Horse Hotel can be seen on the left. The buildings on the left have been demolished and replaced by new buildings, which is called Chariot House. Gran Café Centrale is visible on the ground floor.

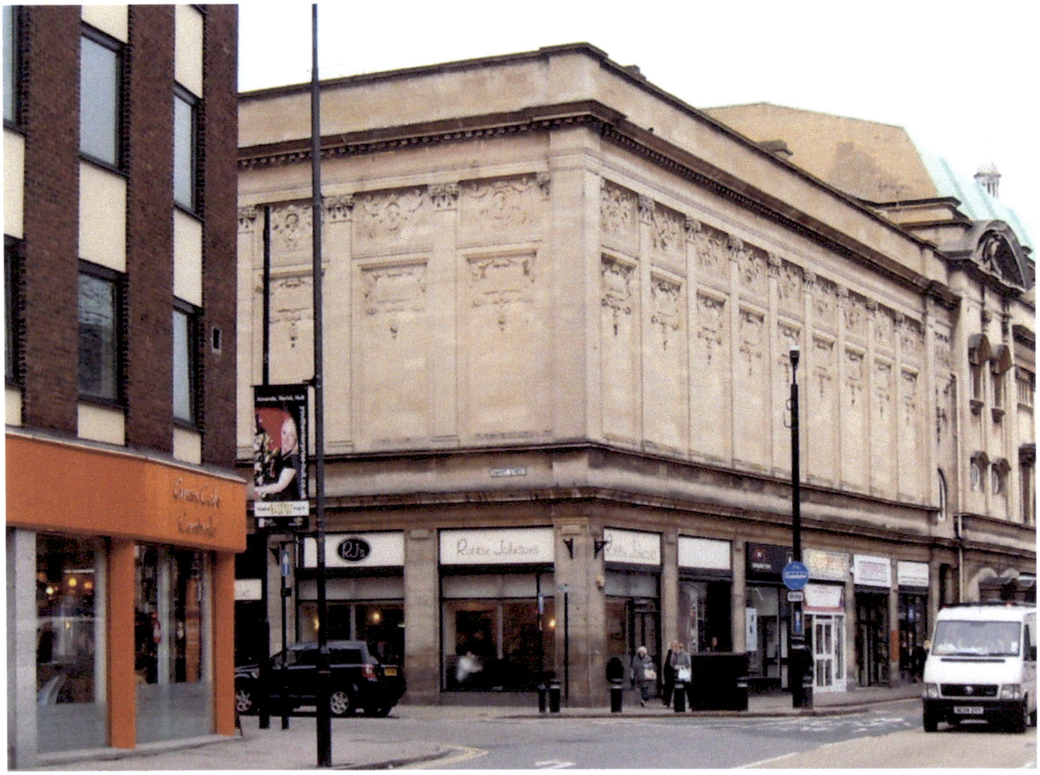

Ferensway Shops

In this photograph, looking across Ferensway, a selection of shops of the 1970s can be seen. On the left of the photograph is a Sports & Leisure shop; next to this is Haller, an exclusive footwear shop, which is having a sale. In the centre can be seen The Model Shop, while next to this is Hullaboo. On the corner of Ferensway and Anlaby Road can be seen Yorkshire Television offices. Over the years many of the shops have changed hands and indeed the type of items they sell. The Model Shop is the only business remaining today.

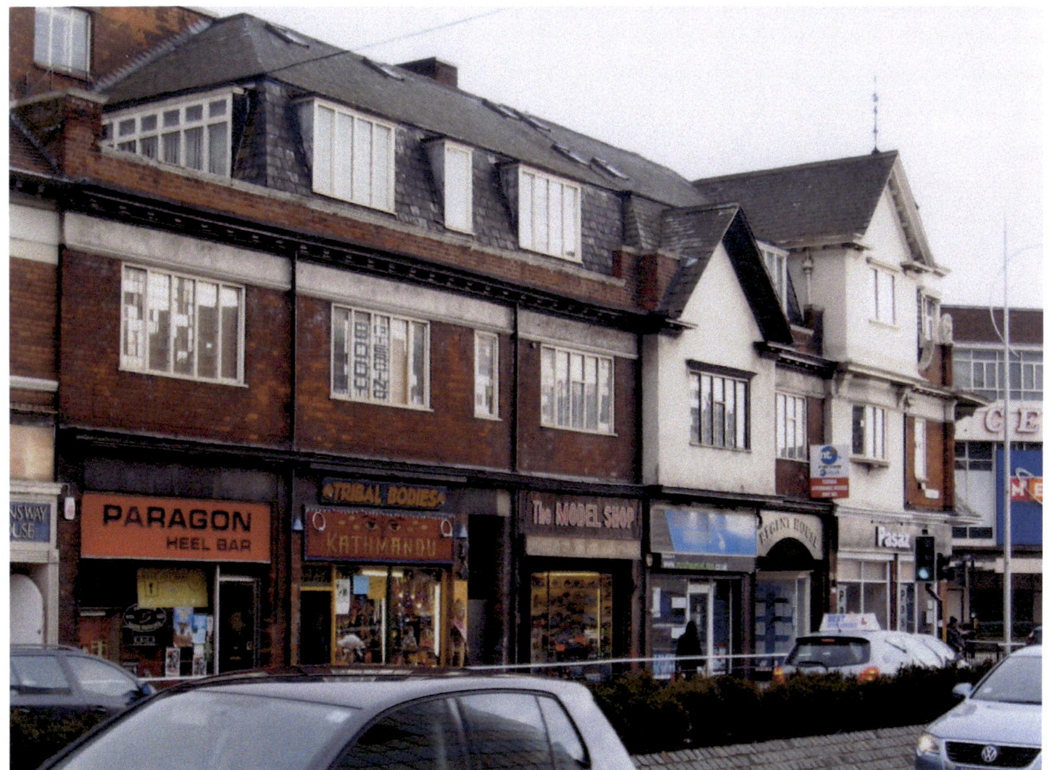

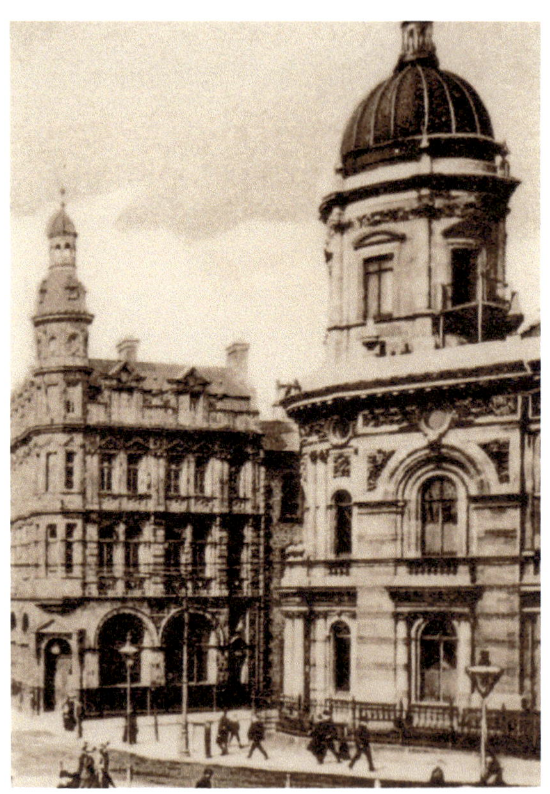

New Cross Street and Yorkshire Bank

The building on the left which is on the corner of Savile Street and New Cross Street is the Yorkshire Penny Bank building, while on the right are the Town Dock offices. A few buildings remained intact after the city centre was blitzed during the Second World War as is visible in the present day photograph. The Bank is now Caffé Nero, while the Dock offices are now a museum.

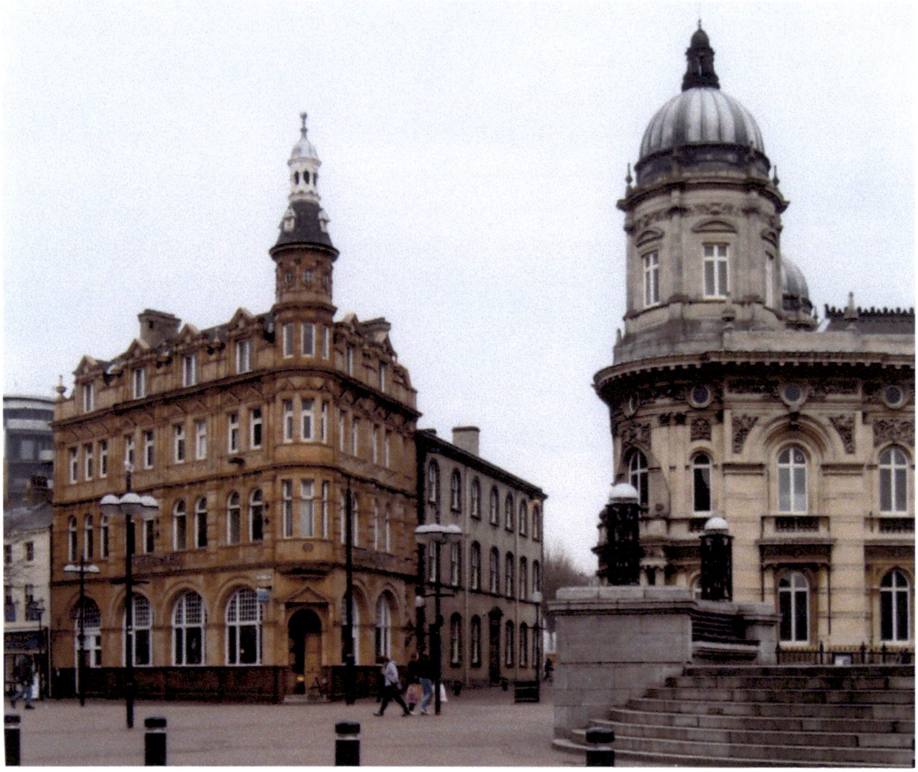

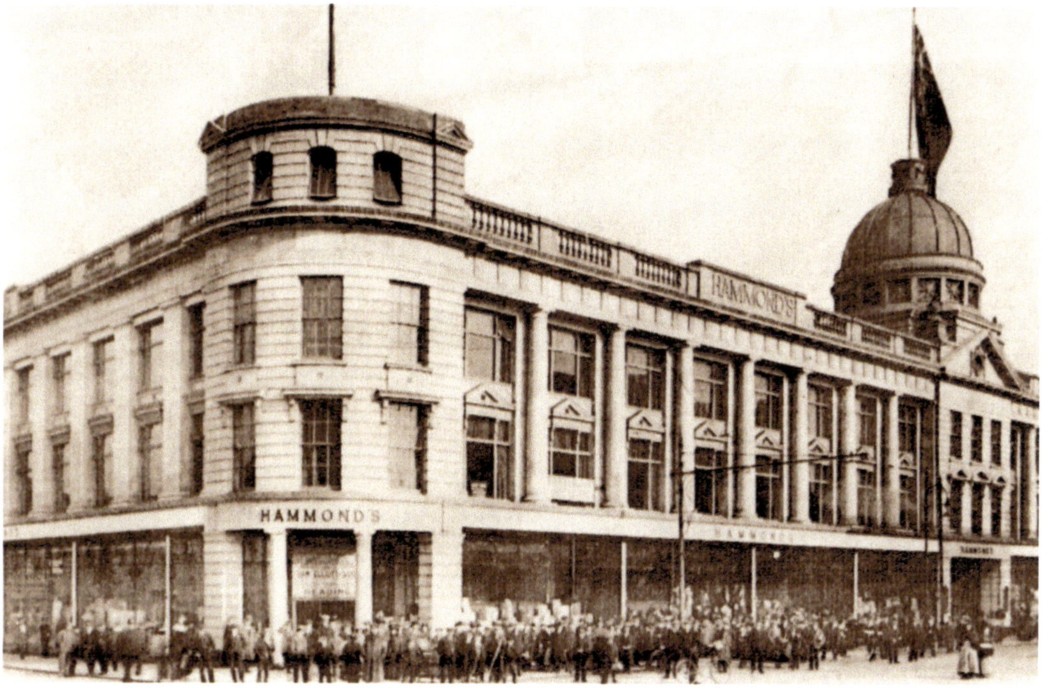

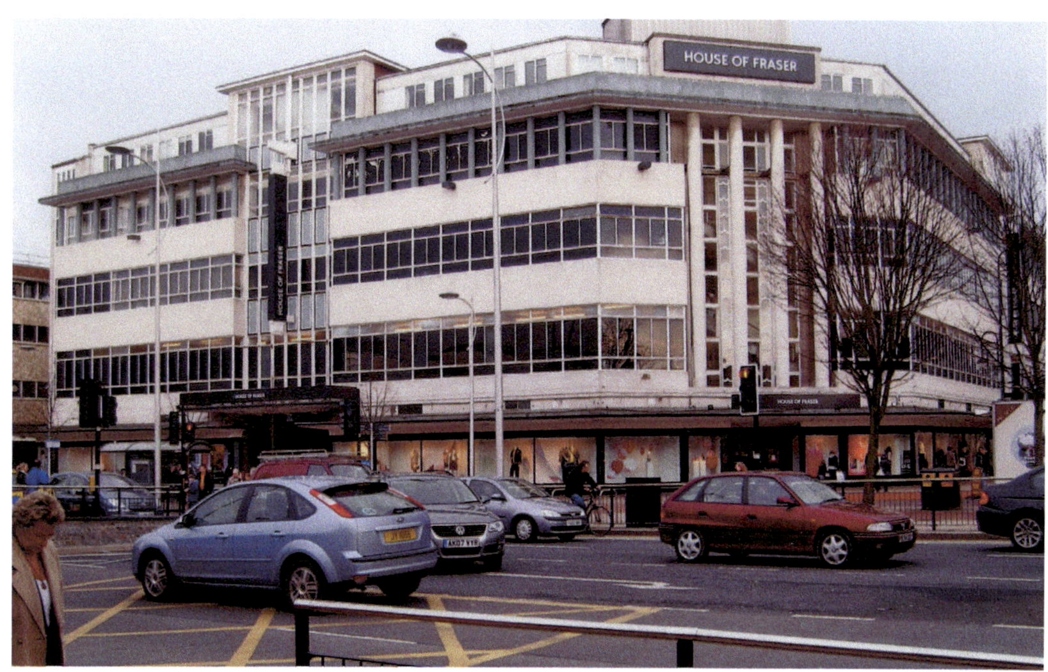

Hammond's Store

The original Hammond's department store in Paragon Square opened in May 1916, replacing an earlier store in Osborne Street. This large, modern looking store stood here for nearly thirty years until it was destroyed by enemy bombs during the Second World War on 7 August 1942. A new Hammond's store was built on the same site after the war and remains little changed since it was rebuilt. Today, Hammond's is now named House of Fraser.

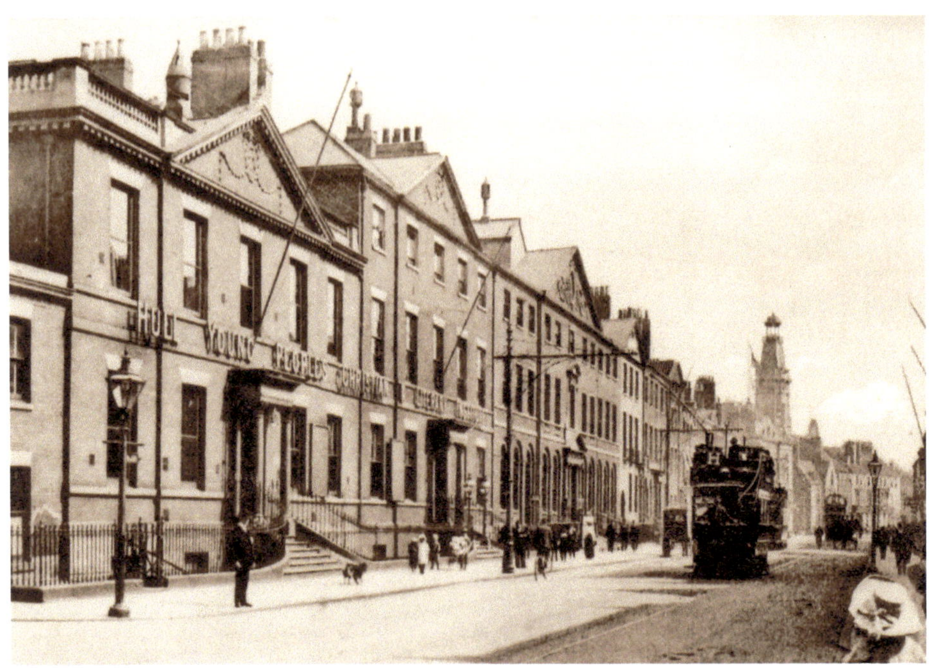

George Street

In this early 1900s photograph looking east up George Street, a stray dog is visible on the pavement on the left. The large building on the left is the Young People's Christian and Literary Association building. George Street is an important road linking the city centre to the east of the city. Two electric trams are seen on the 'H' route to Holderness Road. As can be seen in today's photograph, much of George Street no longer exists.

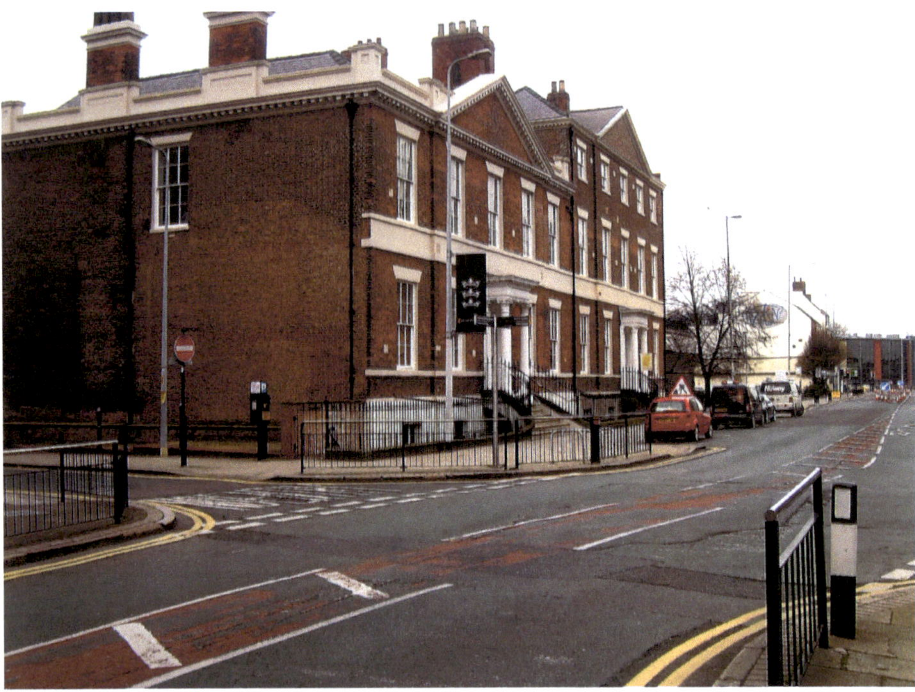

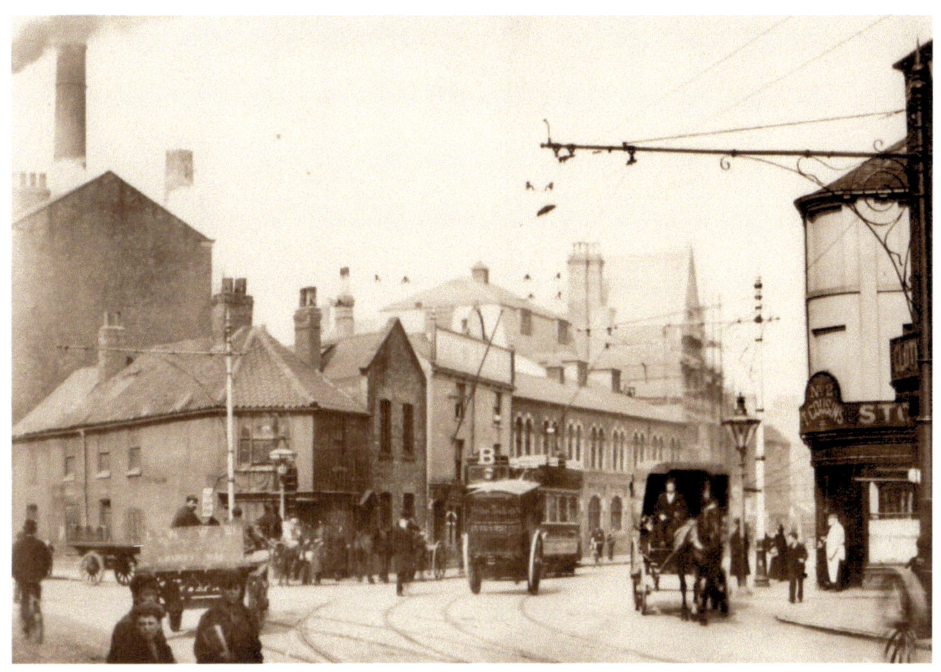

Beverley Road and Spring Bank

There are horse-drawn carts in abundance in this photograph, *c.* 1900, of Spring Bank and Beverley Road. On the left are the works of Blundell, Spence and Co., who were paint and varnish manufacturers. An electric tram is just visible, passing the Zoological public house. On the right is Marlborough Street. Much of this area was completely destroyed during the Second World War. This area for many years was known as Blundell's Corner and many still refer to this area as that. All the buildings in the upper photograph have long gone and the *Hull Daily Mail* offices now stand on this corner.

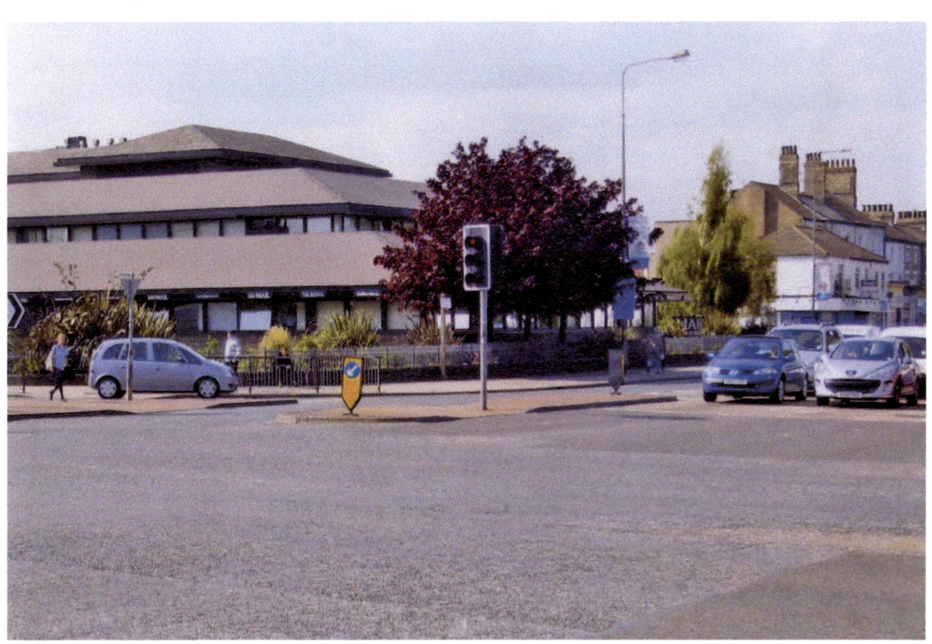

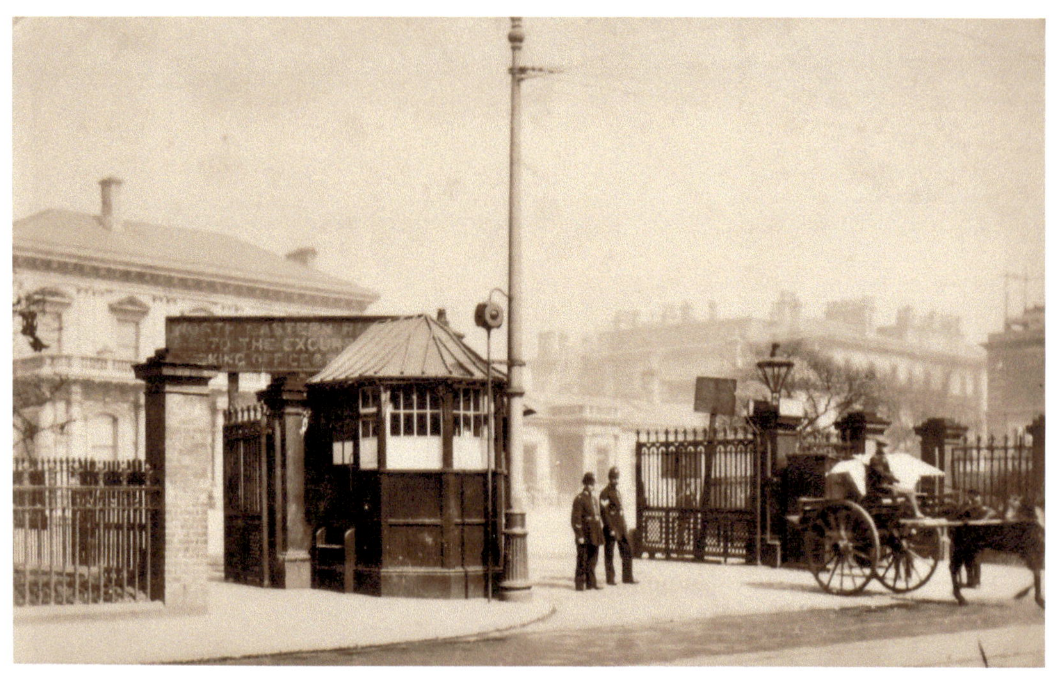

Hull Paragon Station

A horse-drawn carriage is seen leaving the exit which leads to Hull Paragon Railway Station, while a police officer and a police sergeant can be seen at the entrance gates. Part of the railway station is visible in the background in a view from Anlaby Road. The station was built between 1846 and 1848 for the York & North Midland Railway Co.; the station was enlarged in 1903. The Royal Station Hotel, which was built in 1849, is also visible. Parked cars now dominate the forecourt of the railway station.

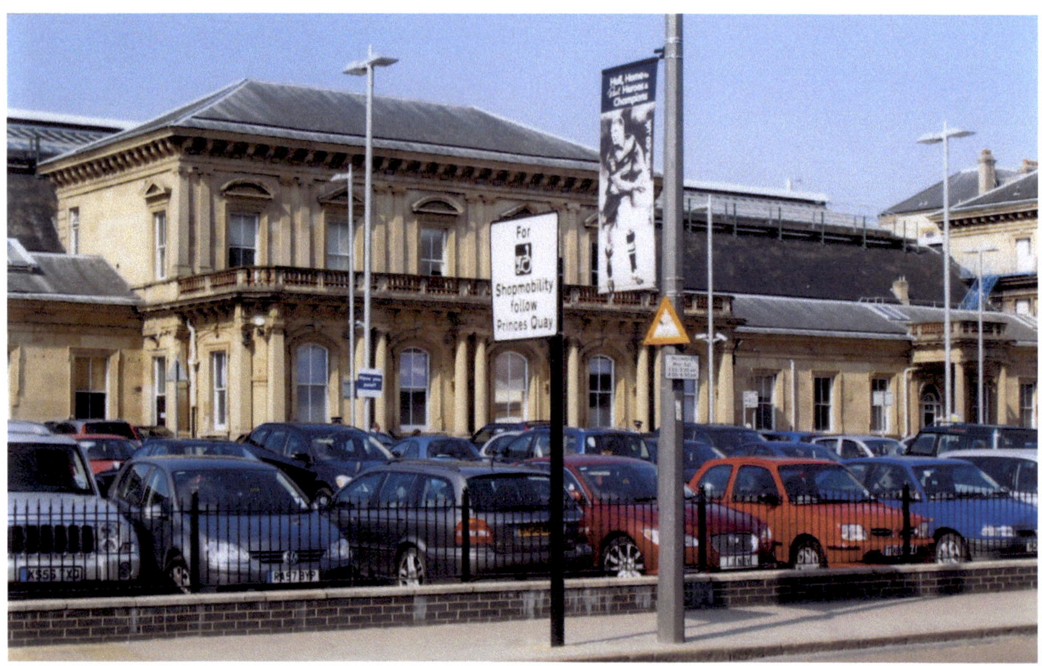

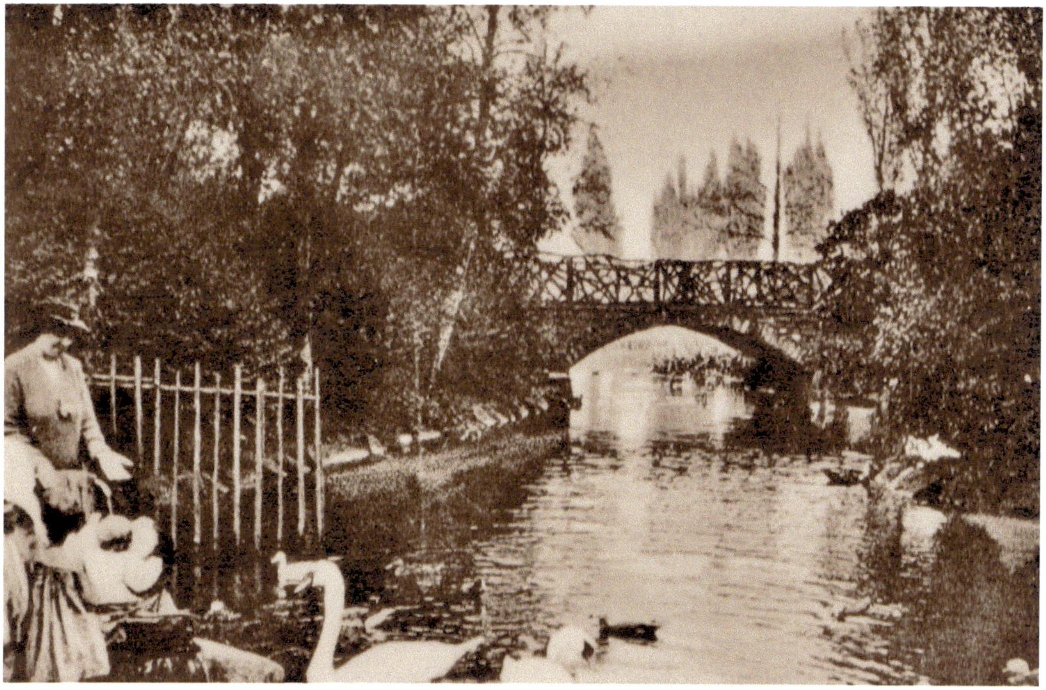

West Park

In 1885, the large site on Anlaby Road and Walton Street was opened as a park; this was to be known as West Park. Seen here is the boating lake, while feeding the ducks and swans was obviously a popular past time. The footbridge over the lake is seen in the background. In today's photograph, the lake is long gone, and visible is the narrow gauge railway. The author's two dogs are seen in the foreground, while in the background can be seen the aviary.

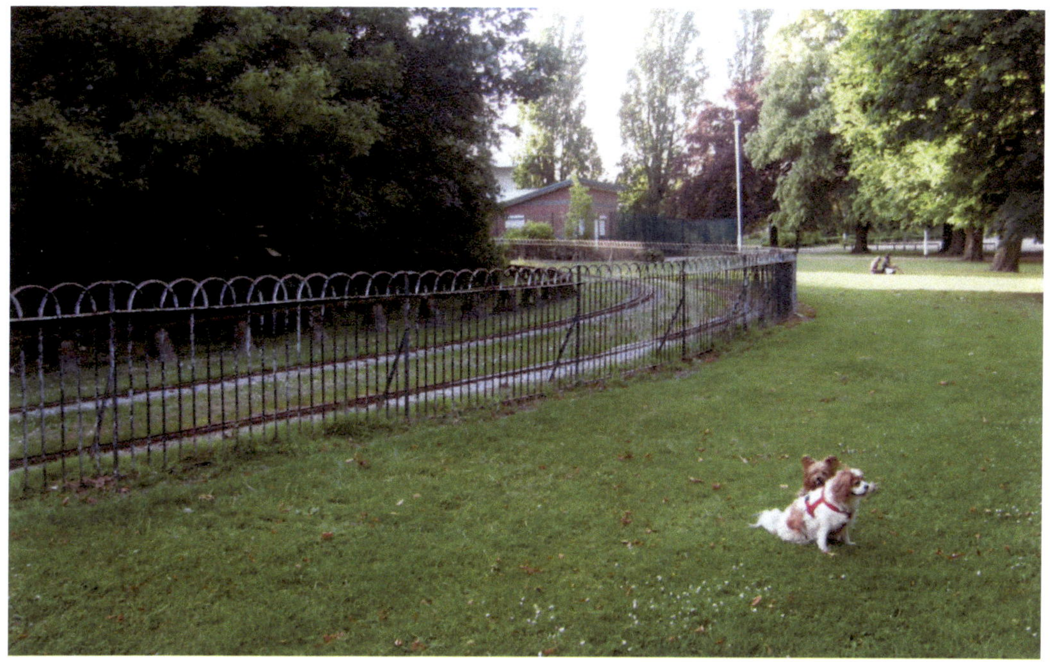

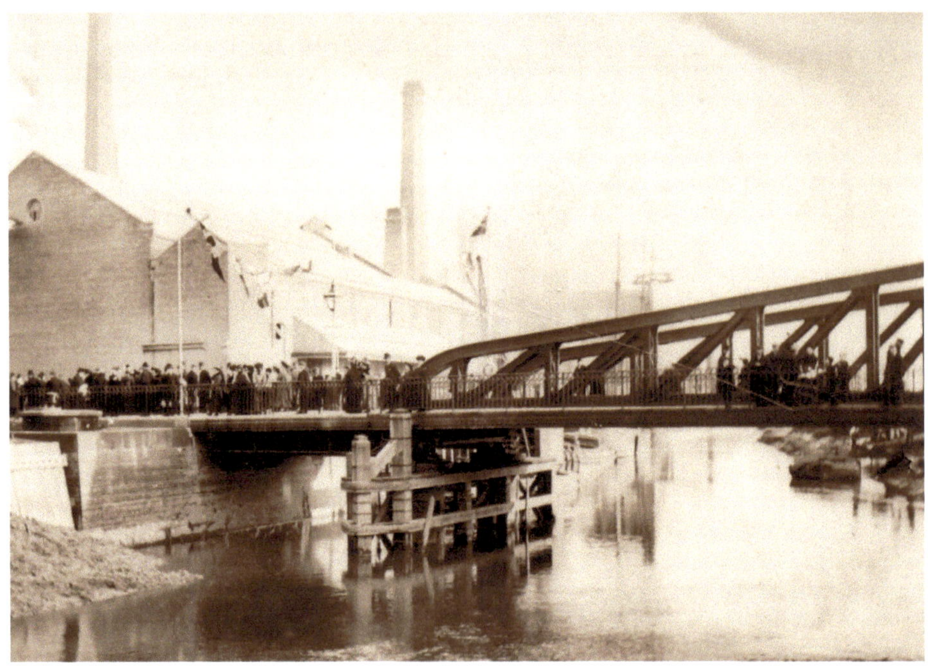

Stoneferry Bridge

In order to cross the River Hull at Stoneferry, it was necessary to take a small ferry. The Stoneferry Bridge was opened in 1905; this replaced the ferry. A large number of people are seen at the opening of the bridge. This narrow bridge, although adequate for horse pulled carts, soon became too narrow for modern day traffic. The old bridge lasted for eighty-six years and was replaced by this new ultra modern bridge, which is actually two separate bridges.

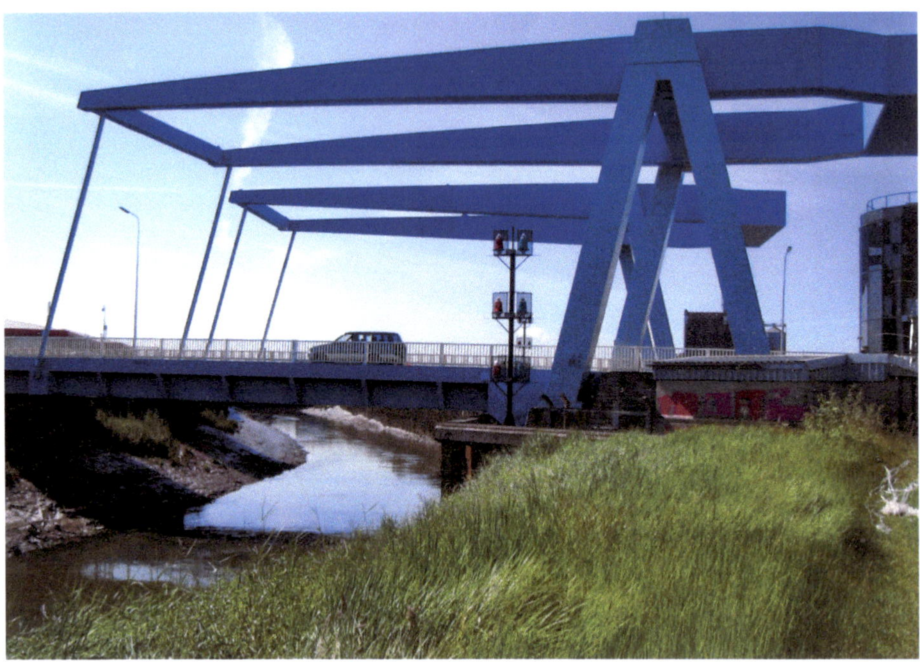

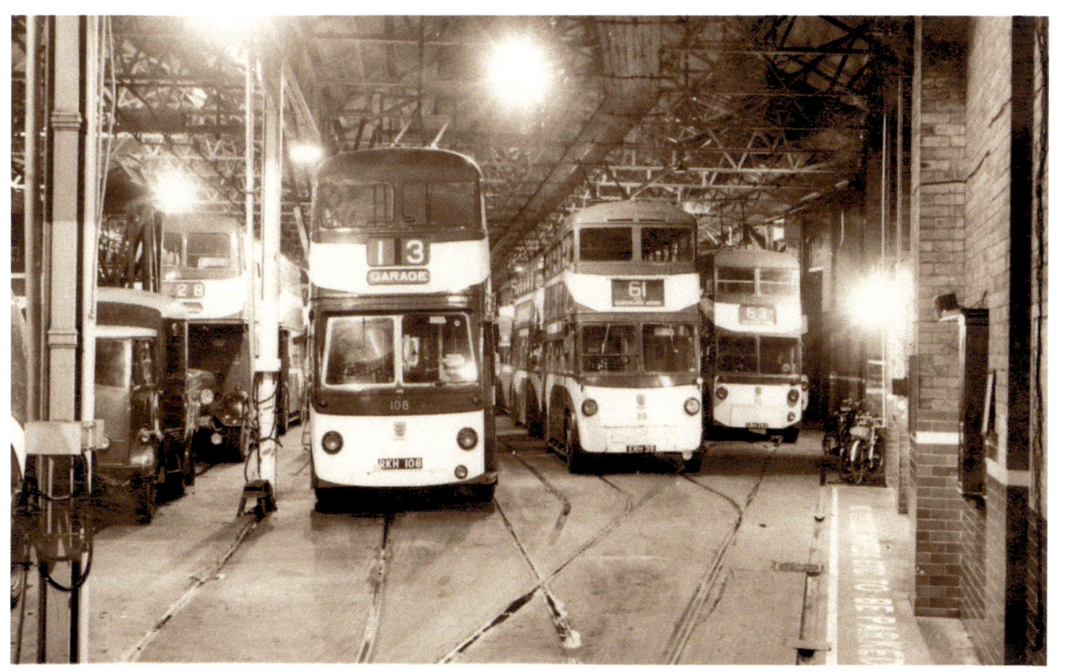

Cottingham Road Tram Depot

In 1909, the Cottingham Road tram depot opened. After the trams were withdrawn, this became a trolleybus and motorbus depot. Trolleybuses including a Coronation class are seen in this evening view, with half cab buses on the left. Note the tram tracks are still visible in the depot. Little now remains of the old tram depot except for the old Corporation Transport offices seen on the left. This site is now occupied by student houses and is named The Trees; each house is named after a different tree, such as Beech House etc.

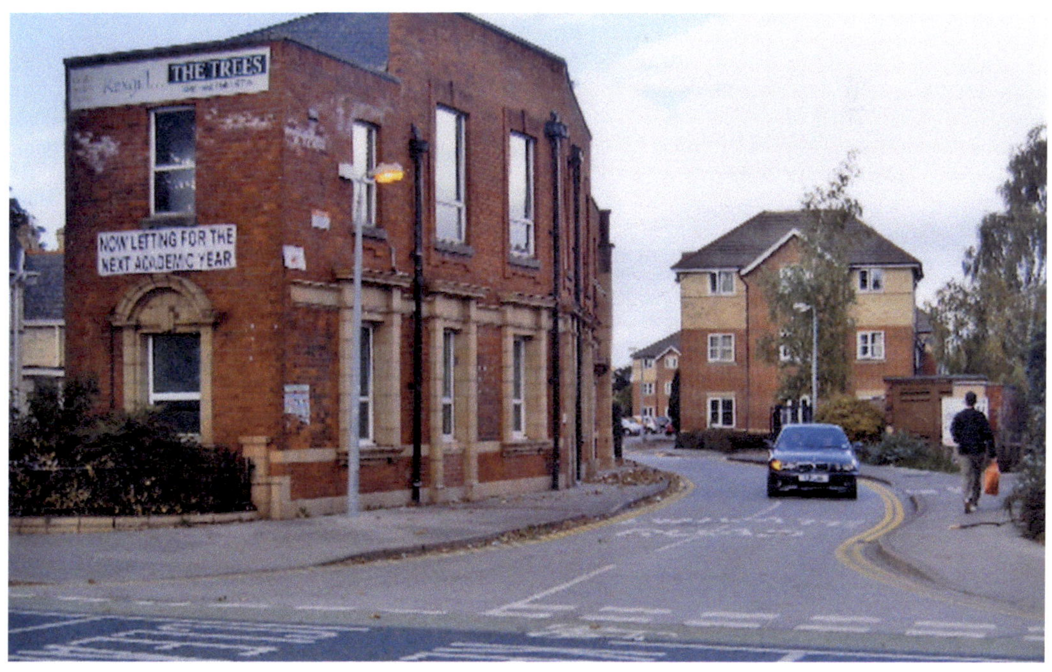

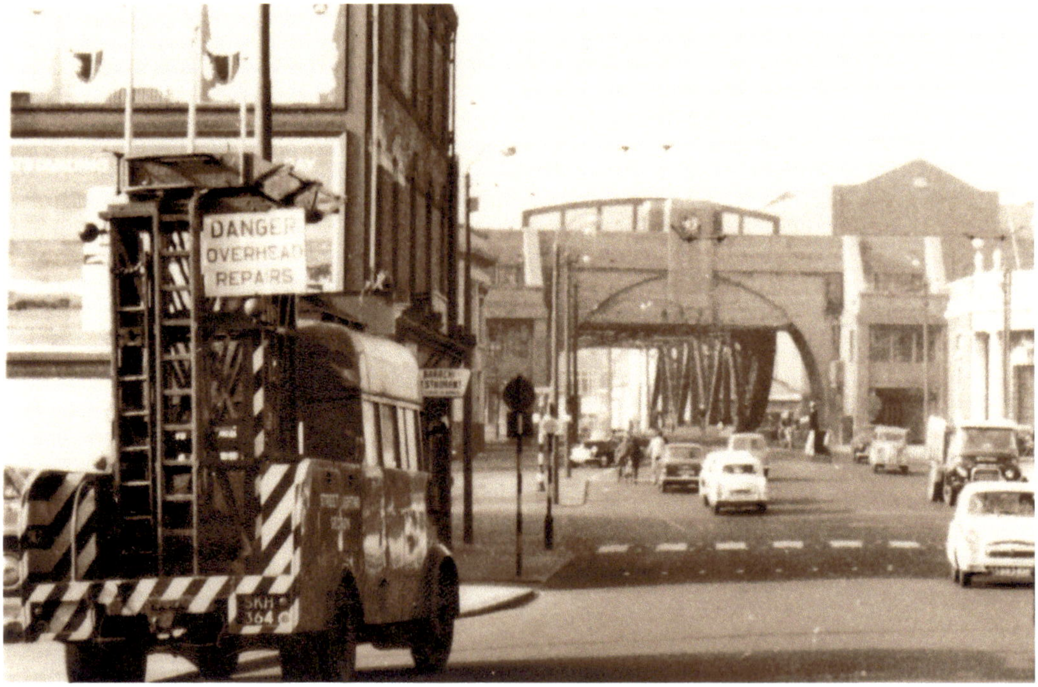

Witham and North Bridge

A Hull Corporation Transport street lighting section vehicle is seen on Holderness Road approaching North Bridge. This is an important bridge as it connects the city centre with Holderness Road and the villages to the east of the city. On the left can be seen Karrachi Restaurant. Note the policeman in the centre of the road on traffic duty. This busy area is now controlled by traffic lights. The Twilight public house is visible on the left.

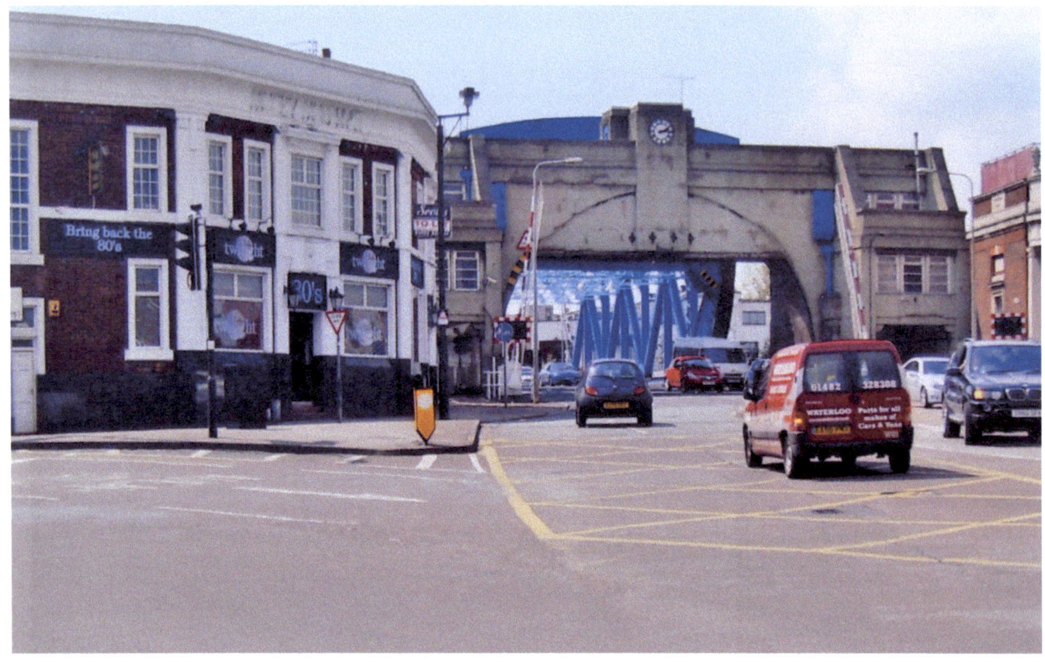

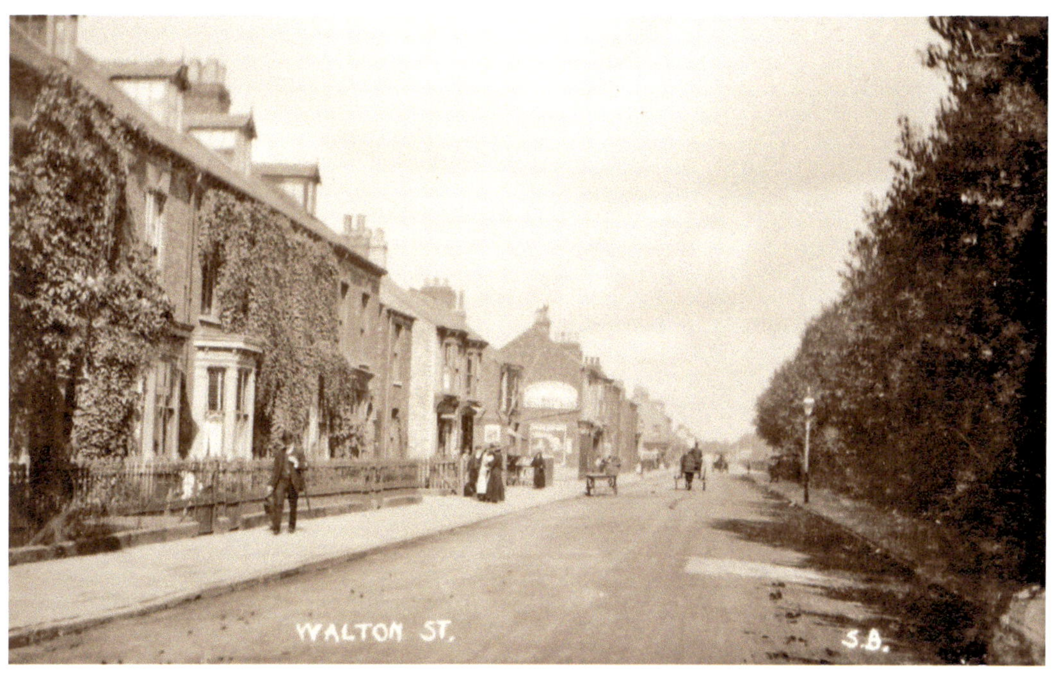

Walton Street

A late 1800s photograph, showing the tree-lined Walton Street, looking towards Spring Bank West, with several small corner shops visible. The site on the left is where Hull fair is situated in October. West Park would be to the near right of this photograph. Today, the area on the right is a car park, while many of the older houses visible in the upper photograph have been demolished and new houses built.

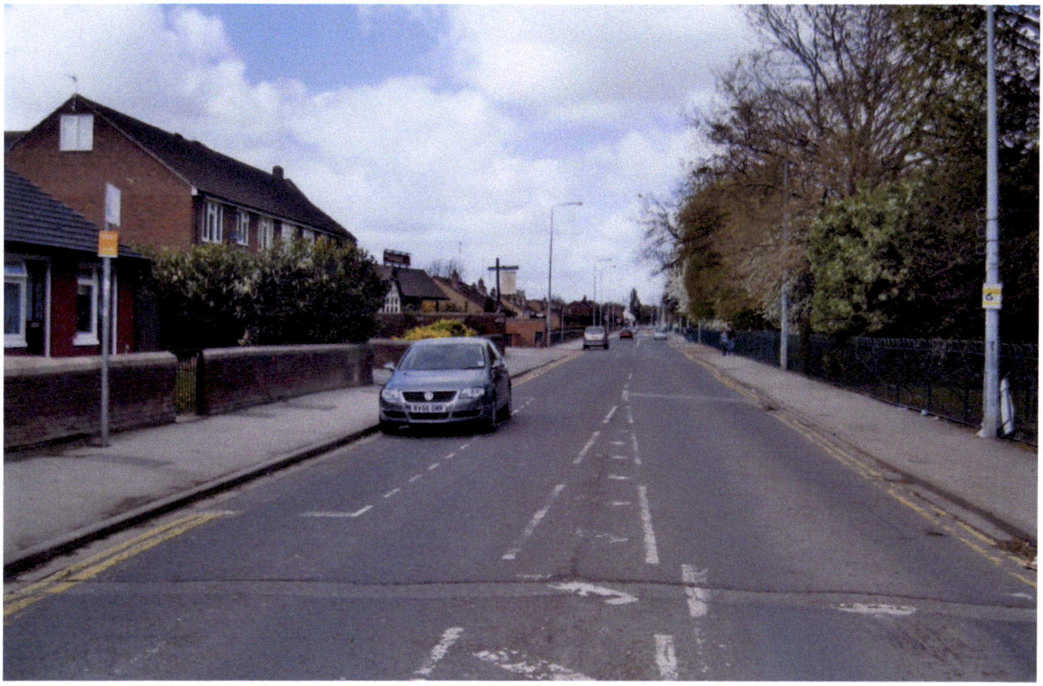

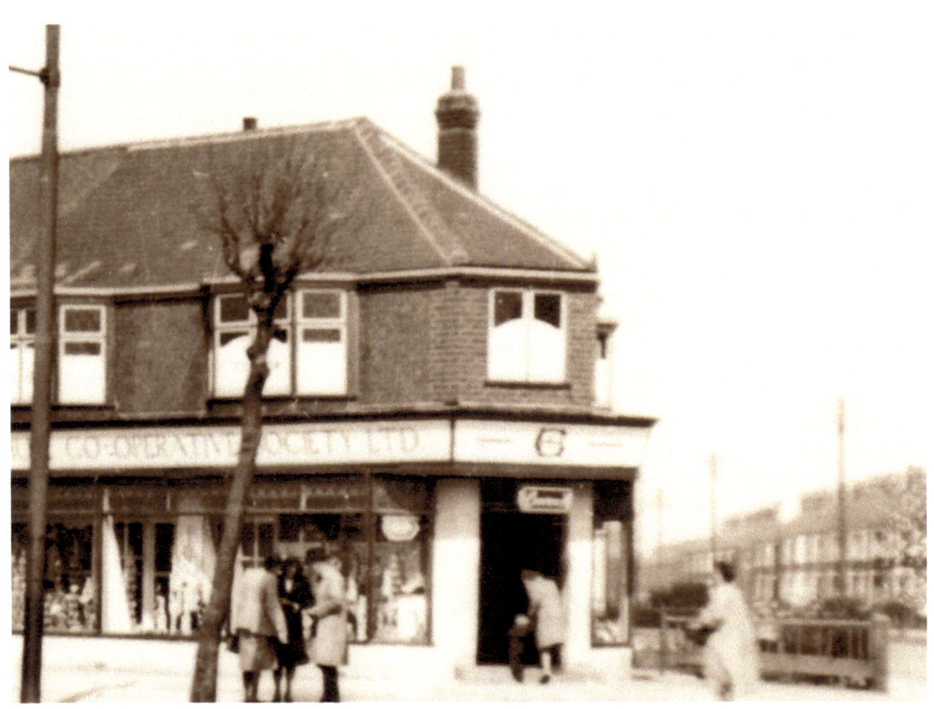

Co-operative Store Anlaby Road

The Hull & East Riding Co-operative Society stores were scattered throughout the city, offering a wide selection of food at reasonable prices and a divvy too. This one is situated on Anlaby Road at the corner of Meadowbank Road. Most of the stores closed in the 1970s and 1980s. Today, the Co-op store is The Floral Lounge, a ladies' hairdresser.

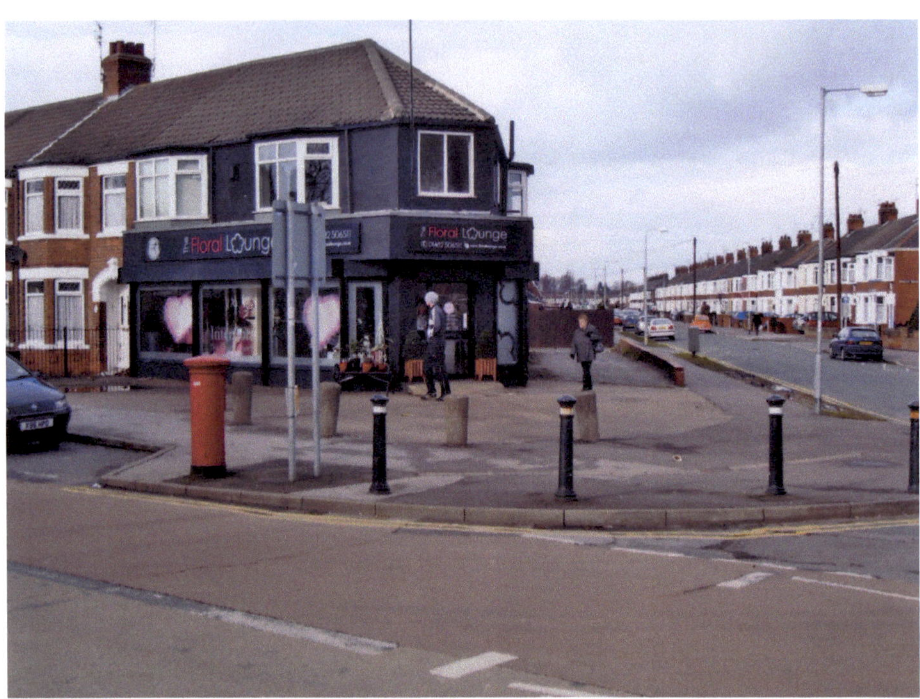

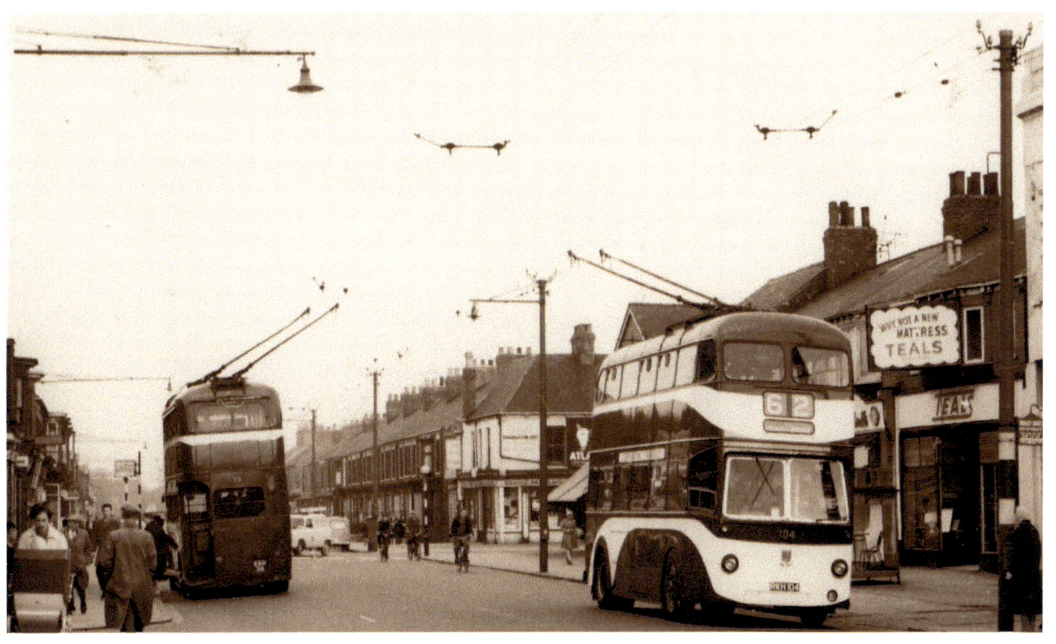

Newland Avenue

A Coronation class trolleybus is seen on Newland Avenue on the 62 service heading back to the city centre, while a much earlier rear entrance trolleybus is seen heading up Newland Avenue. Teals bedding shop can be seen on the right. Alexandra Road is just visible on the right past the trolleybus. Newland Avenue is now a very busy road which can be seen in the modern day photograph. Teals is now St Andrew's Children's Hospice shop.

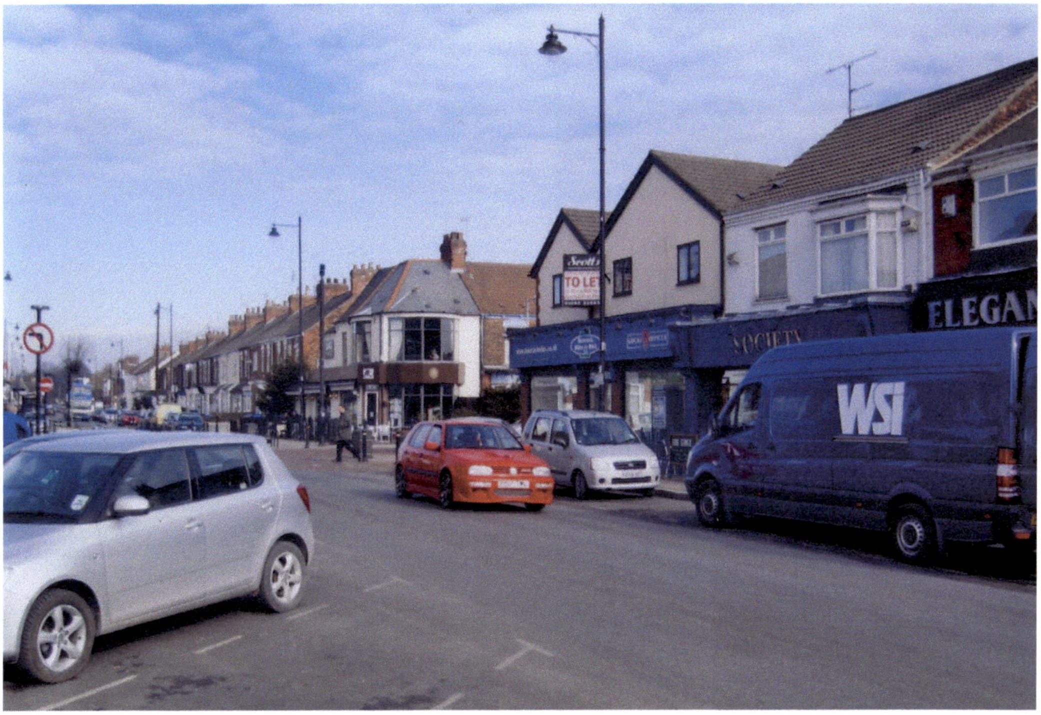

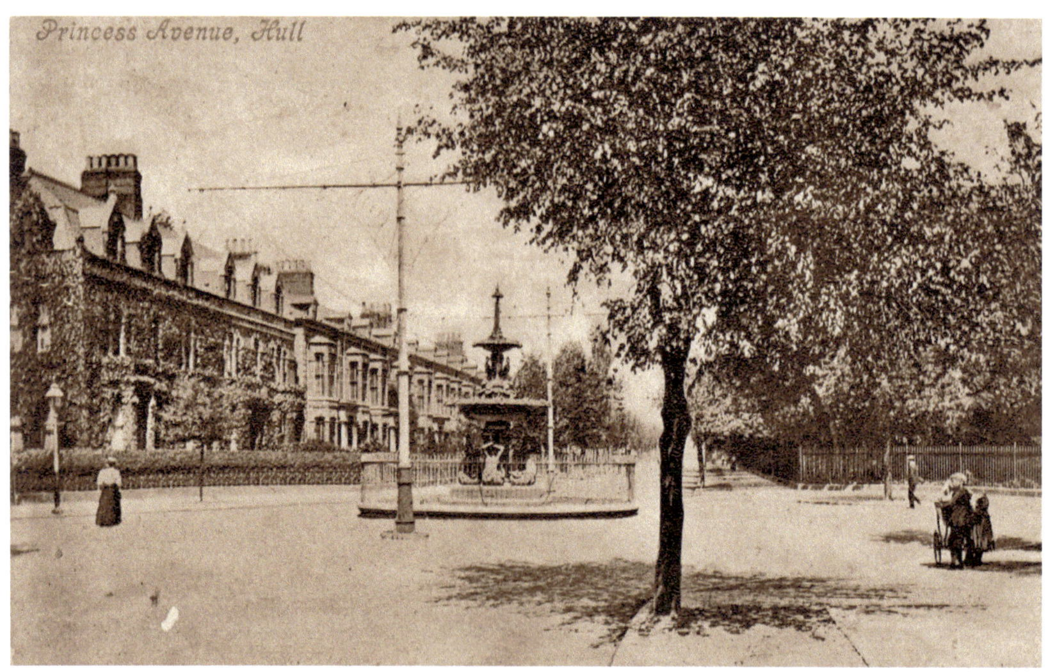

Prince's Avenue

The very elaborate ornamental water fountain is a feature down a number of the Avenues down Prince's Avenue. This one opposite Westbourne Avenue was in the centre of the road facing the Pearson's Park entrance. People had no worries about walking in the centre of the road, as the lady is doing. The water fountain in the present day photograph has gone, but little else has changed. The houses in the background in the upper photograph are still there and have changed very little.

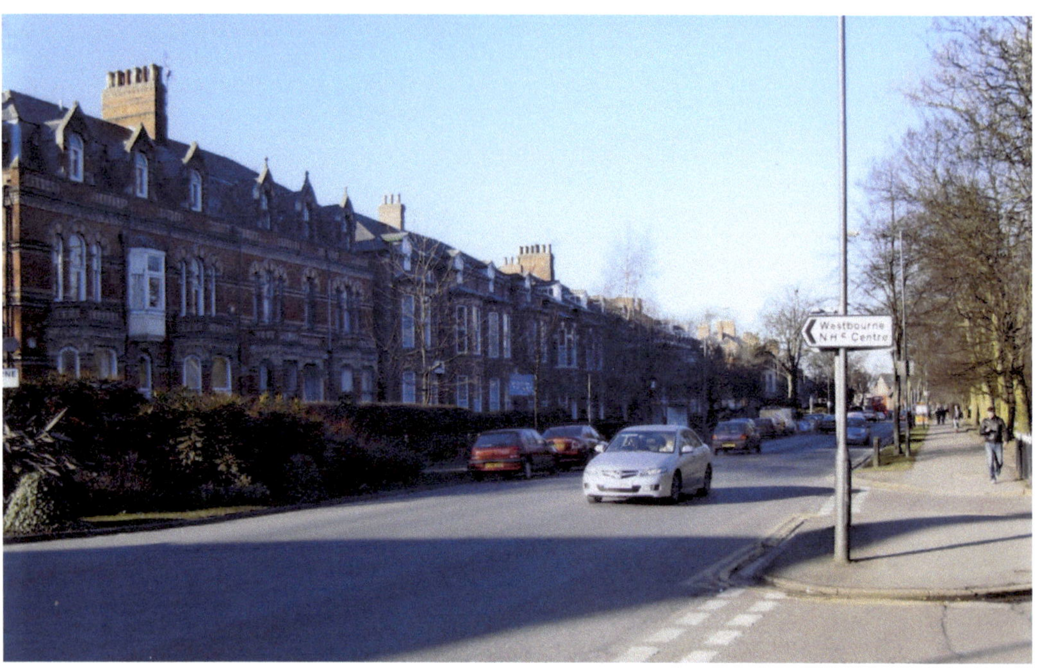

Beverley Road and Endike Lane

Beverley Road is the main road out of Hull city centre heading north for Beverley, York, Newcastle and Scotland. This photograph, taken in the early 1960s, is at the junction of Endike Lane. This was once the terminus for the 63 trolleybus service; later the service 18 motorbus service replaced the trolleybus route. Very little has changed in this later view, except the trolleybus wires have long gone. Also visible is the bus lane. The zebra crossing has now been replaced by traffic lights.

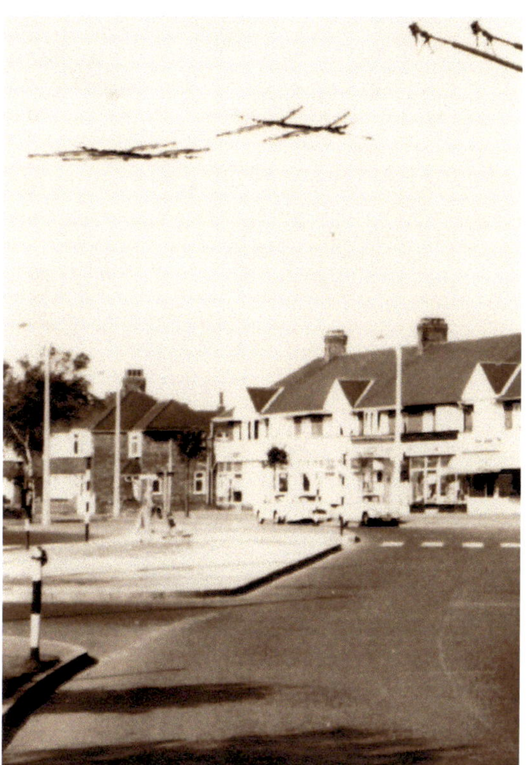

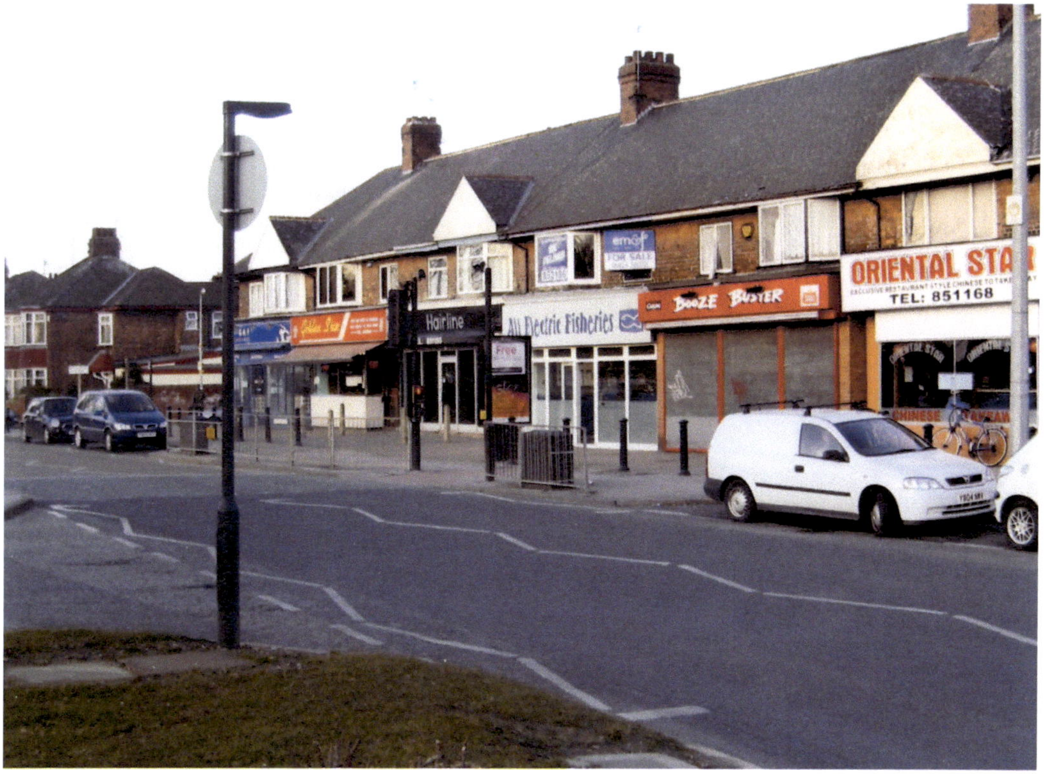

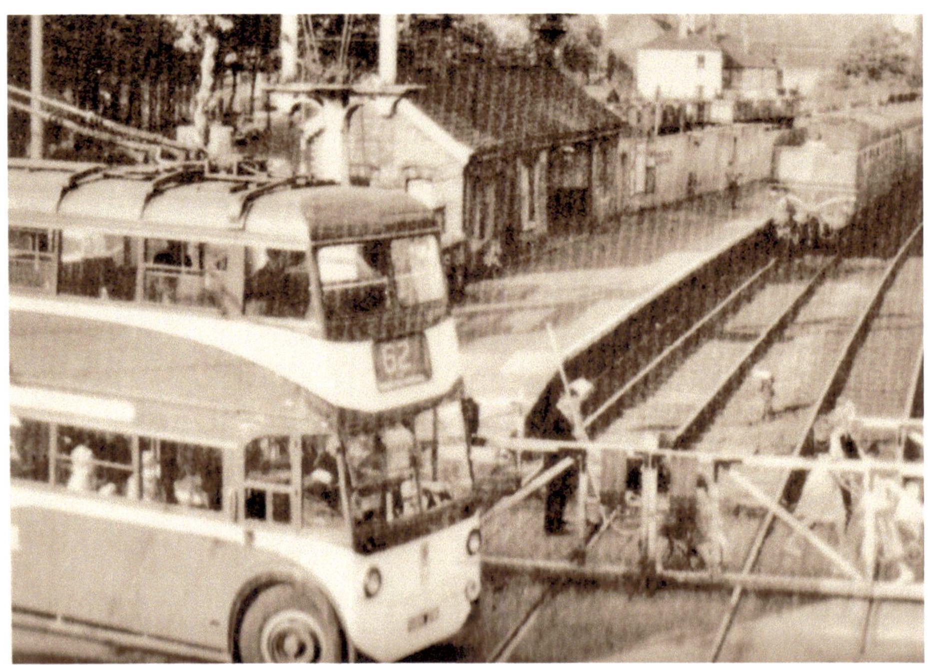

Botanic Gardens Level Crossings

This is an interesting scene at the Botanic level crossings. This is at the junction of Spring Bank and Prince's Avenue. A Hull Corporation trolleybus is seen on the 62 service returning to Hull city centre, while at the station is a Diesel Multiple Unit (DMU). At one time hundreds of passengers would catch trains from this station to Hornsea or Withernsea. The scene at the same location shows no resemblance to the top photograph. Gone is the trolleybus, the level crossings, the station and the train. The Zoological public house now stands on this site.

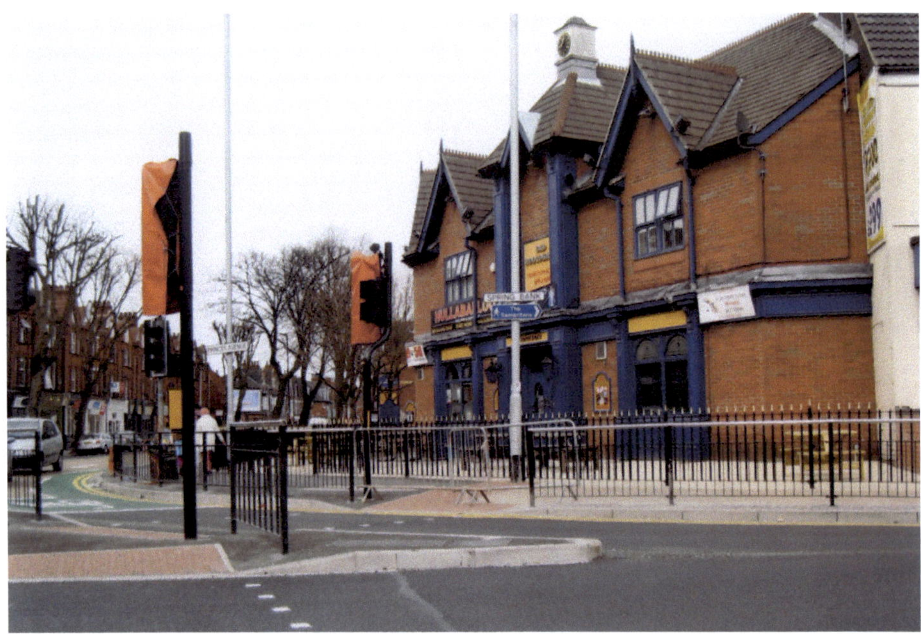

Chanterlands Avenue Railway Bridge

A freight train can be seen crossing the Hull and Barnsley overhead railway bridge on Chanterlands Avenue. The railway lines were built on embankments which did away with the need of level crossings which crossed the main roads. The freight train would have come off the main line and is heading to the docks. The road dipped under this bridge and this area is flooded quite regularly. Murrayfield Road is on the right just by the tree. In the present photograph the houses on the right are now shops, and the building on the corner of Murrayfield Road is now Ken Ellerker cycles. A sign of the times is the graffiti on the bridge.

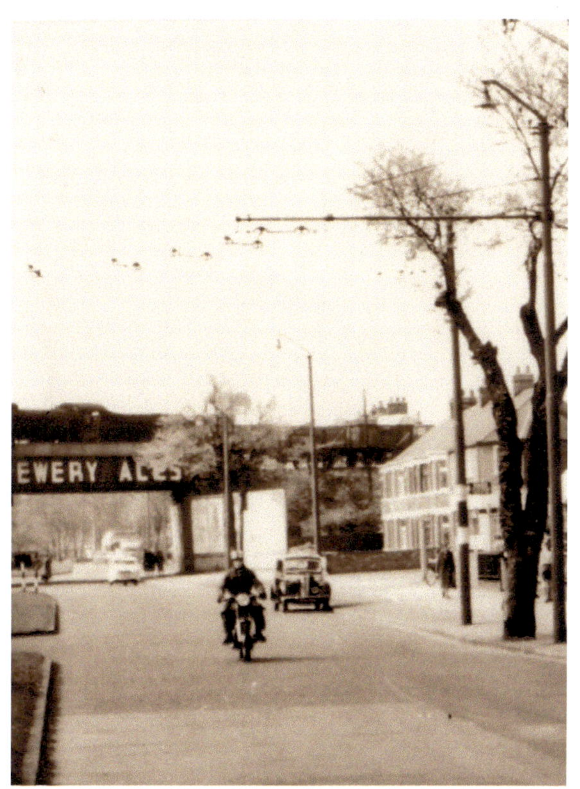

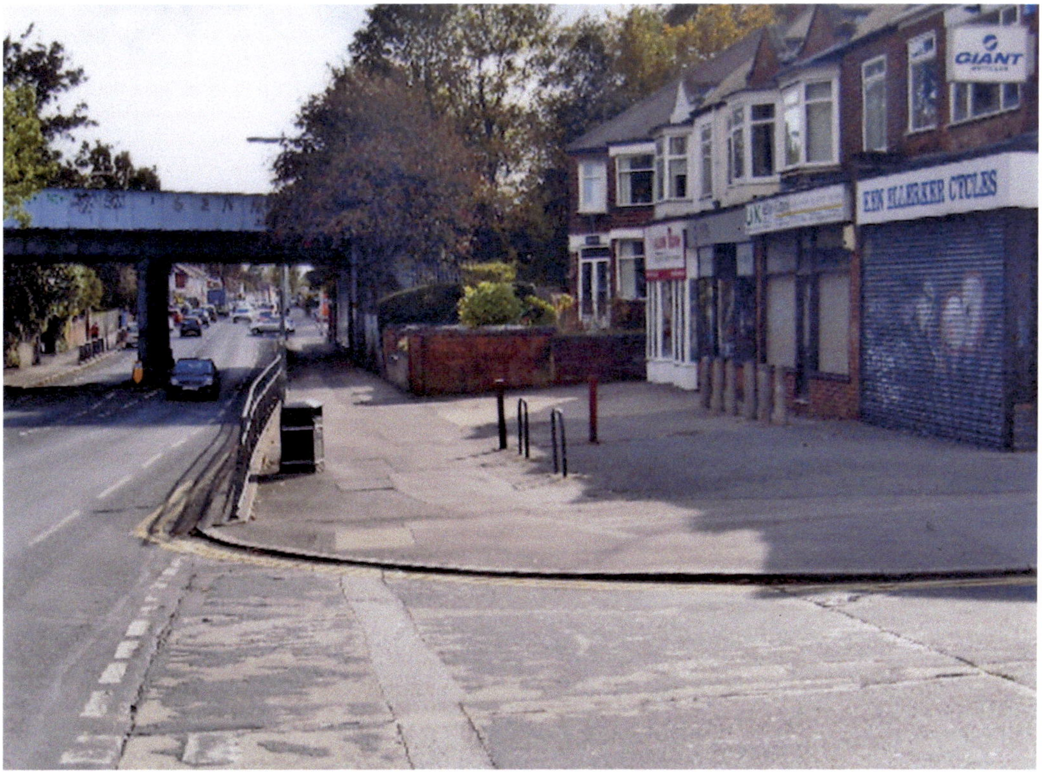

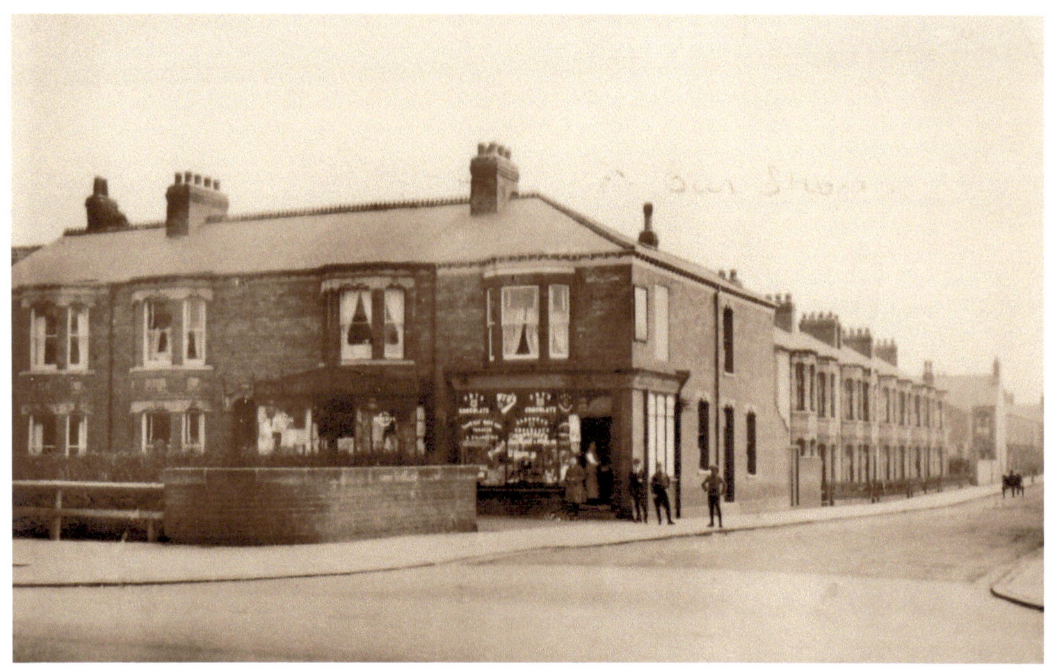

Falmouth Street

The small corner shops were to be found on most street corners of the terraced houses, selling a large variety of groceries, cigarettes and chocolate. This one is at the corner of Cottingham Road and Falmouth Street. Note the drain running in front of these houses on Cottingham Road, once a common sight. Today the local shop is now a student accommodation office, as is the shop next door. The drain has now been filled in, while Falmouth Street is now a dead-end street.

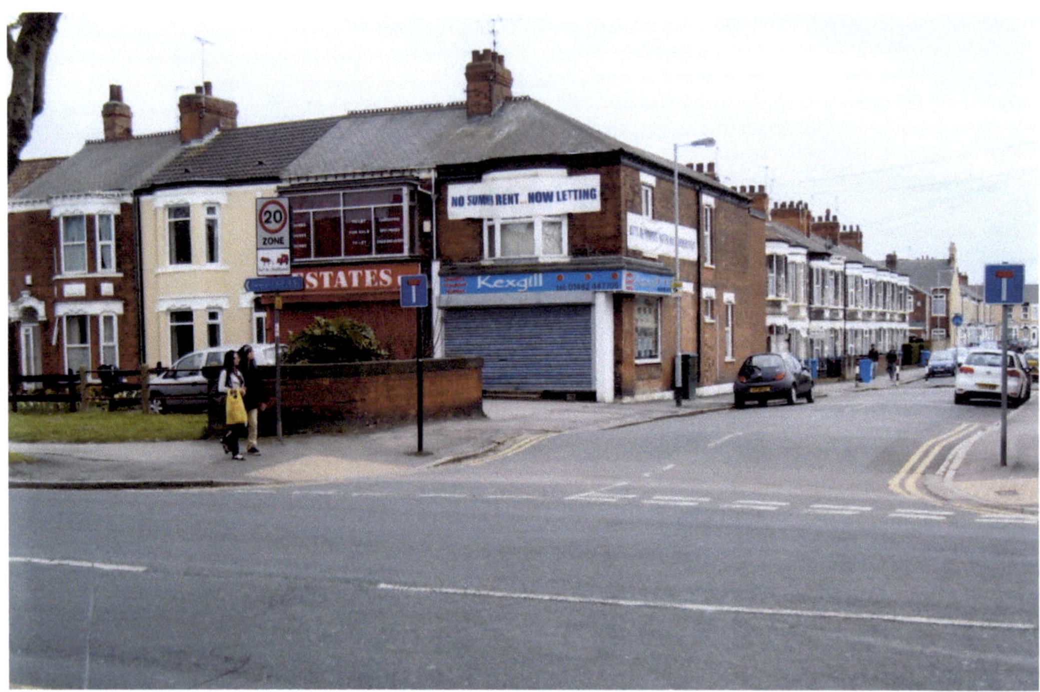

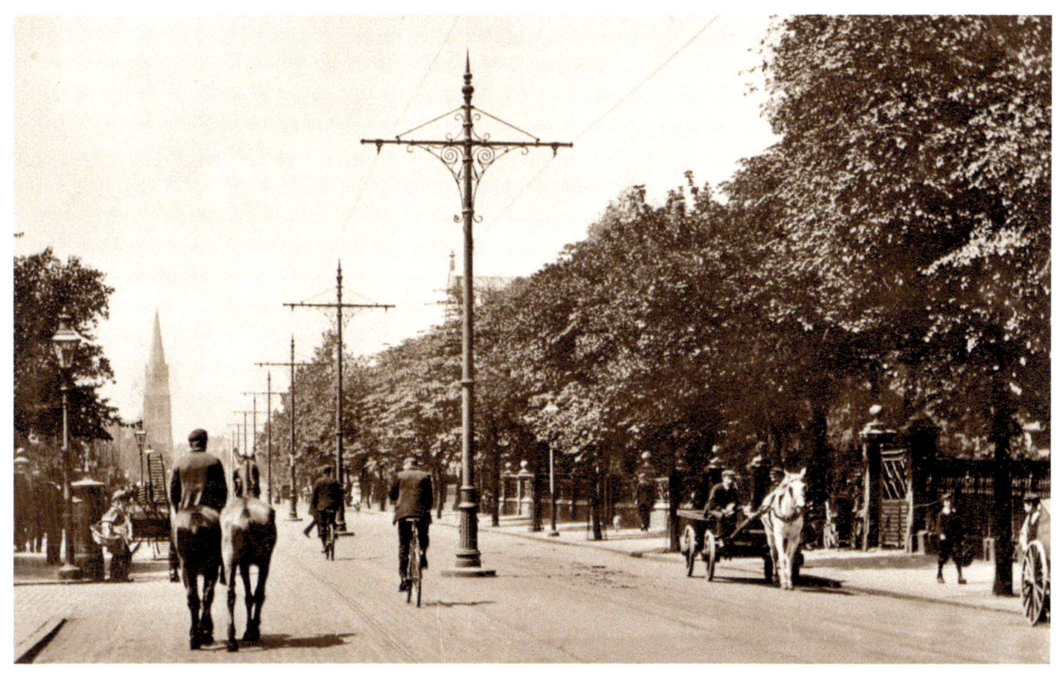

Anlaby Road Looking West

Anlaby Road, at the beginning of the twentieth century, looking west. Anlaby Road at this time was one of the elite areas of Hull with the trees lining both sides of the road. Pedestrians are able to stand in the middle of the quiet road and pose for the photographer. St Matthew's church can be seen in the distance. All the large houses which once stood on the right were demolished many years ago.

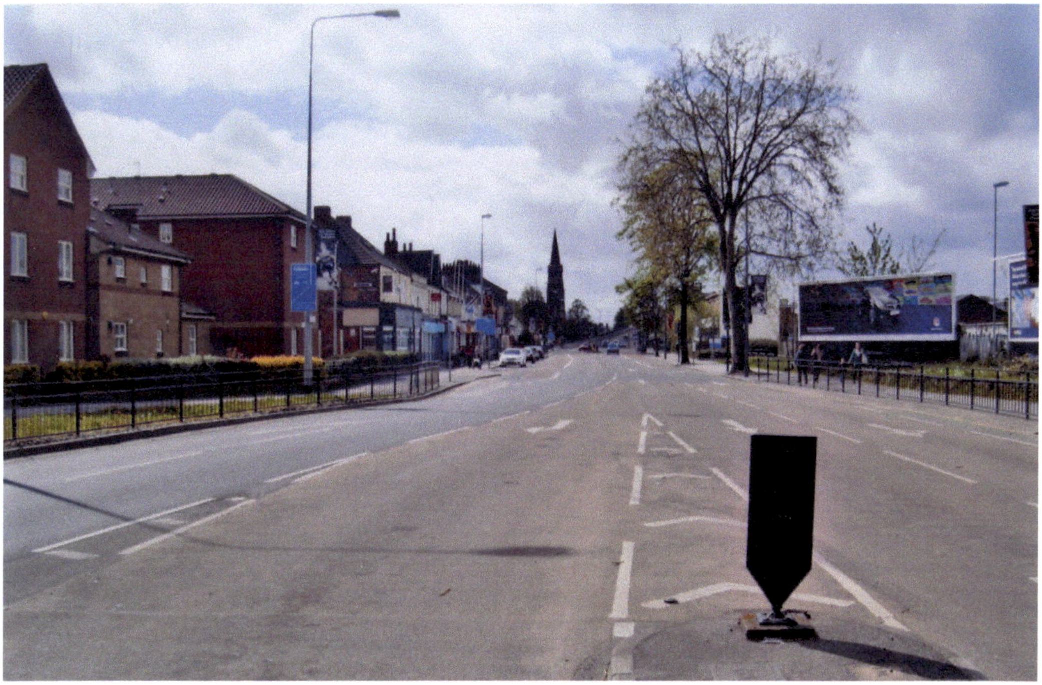

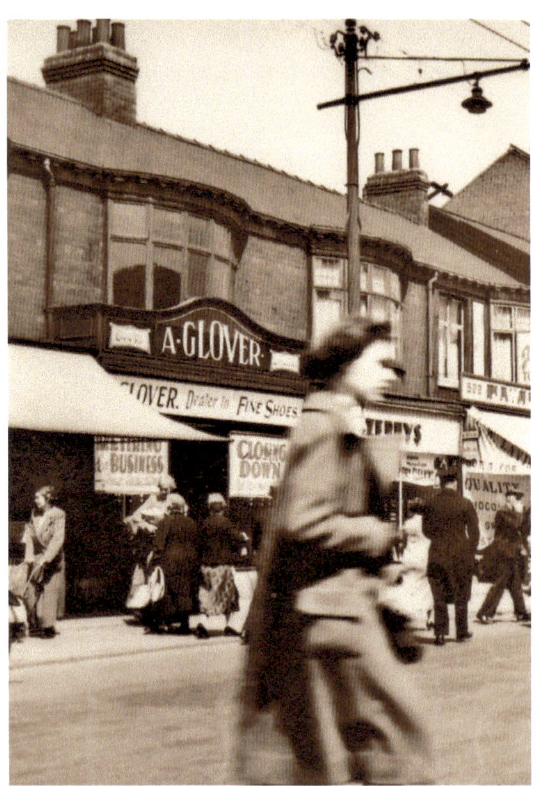

Hessle Road Shops

Hessle Road was, and still is, a thriving road, with a good selection of shops. A youngish woman is seen crossing the road, with several shops in the background, including A. Glover, dealer in fine shoes, which is closing down. Next to this on the right is Zeryns, while No. 522 Hessle Road is a chocolate, sweets and tobacco shop. Note the absence of TV aerials in the upper photograph. Some things do not change and in today's photograph of 522 Hessle Road it is still a newsagent. A sign of the times is the shutters on the shop fronts.

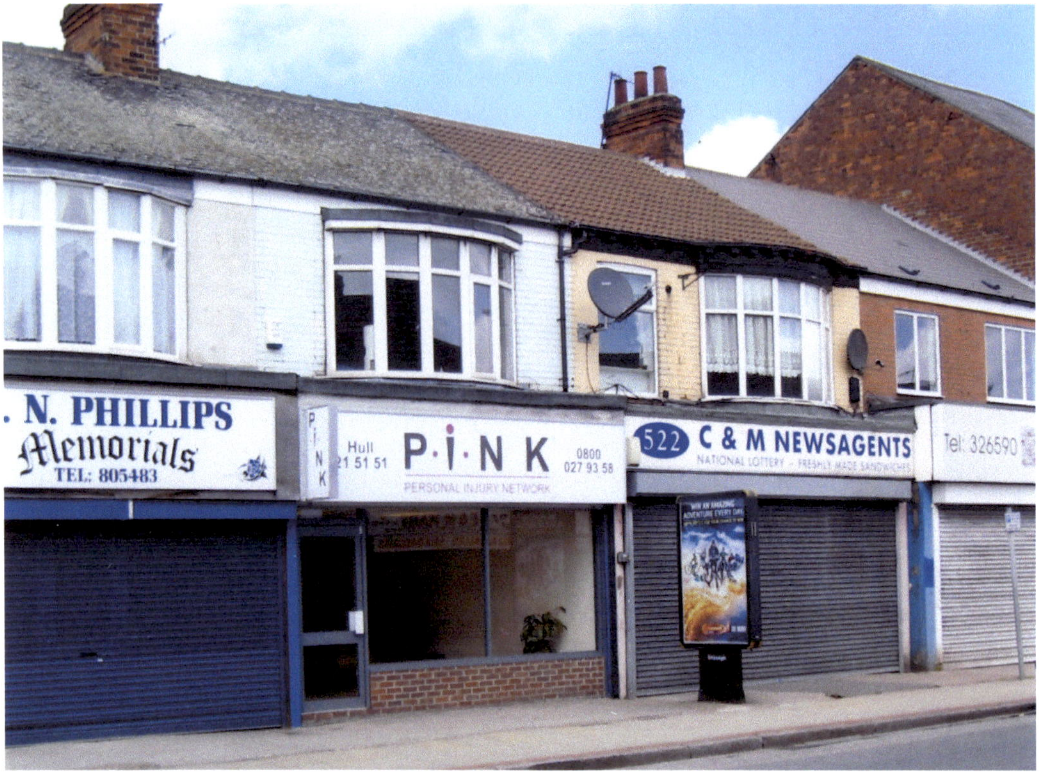

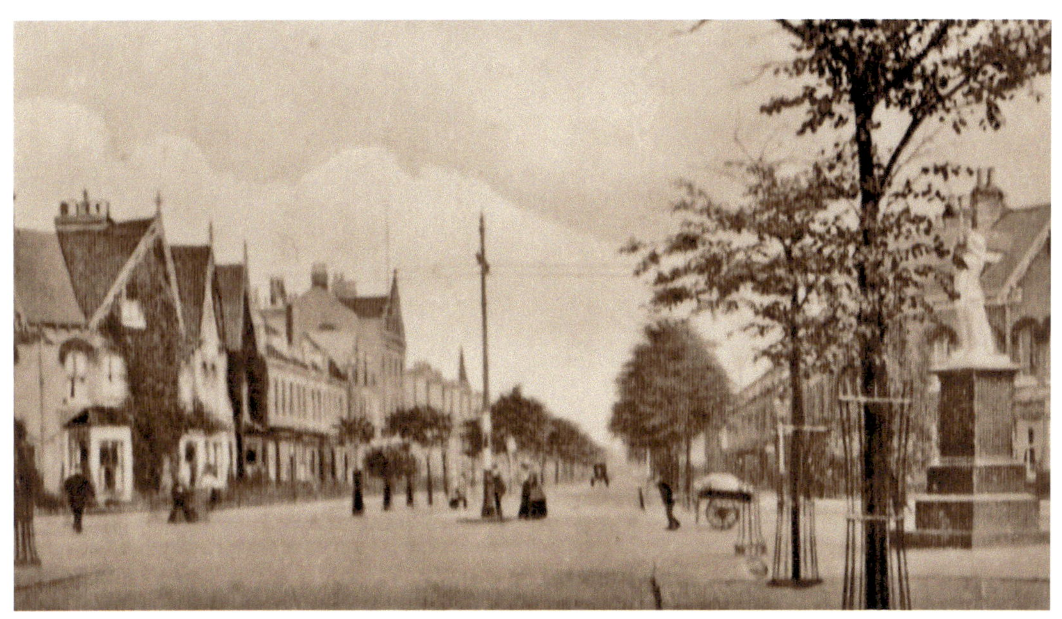

The tree-lined wide road of the Boulevard is clearly visible in this photograph. At one time the wealthier people of Hull lived in this area, including sea captains. In this photograph is the Fisherman's Memorial statue; this is a sculpture of Captain George Smith of the trawler the *Crane*. This memorial was also dedicated to Walter Whelpton, skipper of the *Ming*, who later died on 13 May 1905. The monument was erected in 1905. The inscription also names the others who lost their lives in the North Sea by the action of the Russian Baltic fleet on 22 October 1904.

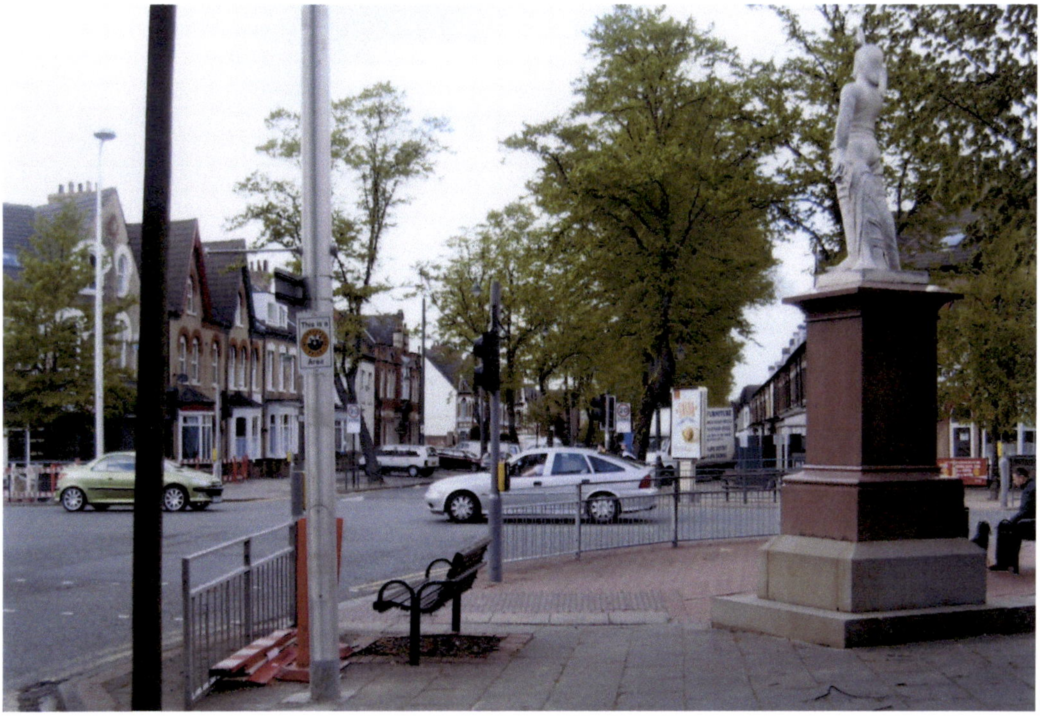

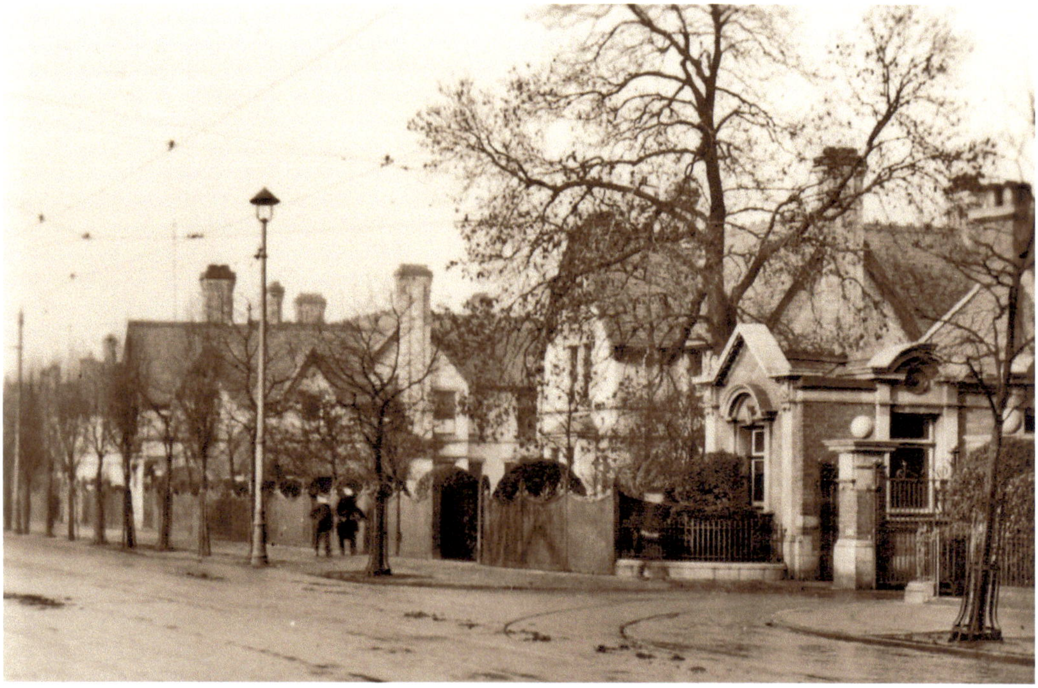

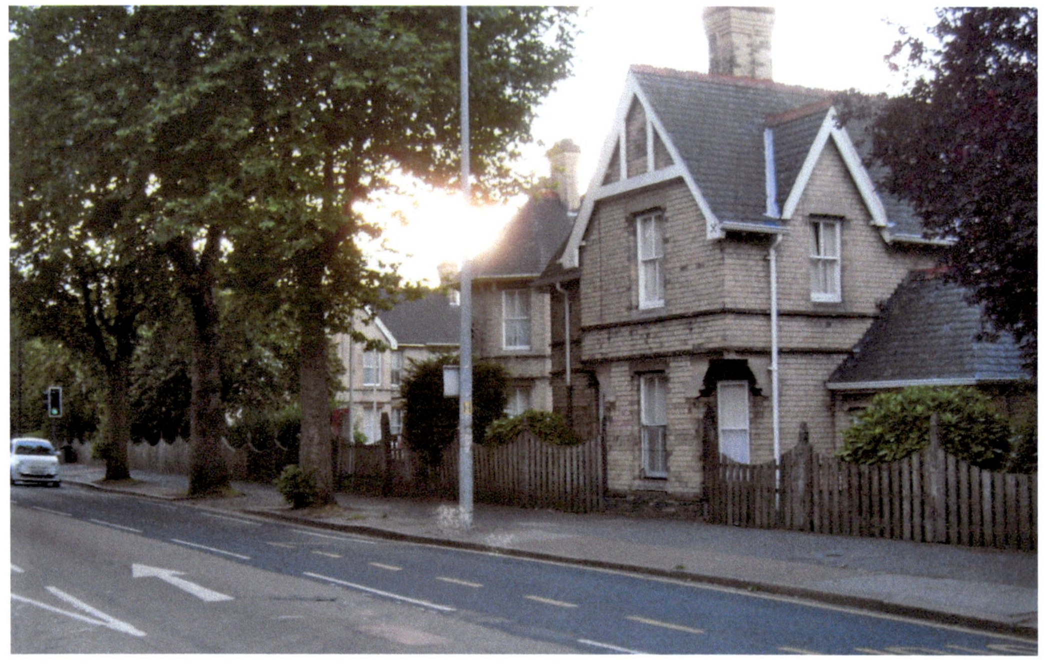

Sailors' Children's Home

The Sailors' Families Society was established in 1821. The houses of the Newland orphanage on Cottingham Road were built in the late 1800s and early 1900s. A number of the houses are seen in this photograph; the one nearest is East Lodge, then Hannah Pickard house (1895), Buxton Brown house (1895) and then Sir James Reckitt house (1896). Also in the grounds was its own school, St Nicholas School. Today, the houses are used to accommodate students.

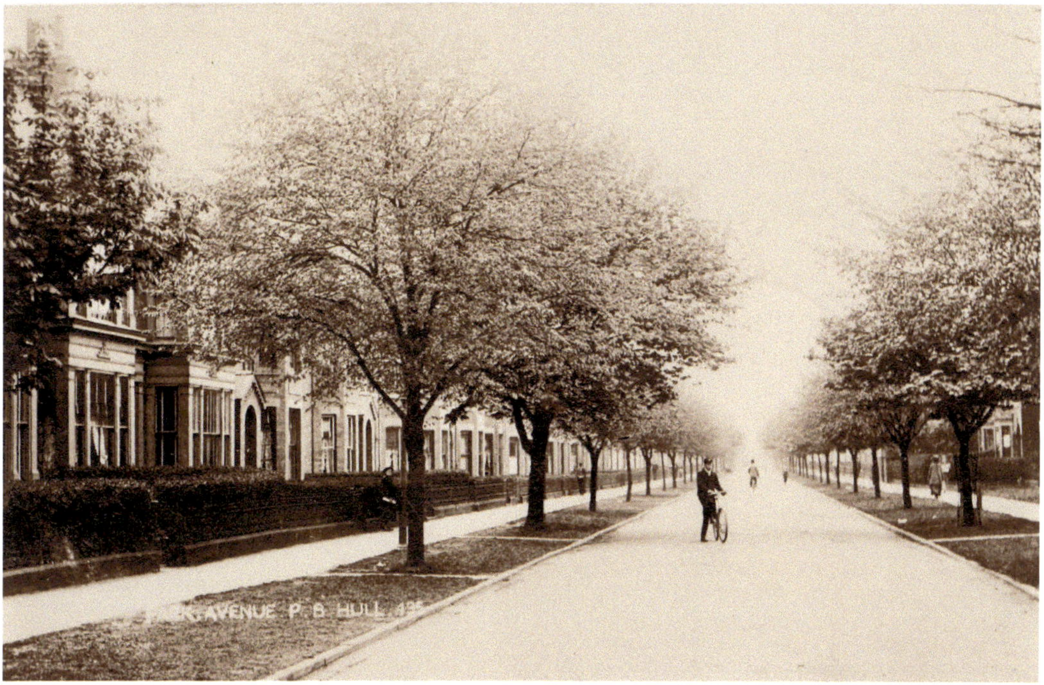

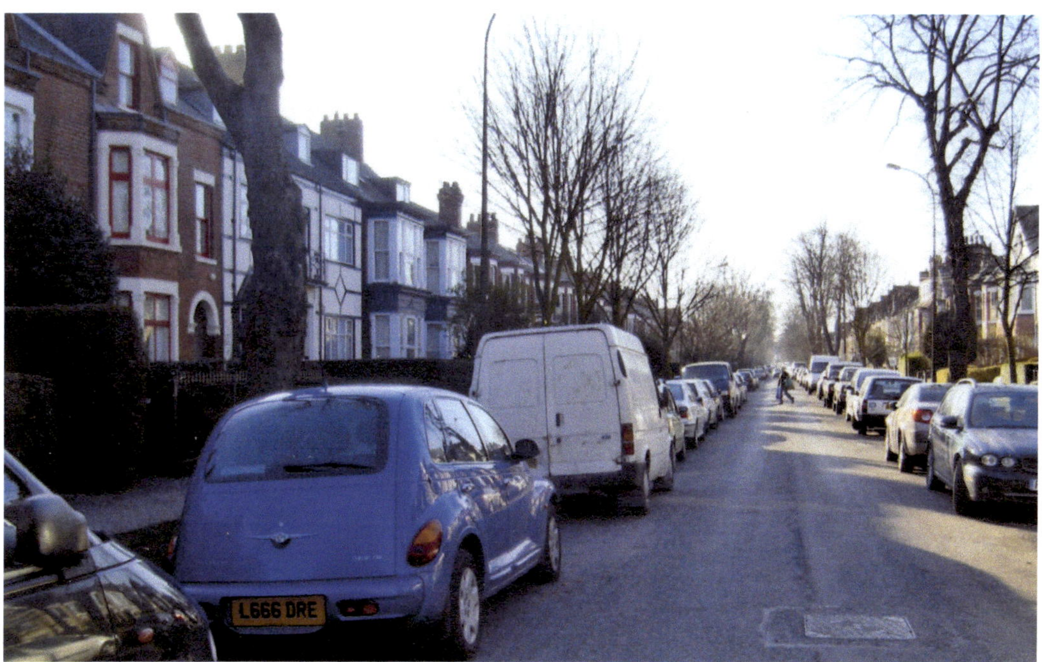

Park Avenue

Once the very elite areas of Hull were the Avenues of Prince's Avenue; these were Victoria Avenue, Park Avenue and Westbourne Avenue, with the very large houses visible in this photograph. This photograph, taken at the beginning of the 1900s, shows Park Avenue with trees either side of the road. A young man poses with his bicycle in the middle of the road. Although perhaps not as elite as it used to be, the Avenues still look splendid and little has changed in over 100 years.

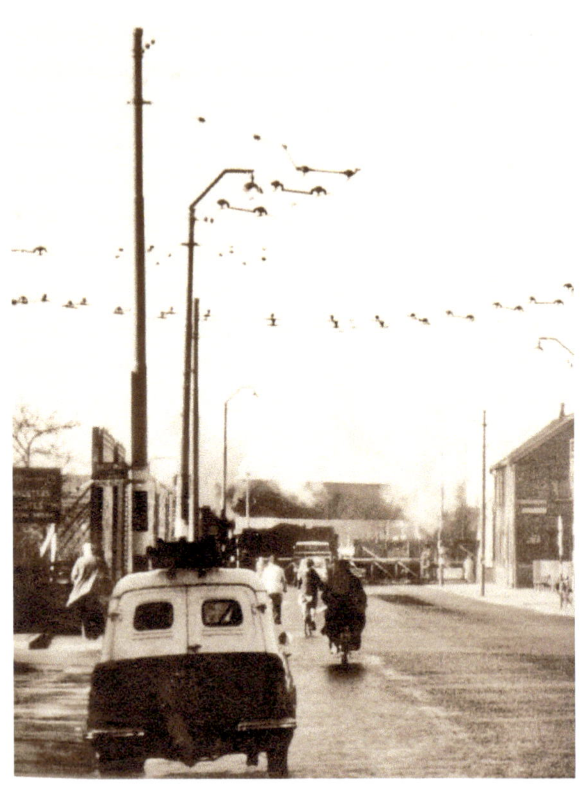

Hessle Road Level Crossing

Up to the 1960s the main railway line into and out of Hull to Sheffield, Manchester, and London etc. had to cross two main roads; these were Anlaby Road and Hessle Road. Railway level crossings had long been a feature of the traffic scene in Hull, which caused delays for the road user as seen in this photograph, waiting for a train to pass by at Hessle Road level crossings. Today, road users use the flyover which eliminates the need to wait for the train to pass. Since the building of the flyover, Hessle Road now detours to the left as is visible in today's photograph.

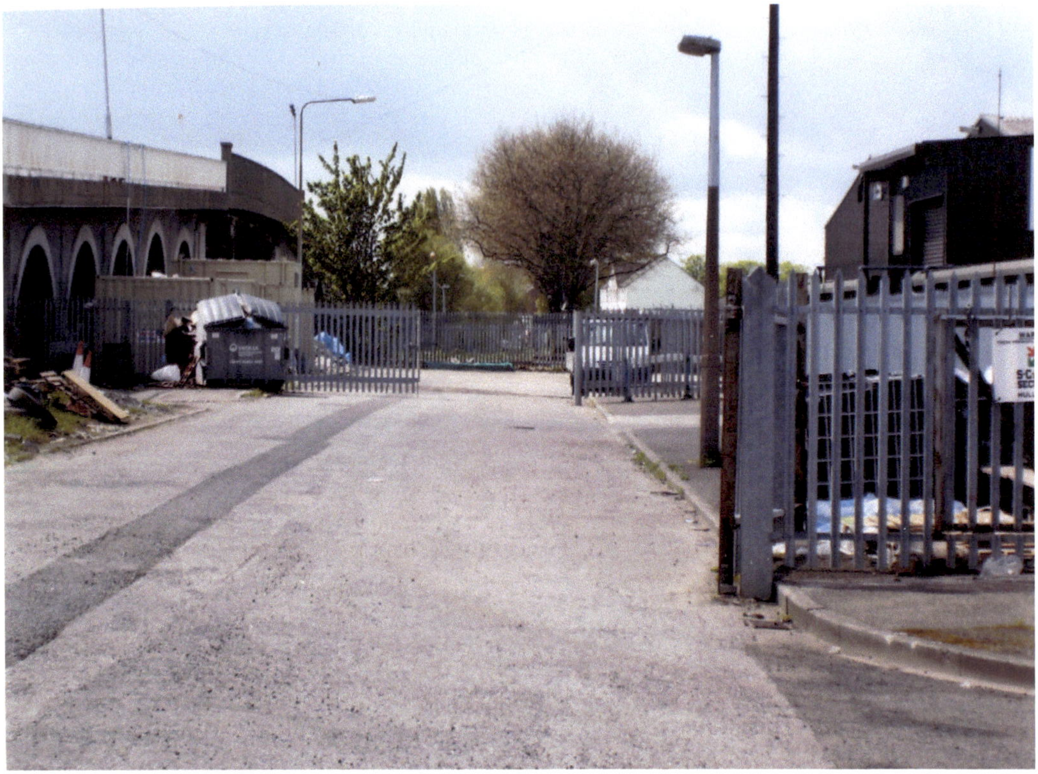

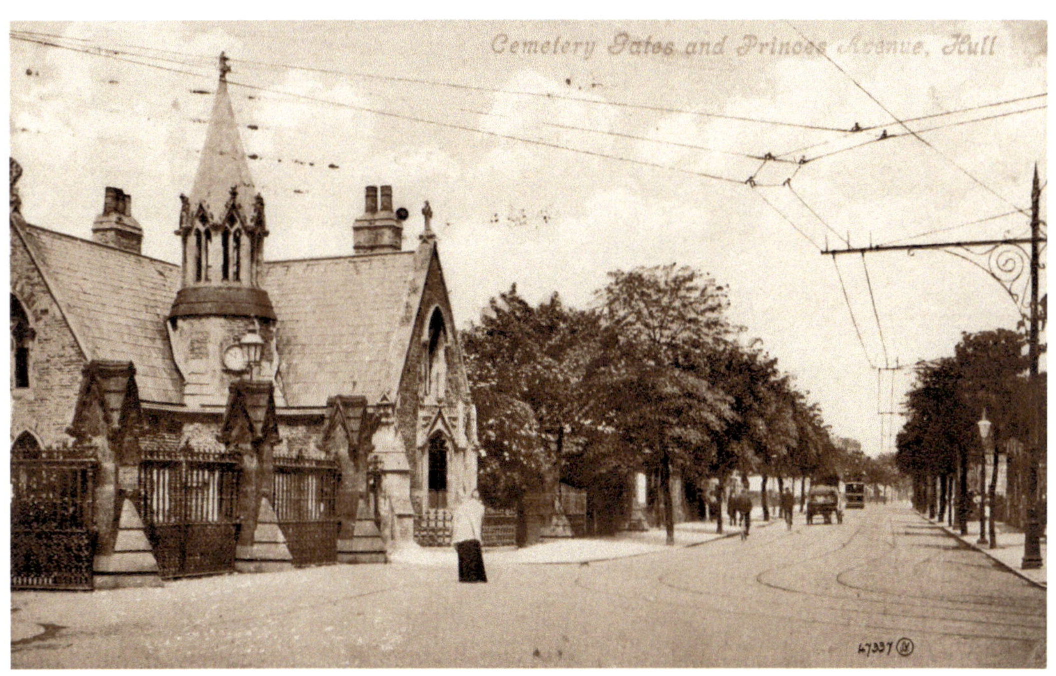

Prince's Avenue Looking North

This is a *c.* 1905 photograph, looking up Prince's Avenue from Spring Bank. Visible are the tramlines and on the left are the old impressive cemetery gates. Botanic railway station is on the right of the early picture. In the present photograph, the cemetery gates, long since demolished, have been replaced by buildings and shops. Traffic lights now control this busy junction; it would be hard these days to walk in the middle of Prince's Avenue.

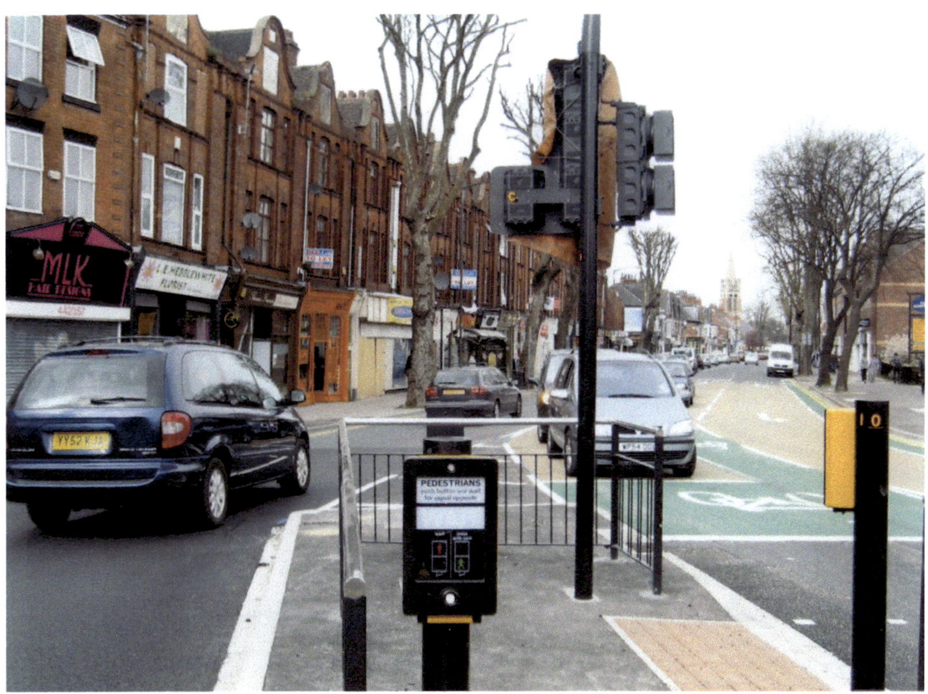

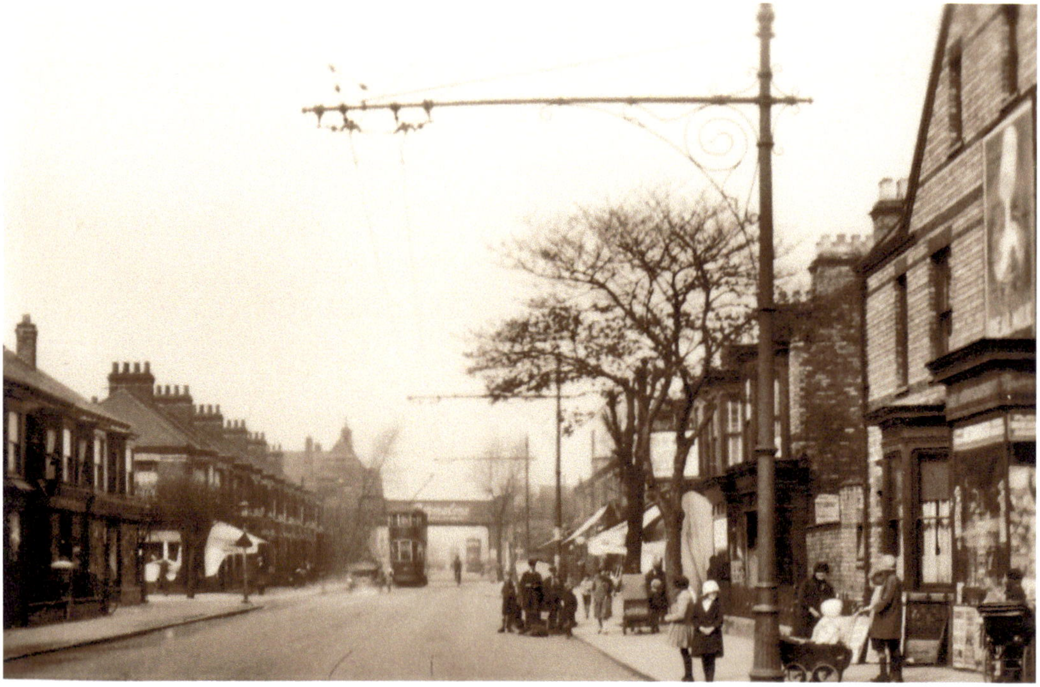

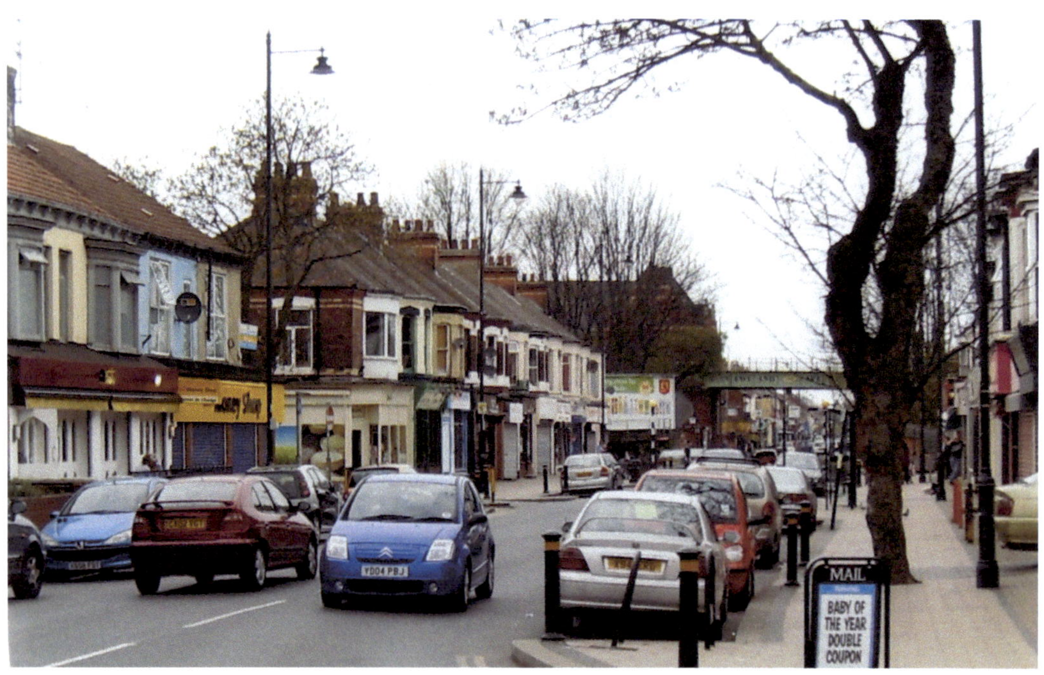

Newland Avenue Looking North

A group of young boys are seen on the road on Newland Avenue. On the right of the photograph is a newsagent and general store. On the left of the photograph is Ella Street. Newland Avenue was built in the 1880s and there are many terraced streets running the full length of Newland Avenue. An enclosed electric tram is seen passing under the overhead railway bridge. Today, many of the houses have been converted to small shops. The shop on the right is still a newsagent shop.

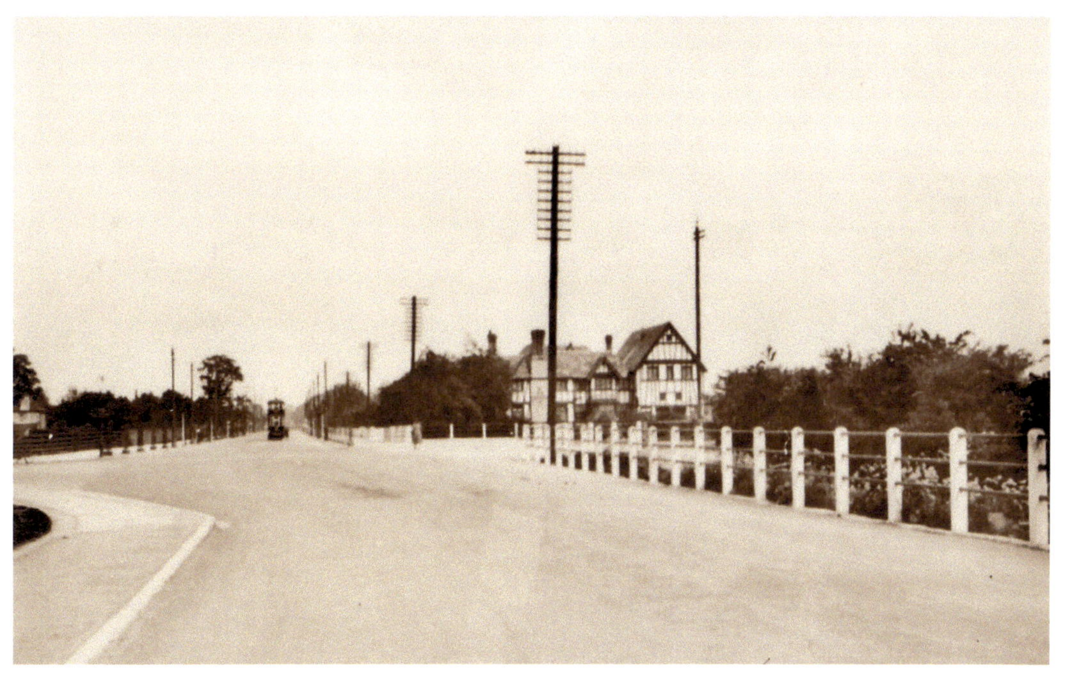

Cottingham Road

With fields on either side of Cottingham Road it has a very rural look to it. The drain can be seen on the right, while also visible on the right is the Good Fellowship Inn, built in 1928. Note how quiet the road is, with only a single enclosed electric tram visible. The Quadrant housing estate (later to become North Hull estate) is yet to be built. Note also the old style telegraph poles. Today, the Good Fellowship Inn can just be seen amongst the trees, while the drain was filled in some years ago.

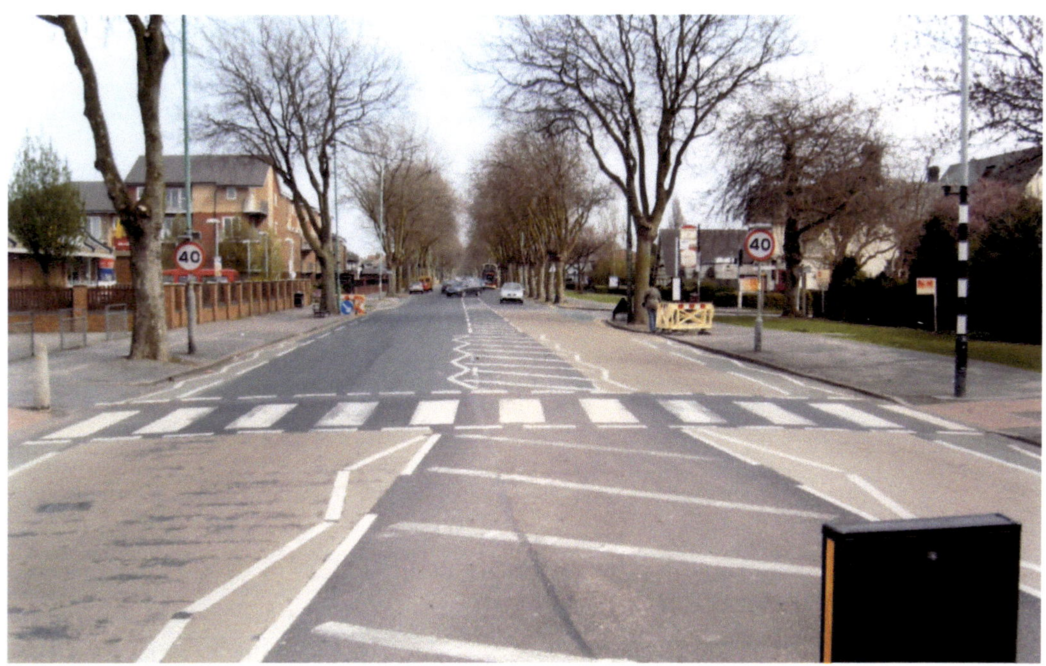

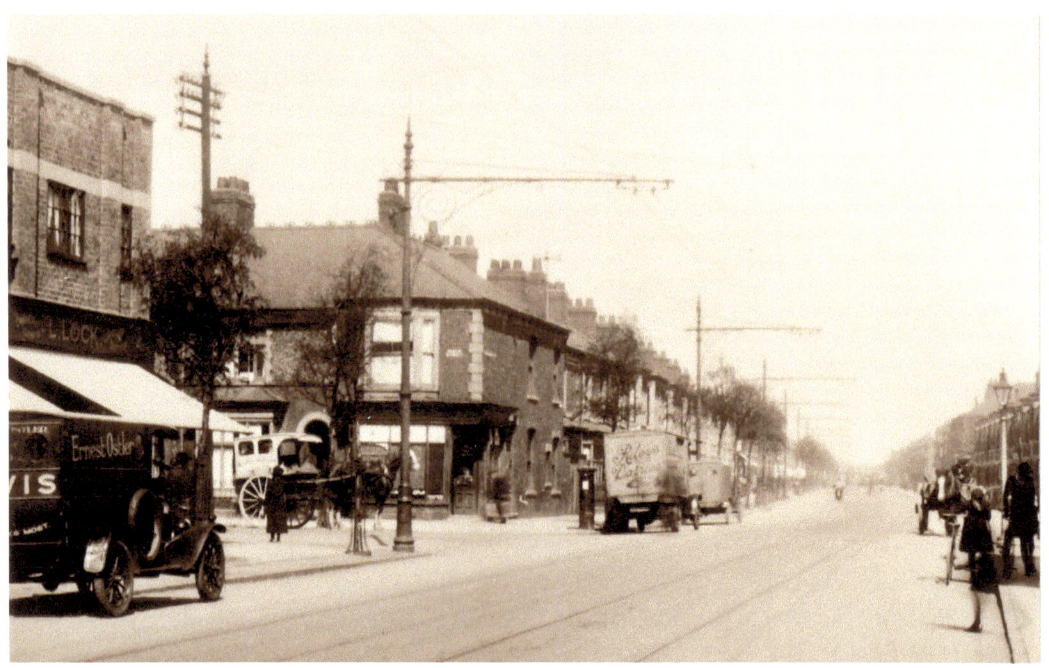

Chanterlands Avenue

A selection of motor vans and horse-drawn wagons are seen in this photograph of Chanterlands Avenue. The shop on the left is L. Lock, with the van belonging to Ernest Ostler. The horse-drawn wagon on Perth Street West belonged to the West Hull Dairy Farm, while the motor van parked alongside the posting box belonged to Riley's Dairies. Although many of the shops have changed hands many times, very little has changed in over seventy years.

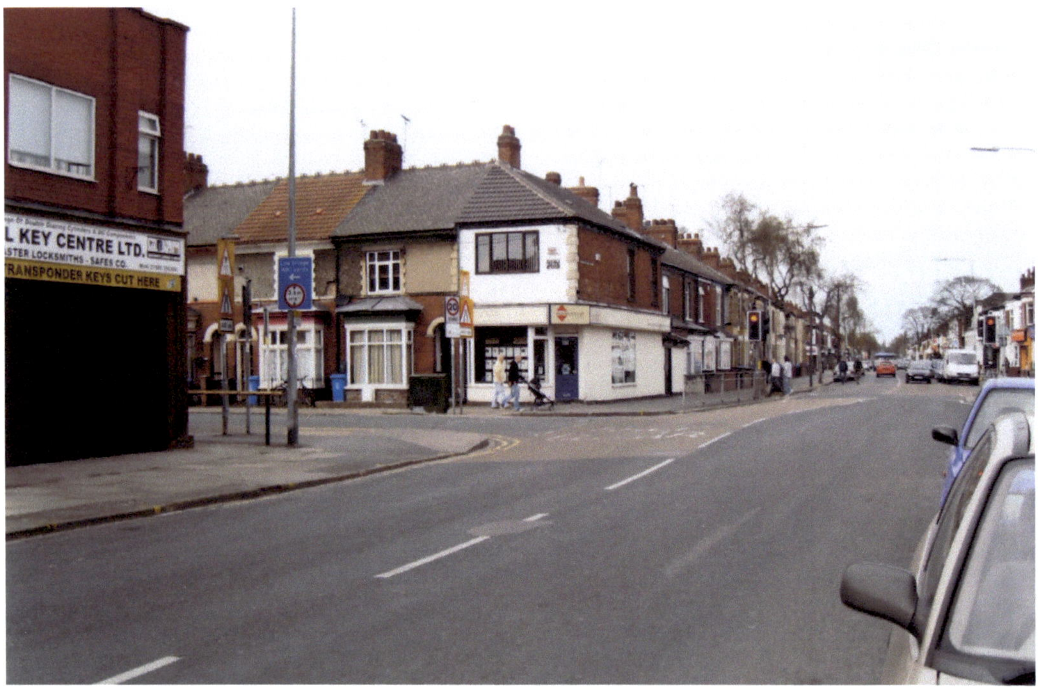

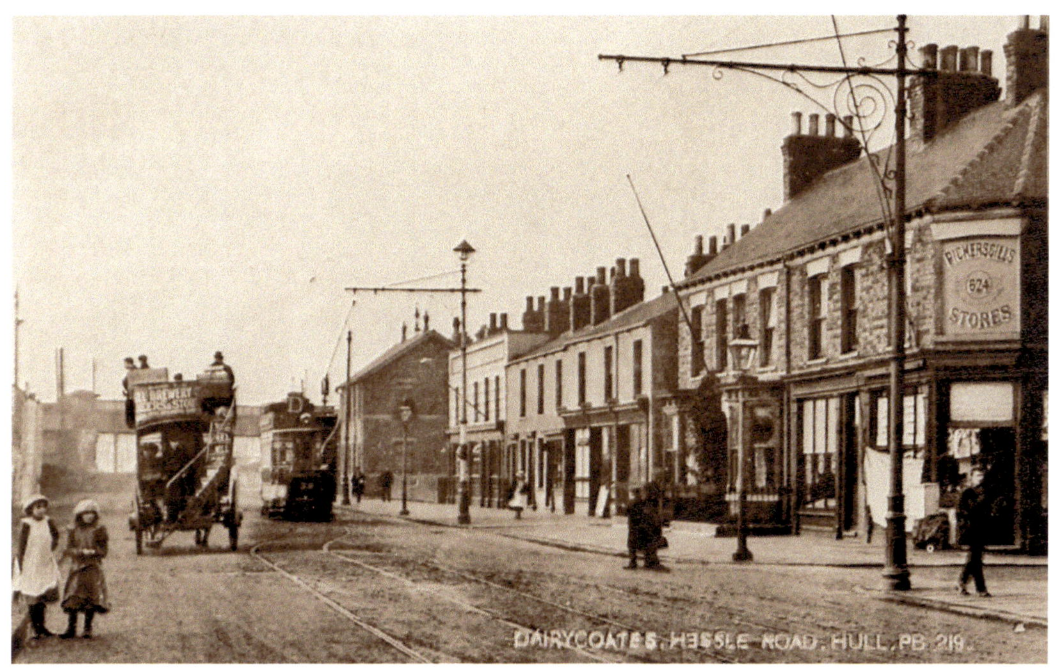

Dairycoates

In this interesting view, transport of yesterday can be seen at Dairycoates, *c.* 1907. On the right is a horse bus on its way to Hessle. In the centre of the photograph is an electric open top tram on the 'D' service, ready for the return journey back to the city centre. On the right is Pichersgills stores of 624 Hessle Road. At this time the electric trams terminated at Hawthorne Avenue. The electric tramway down Hessle Road commenced on 5 July 1899 and was not withdrawn until 30 June 1945. Little now remains of Dairycoates.

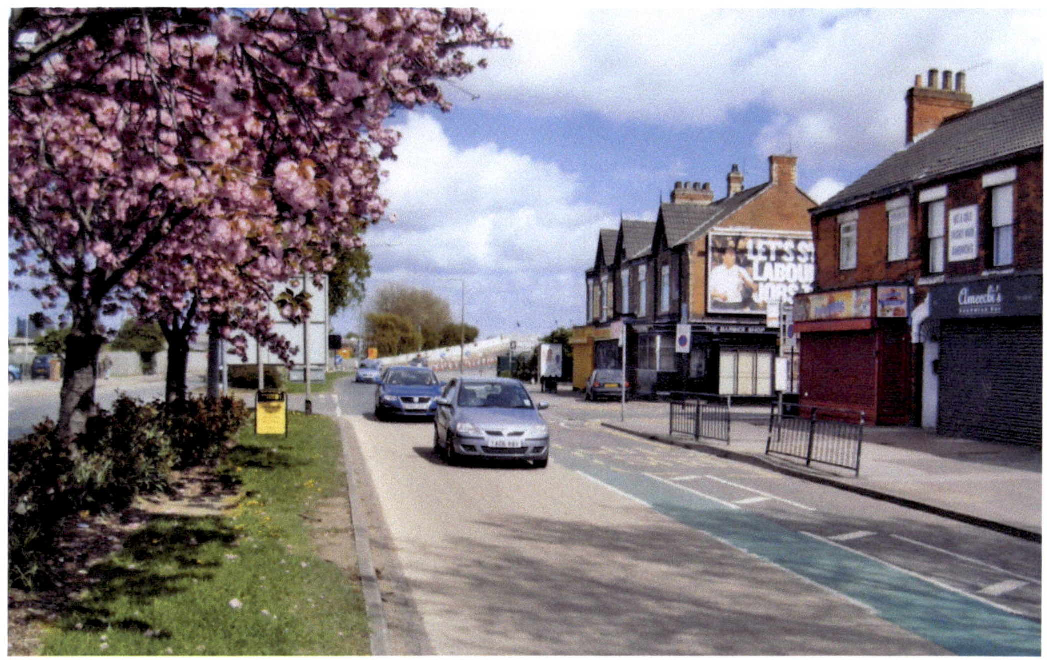

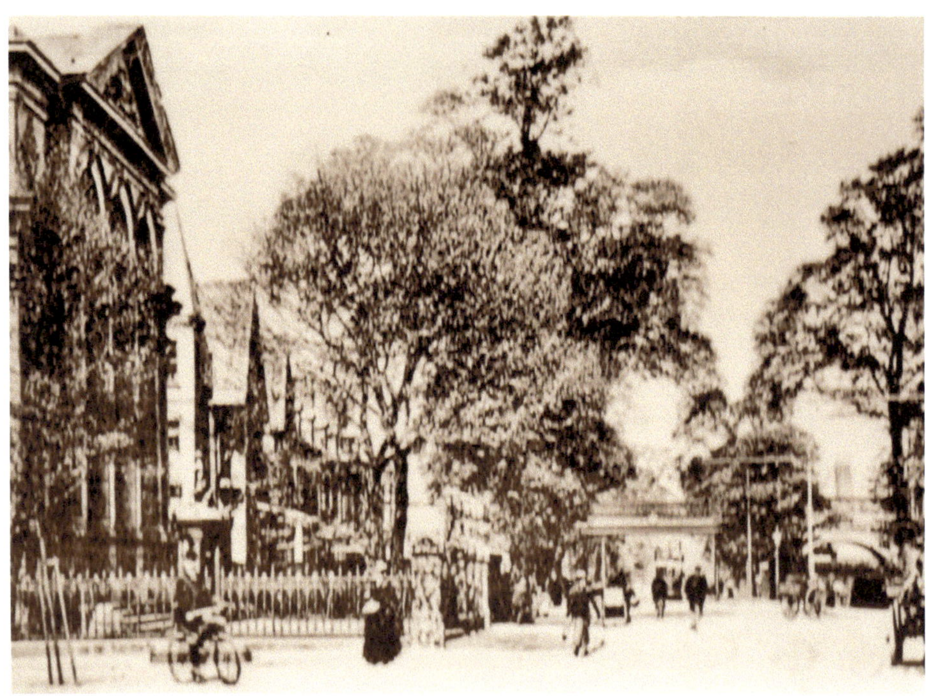

Beverley Road

In the days when the horse-drawn vehicle was the only means of transport for many people, this photograph shows the tree-lined Beverley Road, at the junction of Queen's Road. A lone cyclist can be seen on the left. In the distance can be seen the Hull & Barnsley Railway overhead bridge. It was difficult for the author to stand in the middle of the road with the amount of traffic on this road. The bridge arches are now closed in and the left hand arch is now Newland garage.

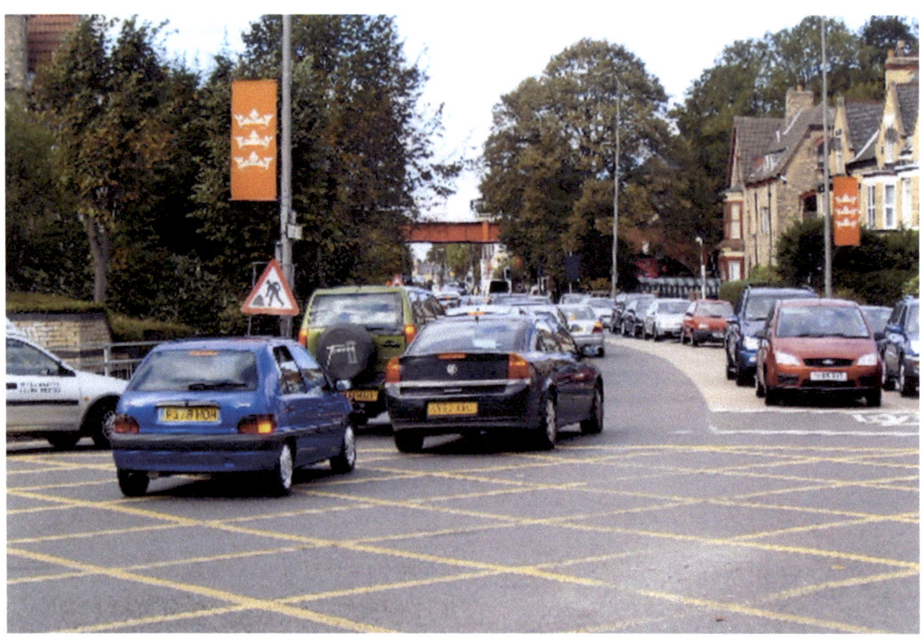

Liverpool Street

Typical of many of the terraced streets on the south side of Hessle Road is Liverpool Street. This area was associated with the fishing industry and many of the families living in this area worked directly or indirectly with the fishing industry. The husbands and sons worked on the trawlers, while the wives and daughters worked in factories processing the fish. The tram depot was on the right of this photograph. Note the Co-operative milk float. Much of Hessle Road over the years was redeveloped, as can be seen in the present day photograph. There is very little that now remains of Liverpool Street.

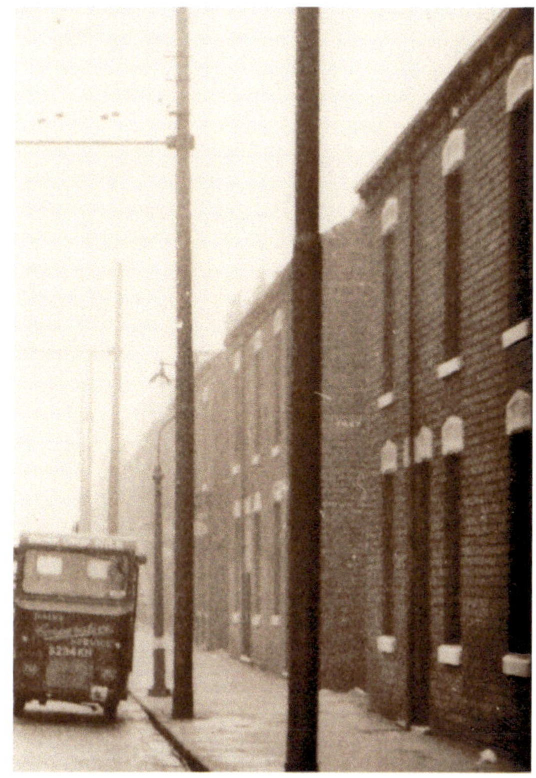

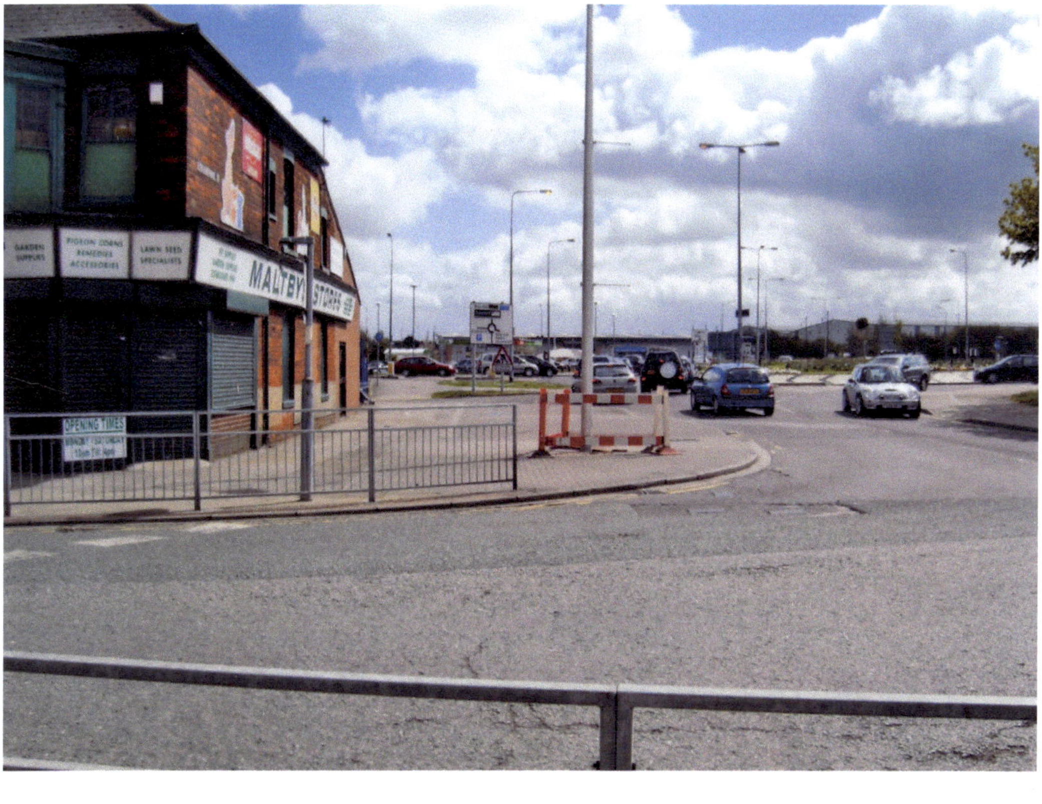

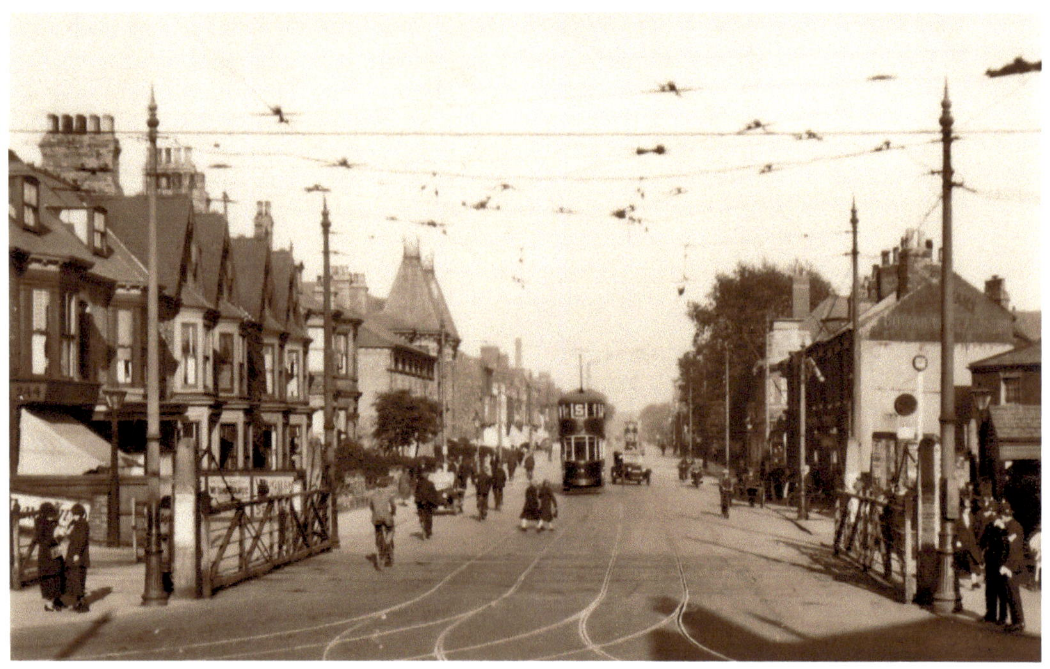

Spring Bank Looking East

A fully enclosed electric tram on the 'S' service is seen on Spring Bank, with the full length of this road visible, looking towards the city centre. Number 244 Spring Bank is clearly visible on the left of the photograph. Derringham Street is on the right with the Polar Bear public house and the Botanic Hotel visible on the right. In the foreground can be seen the Botanic level crossings. Today, this area is undergoing major road improvements and the road has been widened.

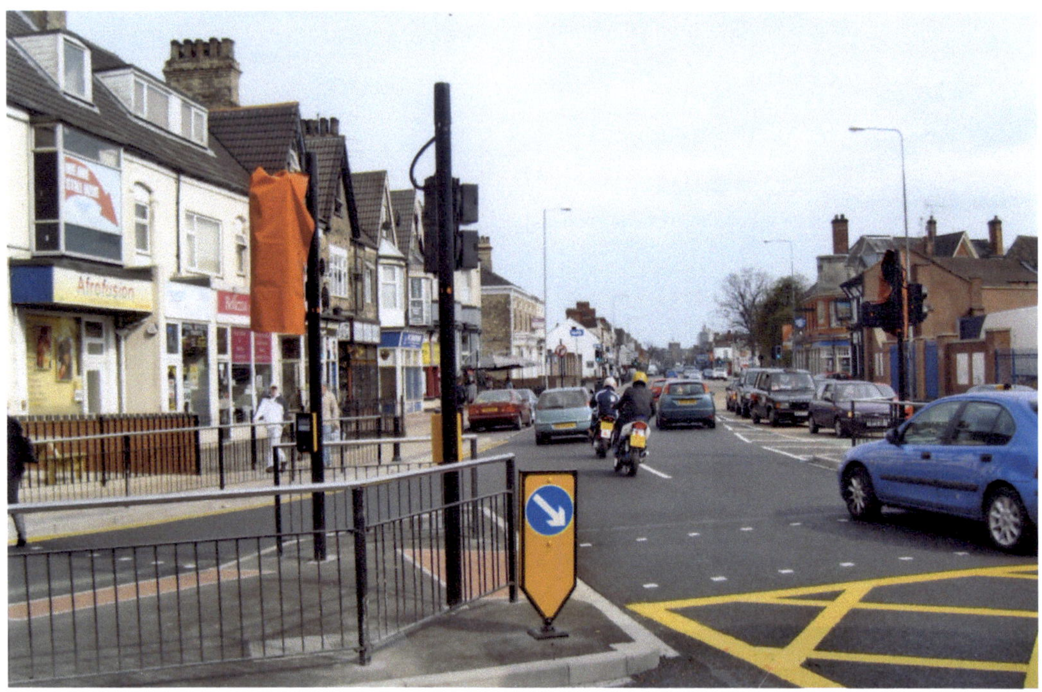

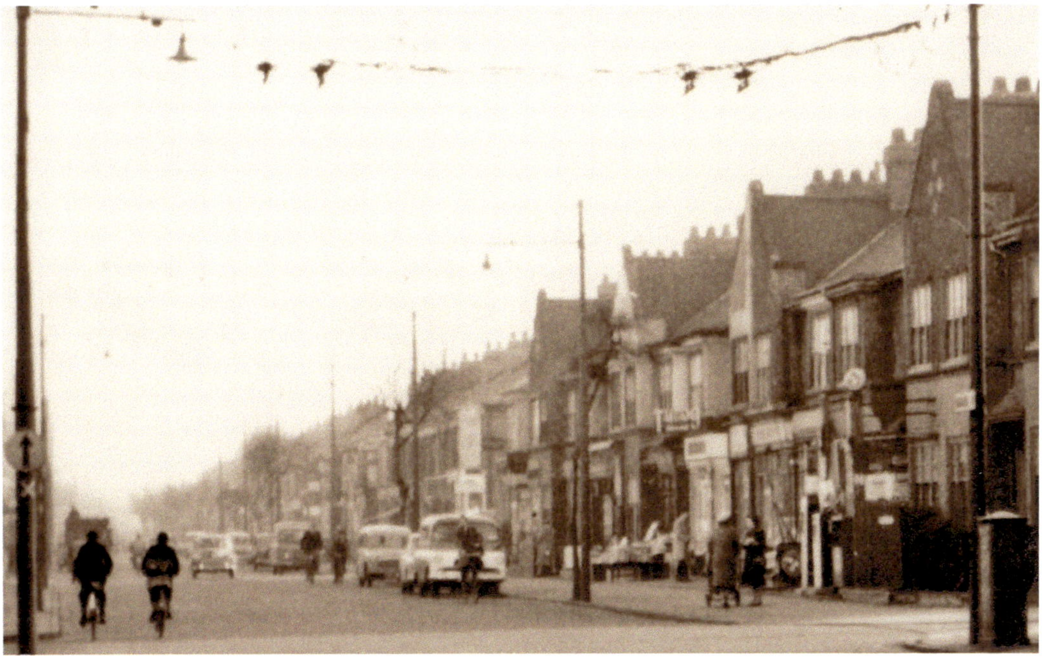

Chanterlands Avenue

Looking down the full length of Chanterlands Avenue, often referred to by many as 'Chants' Avenue. The large selection of small shops is visible, selling a wide range of goods. Note the old-style petrol pumps on the right. Also visible are the overhead trolleybus wires. Today, Chanterlands Avenue is just as busy and still offers a wide selection of small shops, although many have changed the type of items they sell.

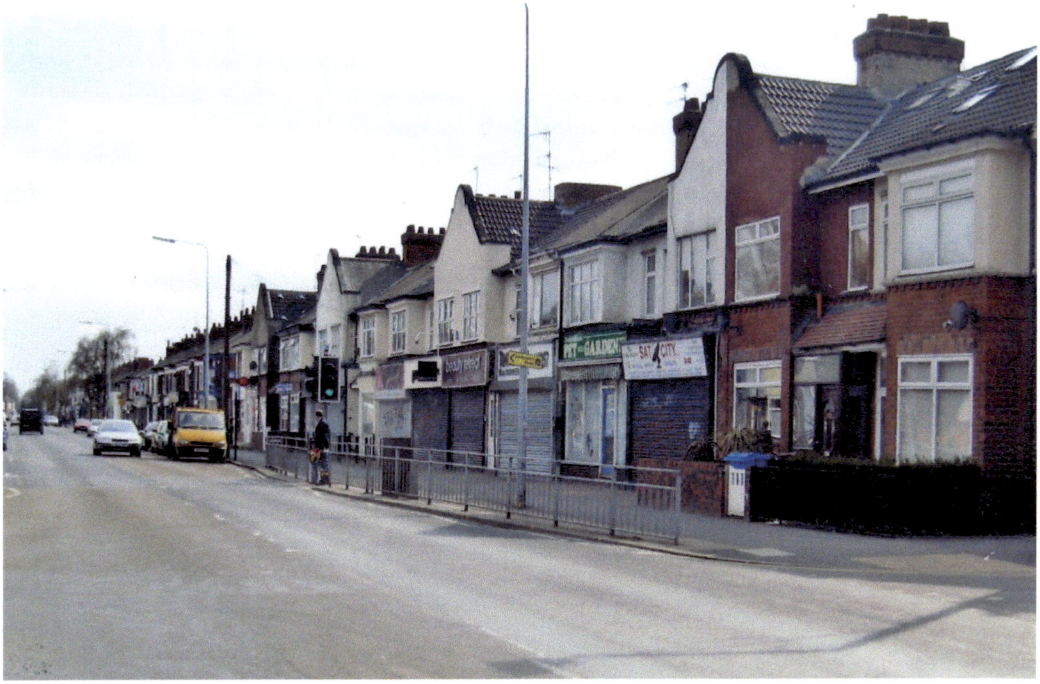

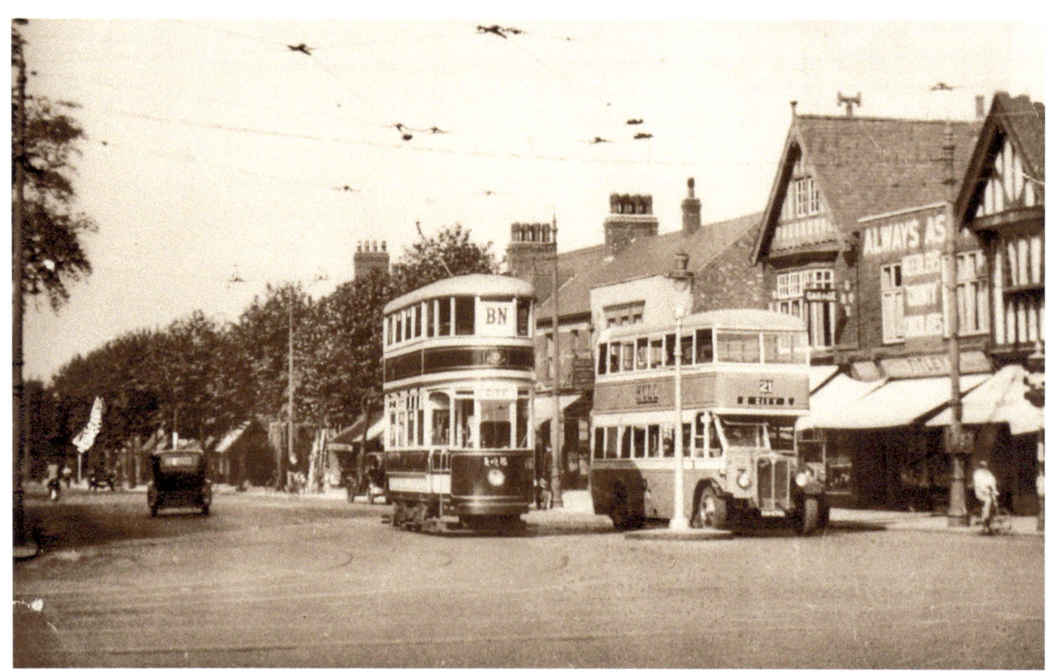

Cottingham Road

A Hull Corporation Transport tram and a Hull Corporation Transport motorbus are seen at the junction of Cottingham Road and Beverley Road. The tram is on the BN route from Newland Avenue corner, heading back to the city centre. The impressive Haworth Arms public house is seen on the right. Tiley's sweet shop is also visible next to Haworth Arms; note the old style traffic lights. Tiley's shop is now a bank. The Haworth Arms Hotel is now painted more brightly.

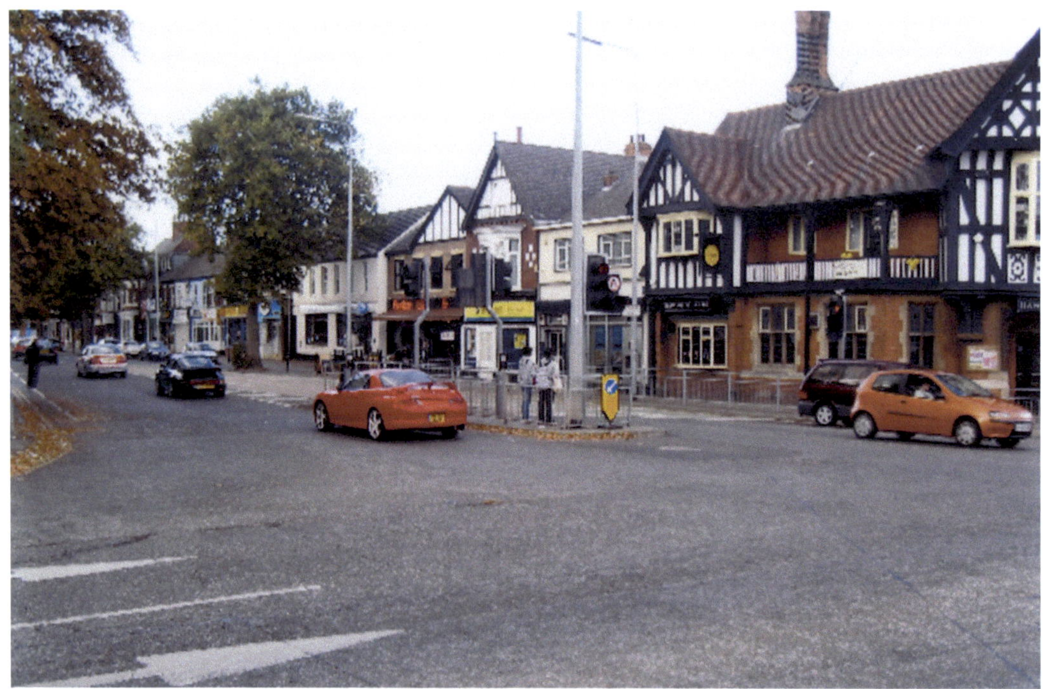

Queen's Hotel, Queen's Road

This is a view of Prince's Avenue looking towards Queen's Road, with Chestnut Avenue directly in front of us. The Queen's Hotel, which was built in the 1800s, is clearly visible in this photograph. Note the selection of classic cars of the day, including a Morris Minor. Today, the Queen's Hotel still stands and is still a public house. Note that the Queen's name has been moved to the other side.

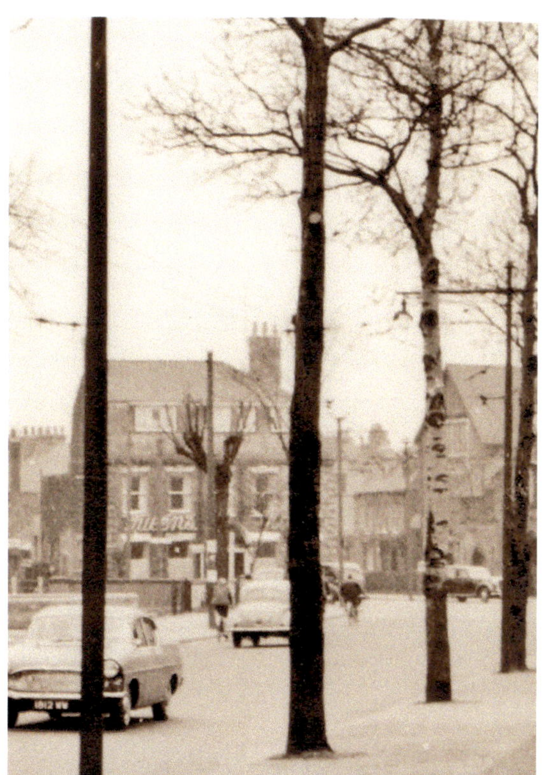

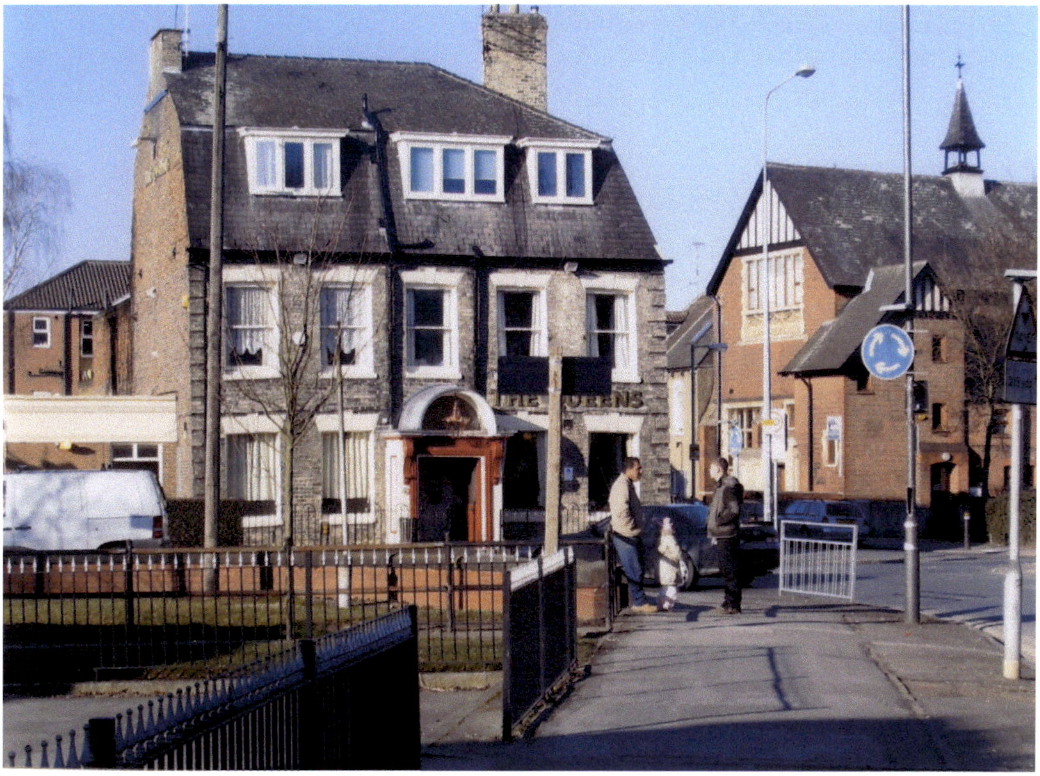

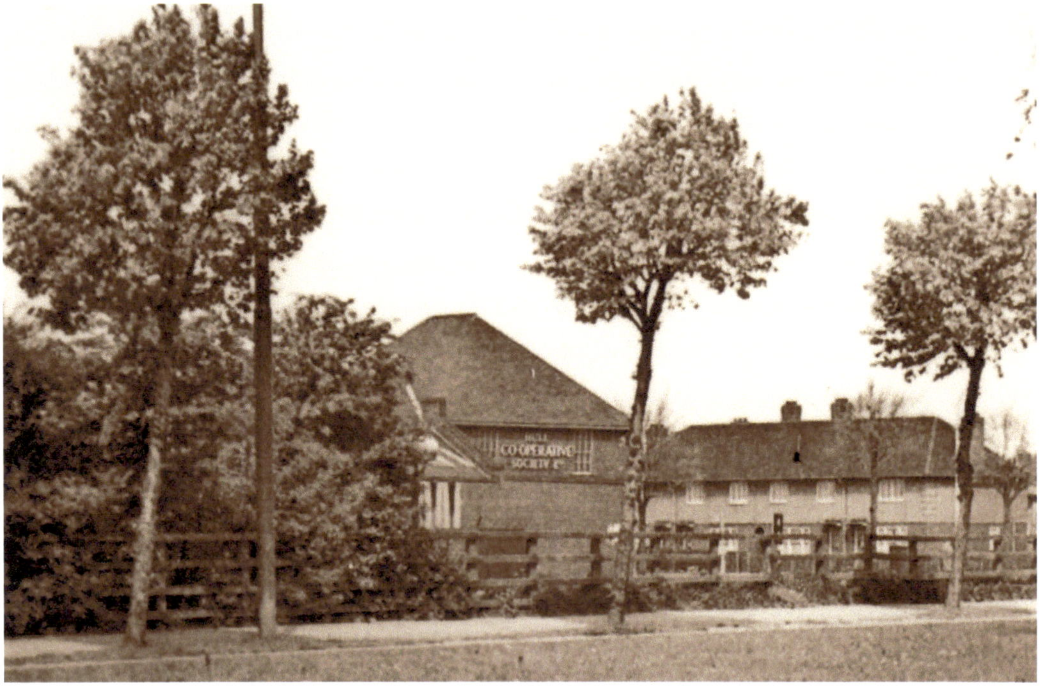

Greenwood Avenue and Beverley Road

Greenwood Avenue can be seen on the right of the photograph, in this view from Beverley Road. The Hull Co-operative store is visible in the centre of the photograph. This was demolished some years ago. Today, the Pilot public house stands on this site.

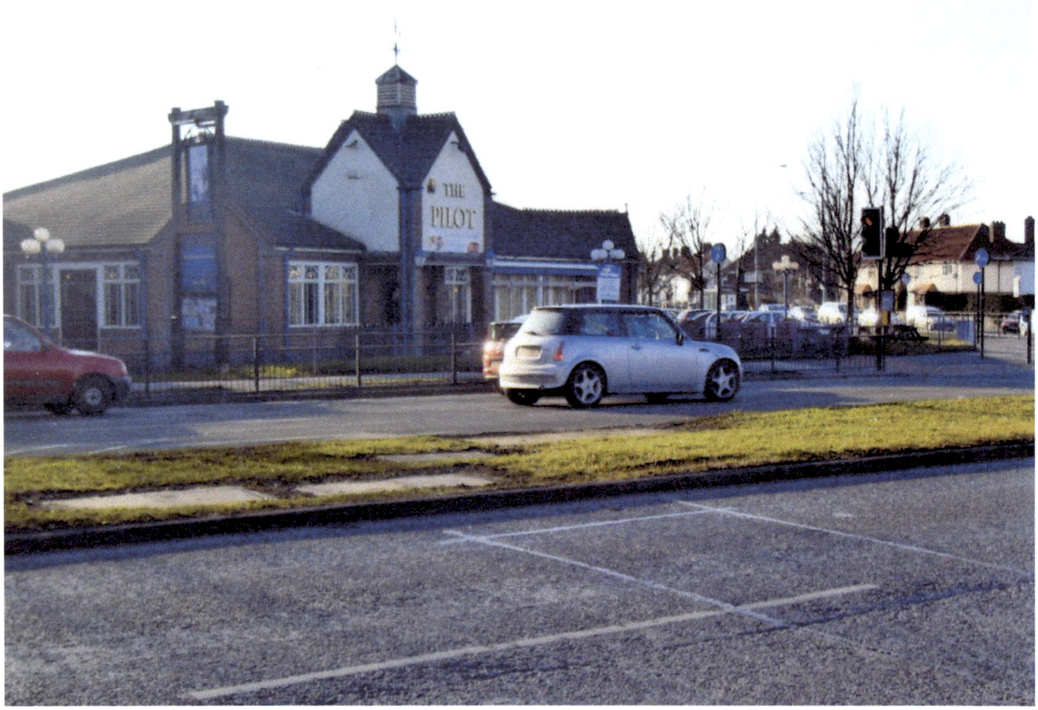

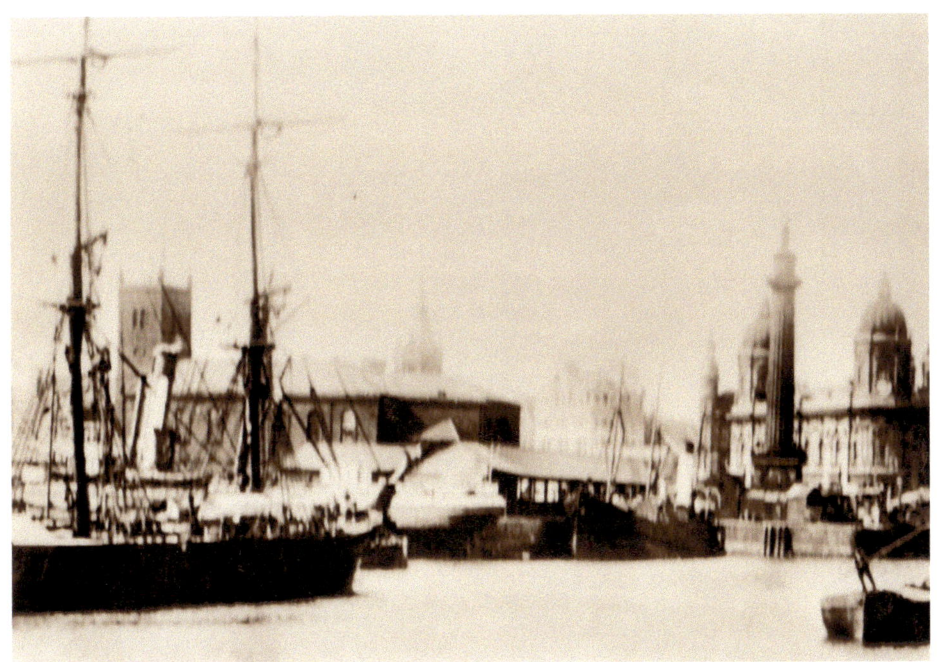

St John's Church

A selection of sailing ships can be seen in Prince's Dock. This was originally called Junction Dock. At one time, this was a very important and busy dock and linked the Old Dock (now Queen's Gardens) with the Humber Dock and the River Humber. Visible is St John's church, the Town Dock offices, with William Wilberforce's Monument standing in front of the Dock offices. The very top of the Prudential building is just visible in the background. Today's photograph is very much different, with the Prince's Quay shopping centre now taking up much of the photograph. The Ferens art gallery now stands on the site of St John's church, while William Wilberforce's Monument now stands in Queen's Gardens.

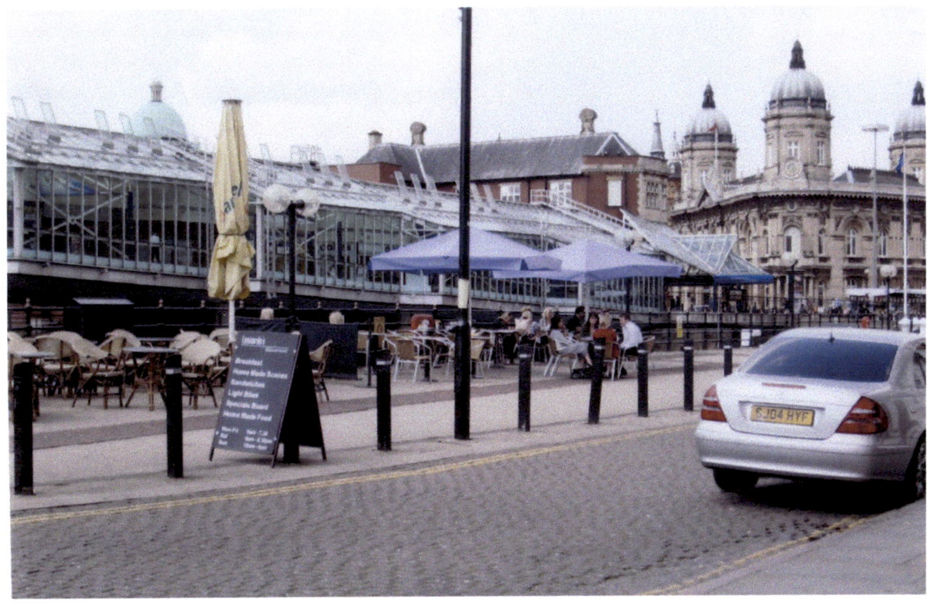

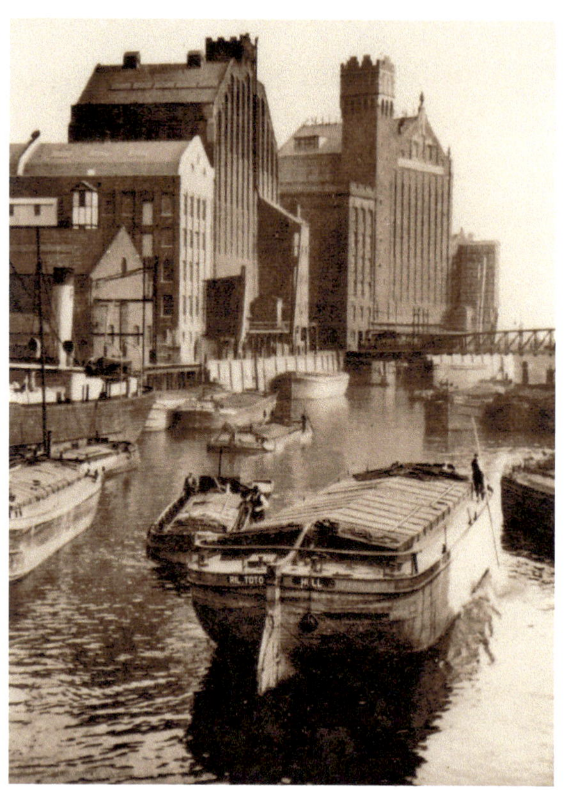

The River Hull

The River Hull as photographed in the late 1930s. The River Hull was always busy with barges of different sizes carrying a variety of goods. Large boats too were a common sight on the river. The barge in the foreground is the *Ril Toto*. In the background can be seen the old Drypool Bridge and on the left the flower mills. These days little traffic is carried by barges up and down the River Hull. The flower mills of Rank Hovis have now closed, while the old Drypool Bridge was demolished and replaced by a new bridge in 1961.

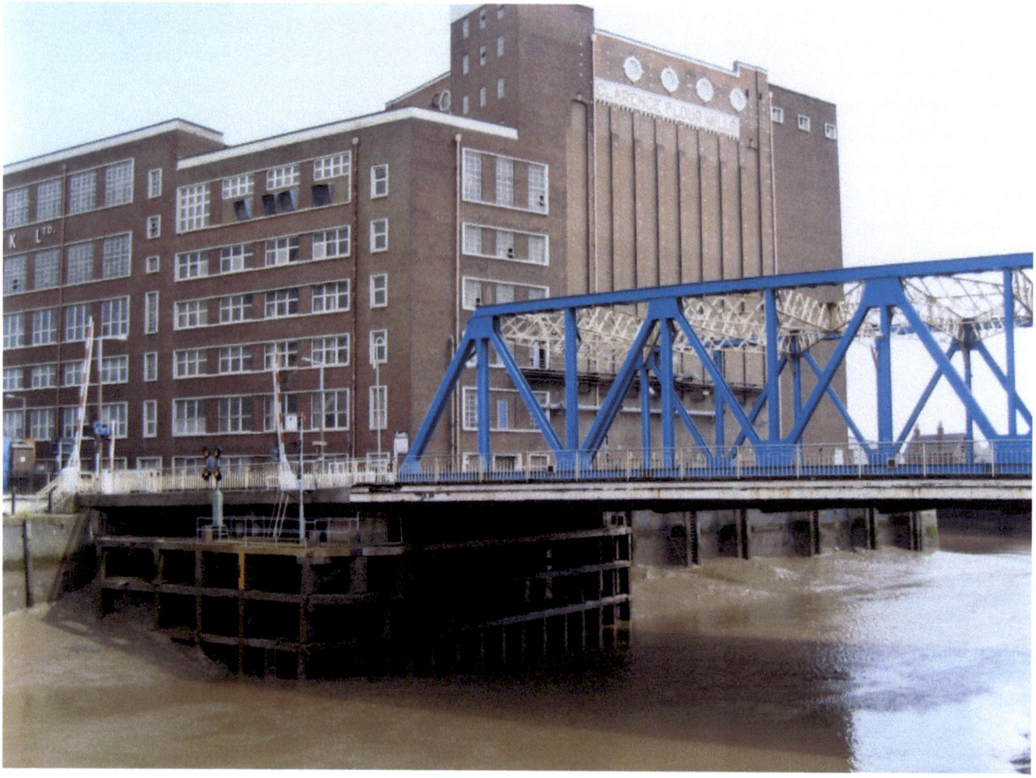

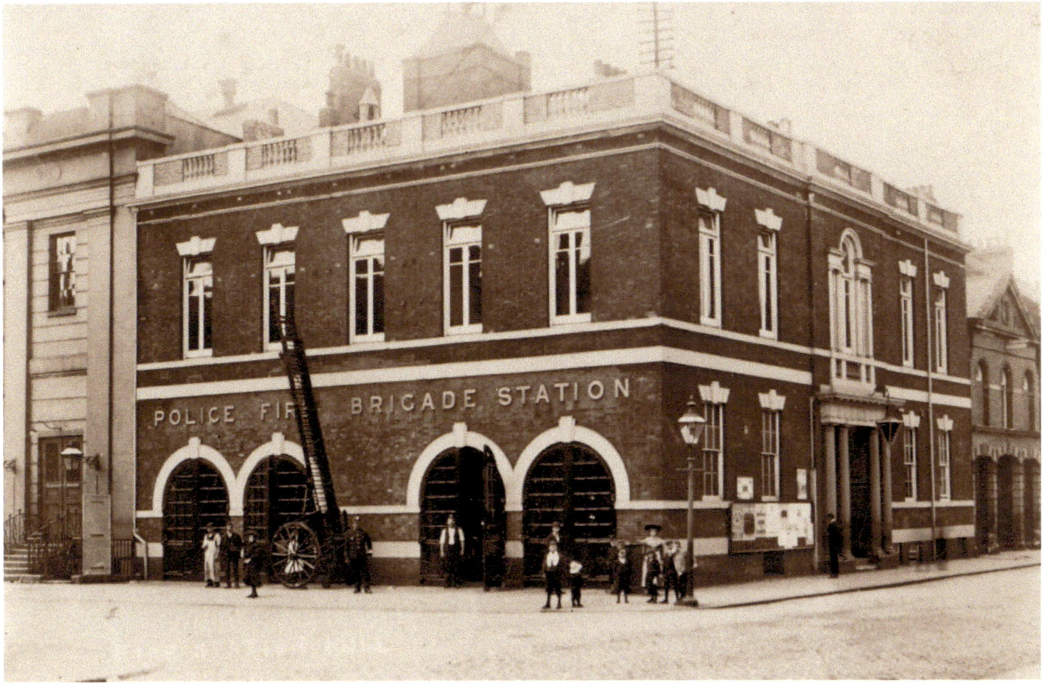

Hull Central Fire Station

The central fire station of the Hull fire brigade is seen in this photograph. It is at the corner of Worship Street and Jarratt Street. The Hull police force was also stationed in this building. Note the escape ladder. Next to this building was the Assembly Rooms. The new central fire station is seen in today's photograph with the Hull Theatre on the left.

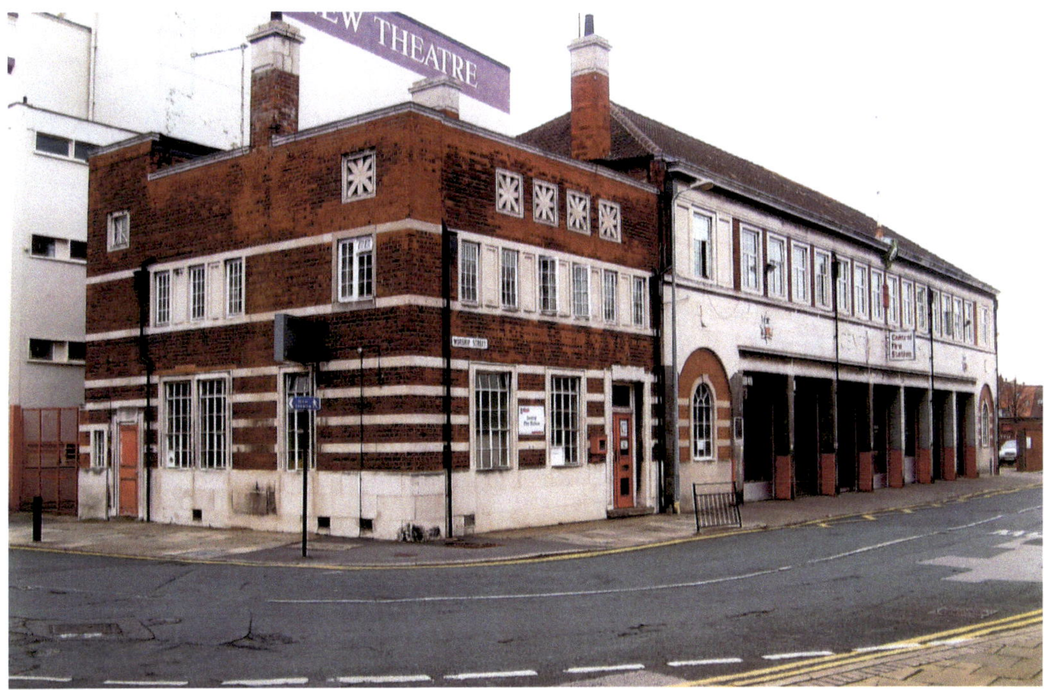

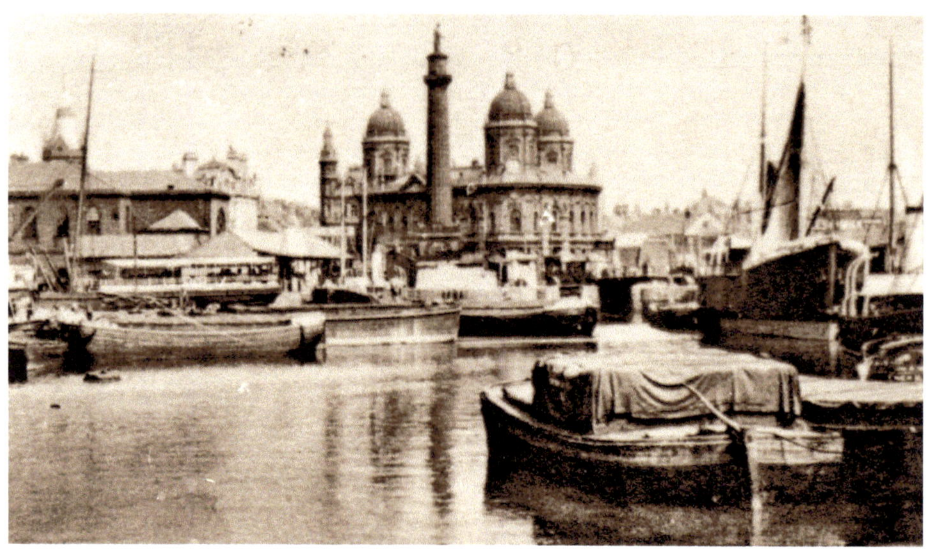

Junction Dock and Prince's Dock

A view looking across Junction Dock, renamed Prince's Dock in March 1855, after a visit by Queen Victoria and Albert. The dock was opened in 1829 and was closed in 1967. The Dock offices are clearly visible as is William Wilberforce's Monument. To the right of the offices are Monument Bridge and Queen's Dock; originally named Old Dock or the Dock, this was renamed at the same time as Junction Dock. It was closed in 1930 and later filled in to become Queen's Gardens. Today, the Prince's Quay shopping centre stands on this site of the former Prince's Dock.

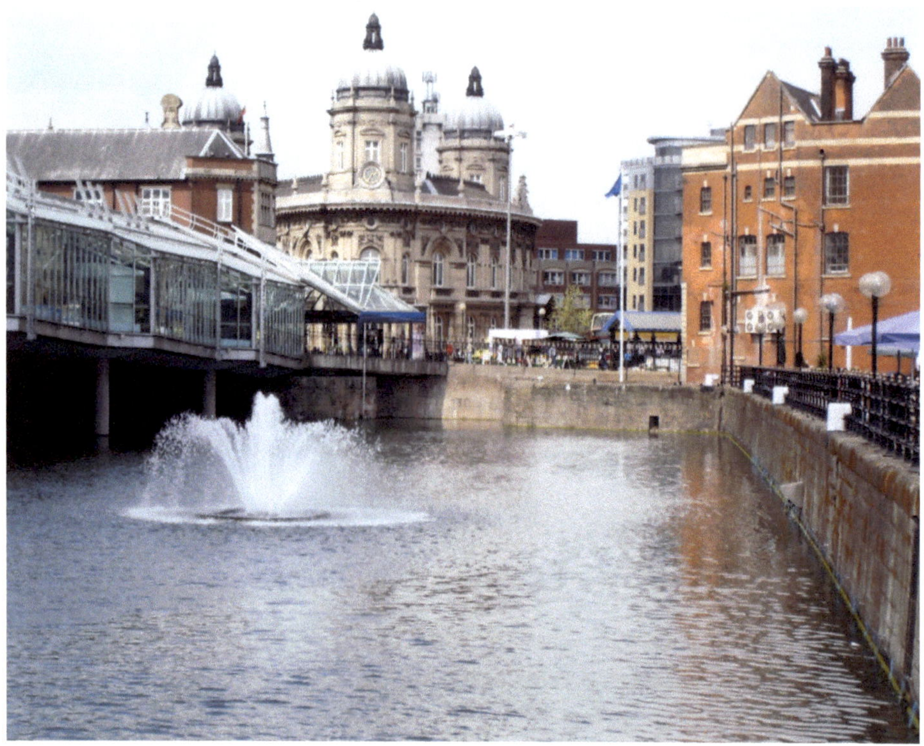

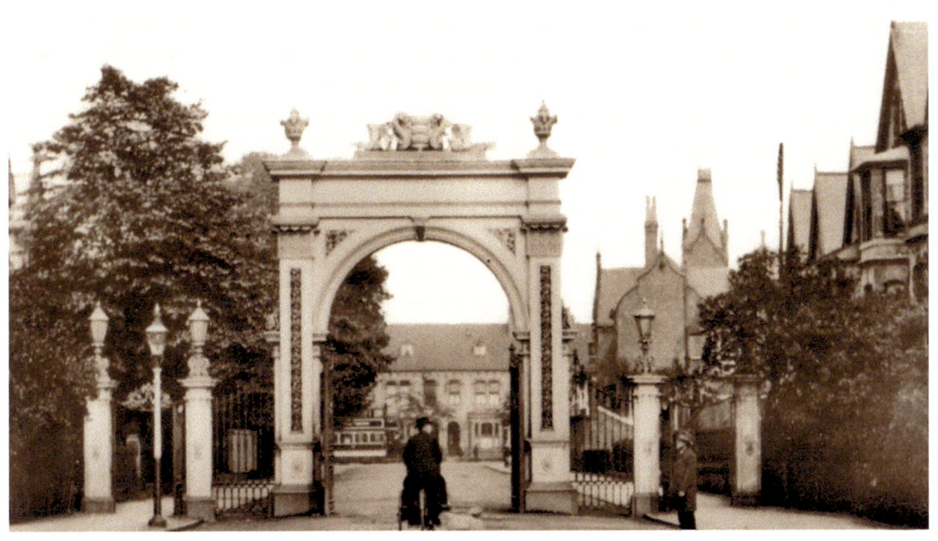

Pearson's Park Gates

The elaborate gateway to the entrance of Pearson Park from Beverley Road. The houses seen on the right of the photograph were indeed for the very well off people of Hull. An elderly gentleman is seen passing under the archway, while an open-top electric tram is just visible in the background. Little has changed in the last hundred years or so.

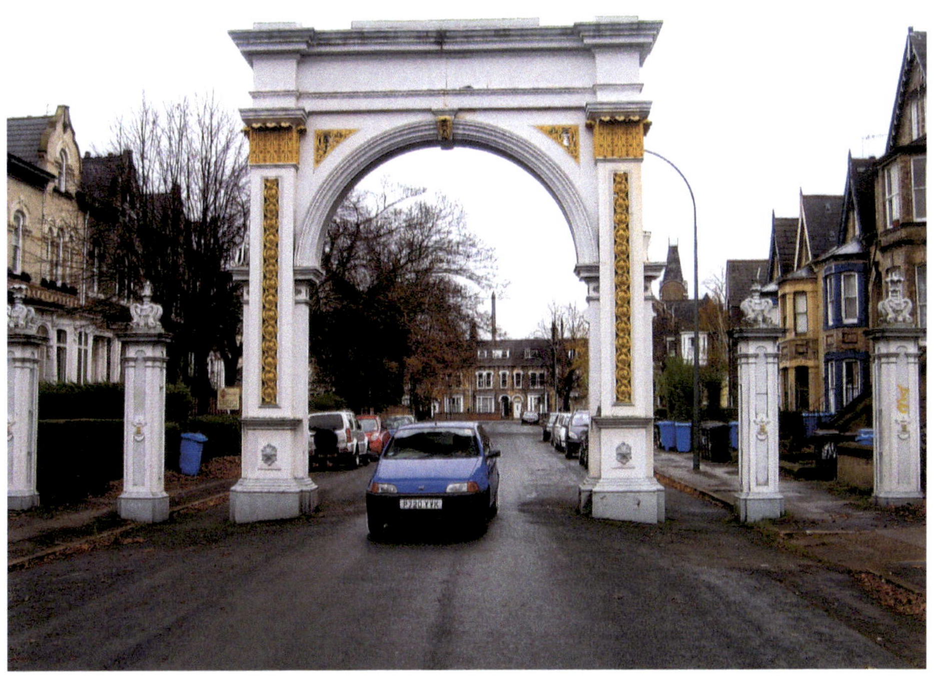

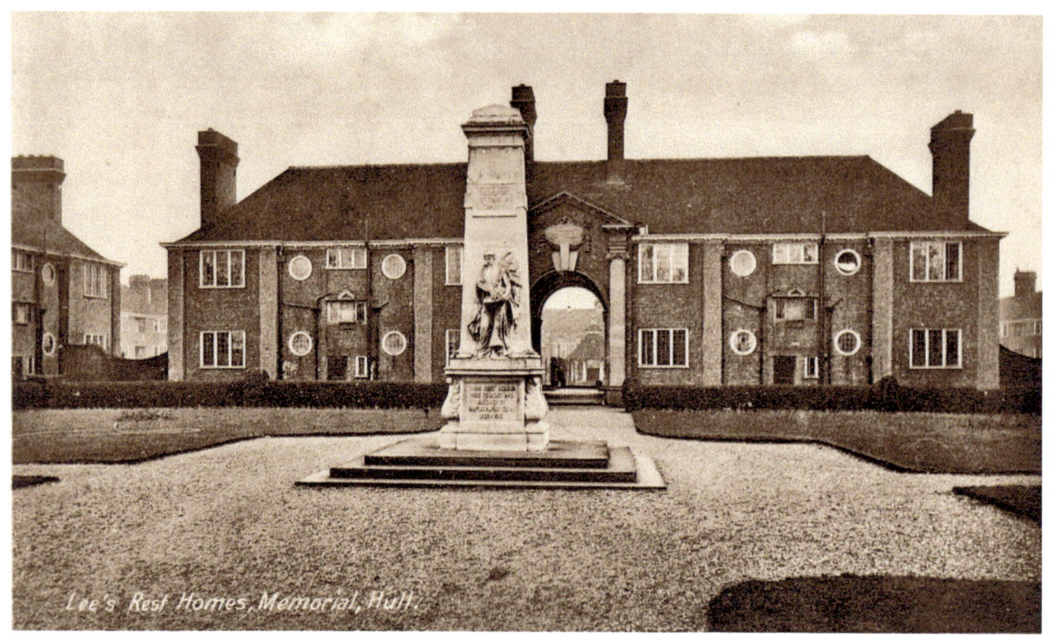

Lee's Rest Homes

Lee's Rest Homes on Anlaby Road were founded and endowed by Charles Alfred Lee MD (1825-1912). They were built between 1914 and 1915 and contain sixteen detached blocks of buildings, while each block contained eight flats and were intended for the better well off people who, through sickness or for other reasons, had been reduced to poverty. This view shows the central pavilion and the Memorial. Very little has changed in the photograph of today, except that a number of trees were later planted.

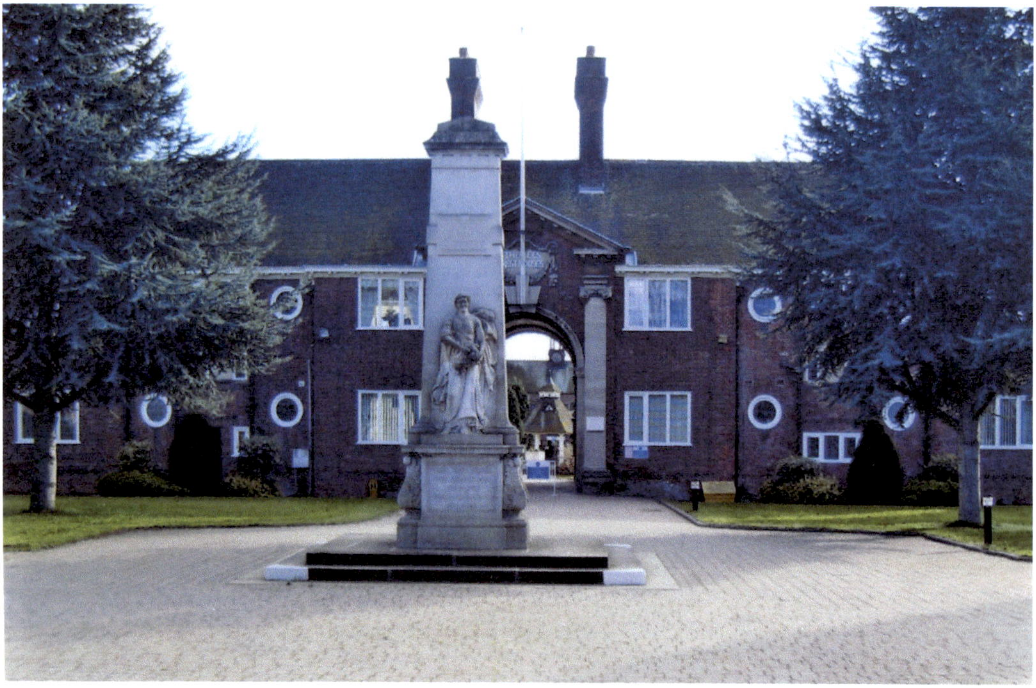

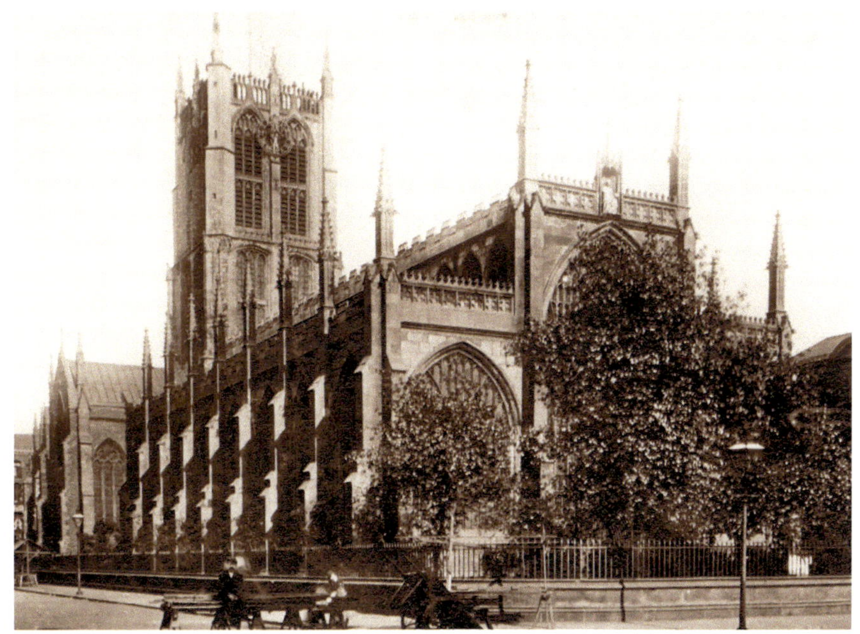

Holy Trinity Church

For well over 400 years, the very impressive Holy Trinity church has long been a feature of the city landscape. Holy Trinity church was built on the site of an earlier church. In the 1290s, the transept of the building was started. The windows in the transept were fitted between 1315 and 1320. The impressive tower was built in three stages. The first stage was built in the early fourteenth century. Work on the church was completed between 1520 and 1529. The open market once formed part of the churchyard. William Wilberforce was baptised at Holy Trinity church.

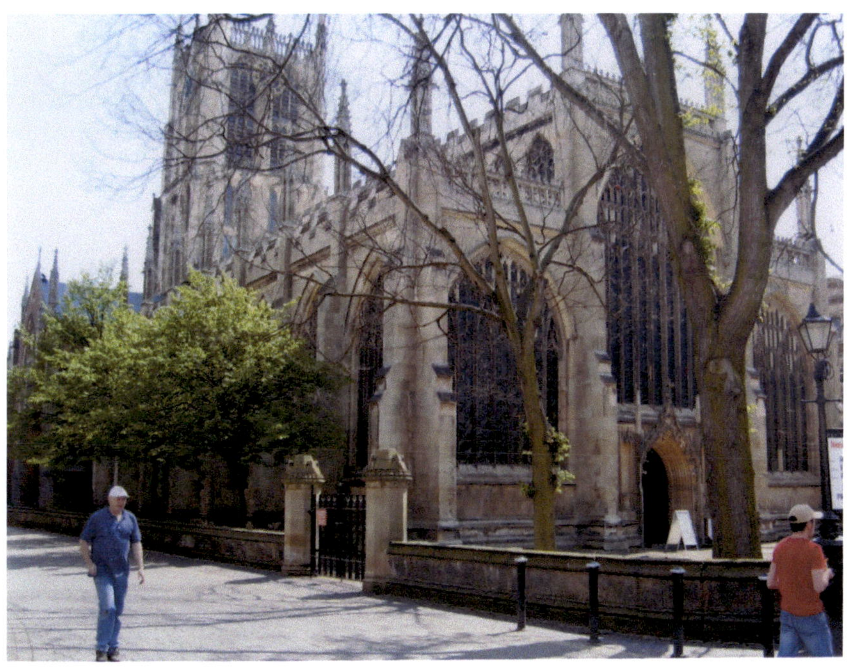

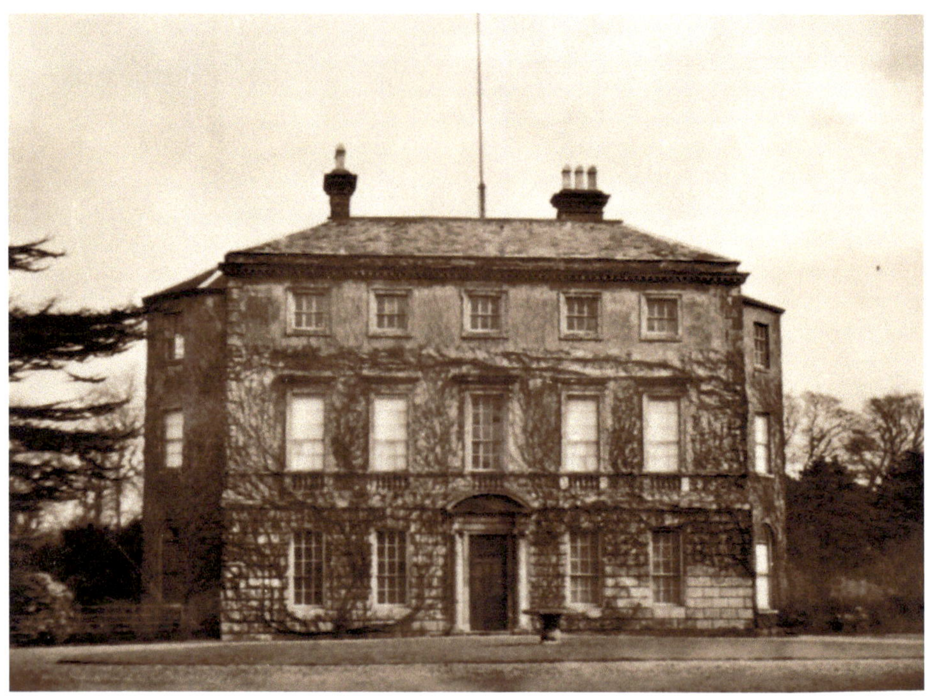

Haworth Hall

Built in the early eighteenth century, this is the impressive Haworth Hall, originally named Hull Bank House. The Burton family, who were wealthy landowners, owned the Hull Bank House in the 1740s. Much of the estate which stretched from the River Hull to Cottingham has been sold off for housing, including: North Hull Estate, Orchard Park Estate and later Haworth Park Estate. Cars now park where, at one time, horse-drawn carriages would turn round. A sign of the times is the visible security cameras. The house is now apartments.

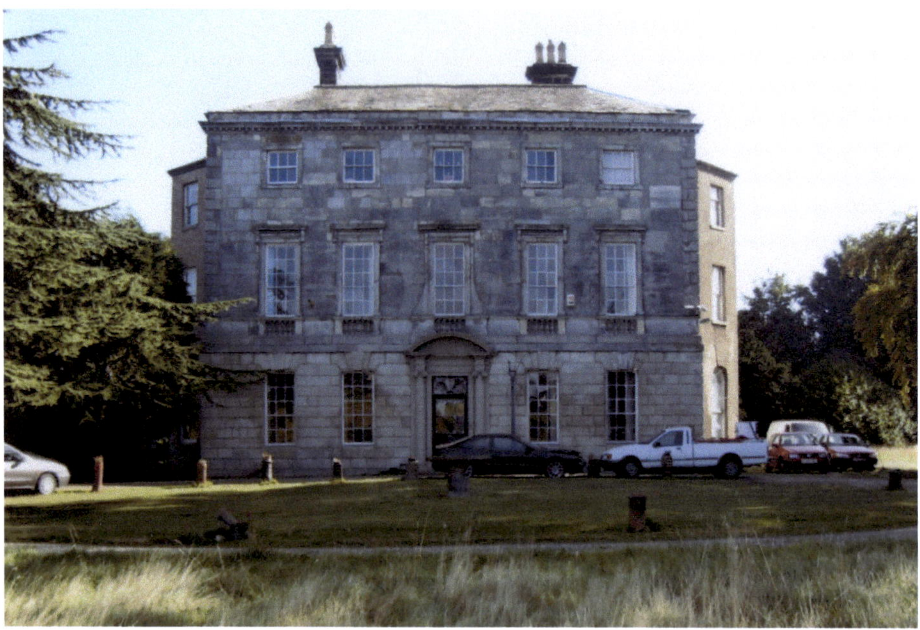

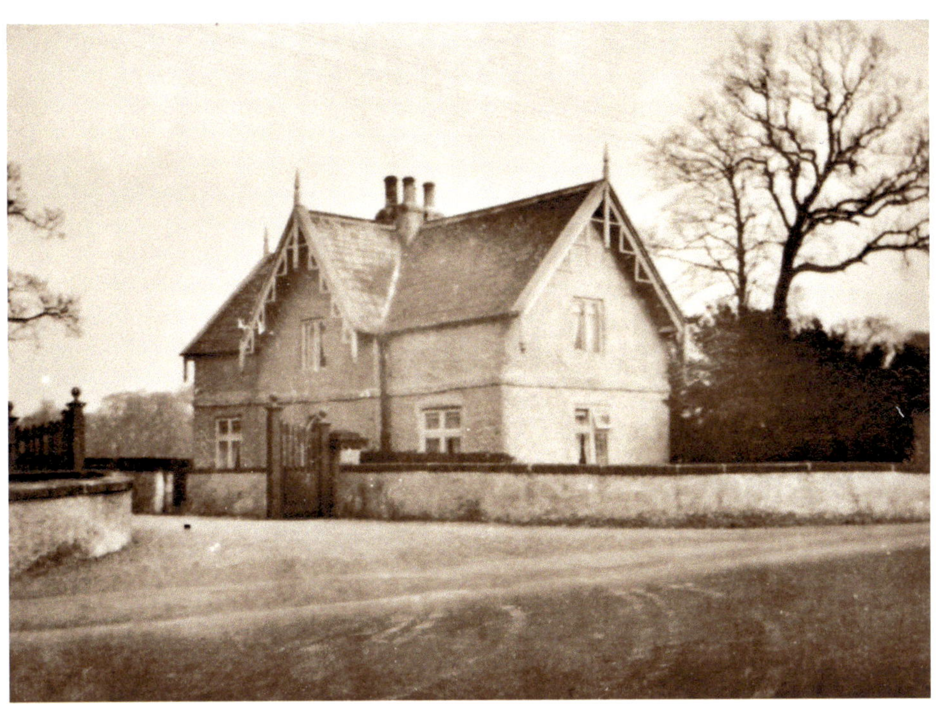

Haworth Lodge

The impressive Haworth House stands in acres of land. The main entrance to the house was by way of a track. The entrance was dominated by the impressive Haworth Lodge. This view was taken in 1928 and shows the wall around the estate, and also visible are the gates, as seen on the left. Haworth Lodge was sold off some years ago and is now under private ownership; it is now the business of Haworth Builders.

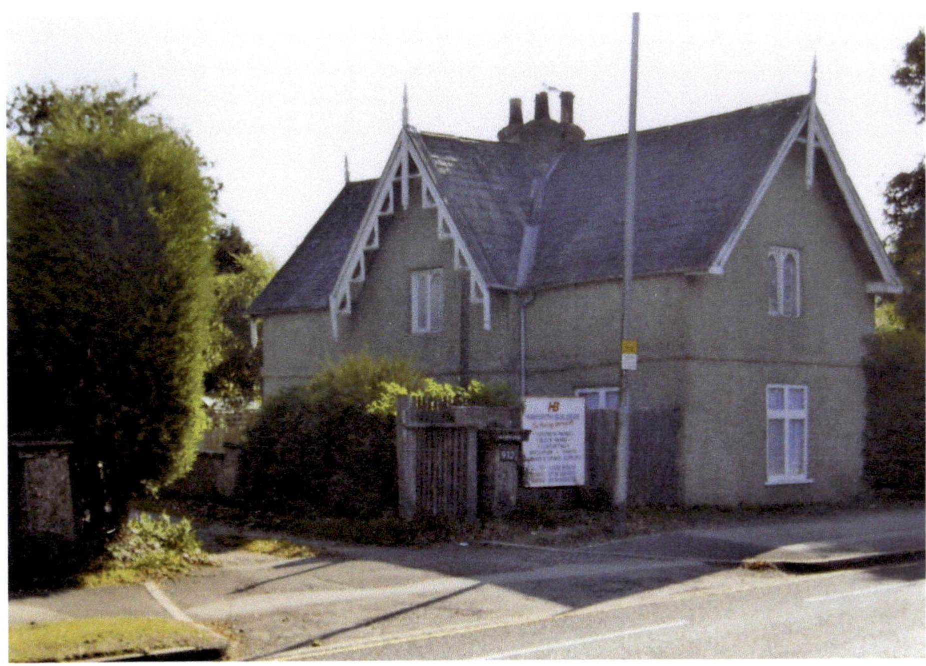

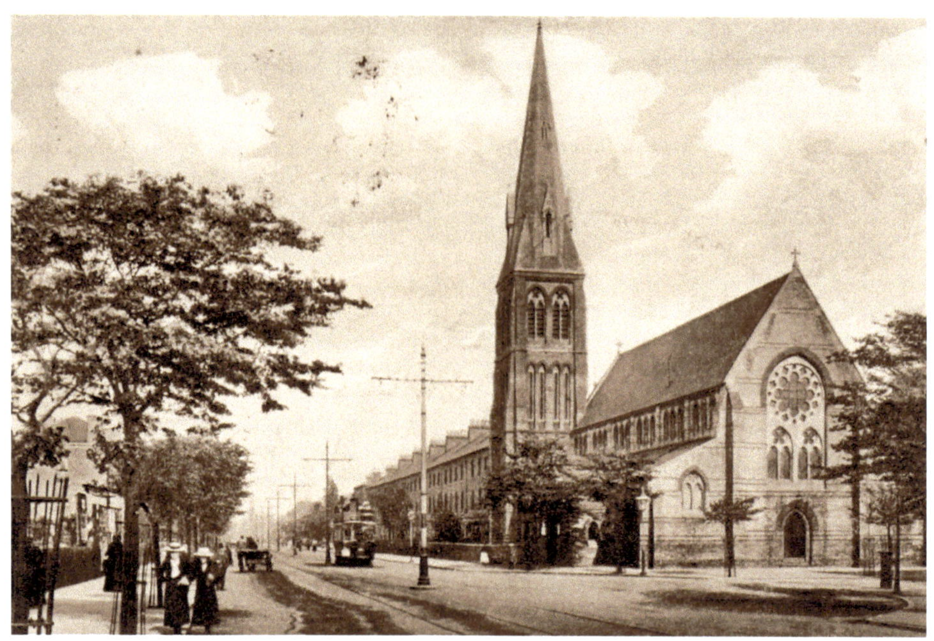

St Matthew's Church, Anlaby Road

In this *c.* 1915 postcard looking down Anlaby Road, the large Victorian spiral of St Matthew's church can be seen on the right at the corner of The Boulevard. This impressive looking church was built in 1870. An open-top electric tram is just visible in an otherwise quiet road. Also just visible is a horse-drawn vehicle. The buildings on the left were demolished for the building of the Anlaby Road flyover, just visible in today's photograph on the left.

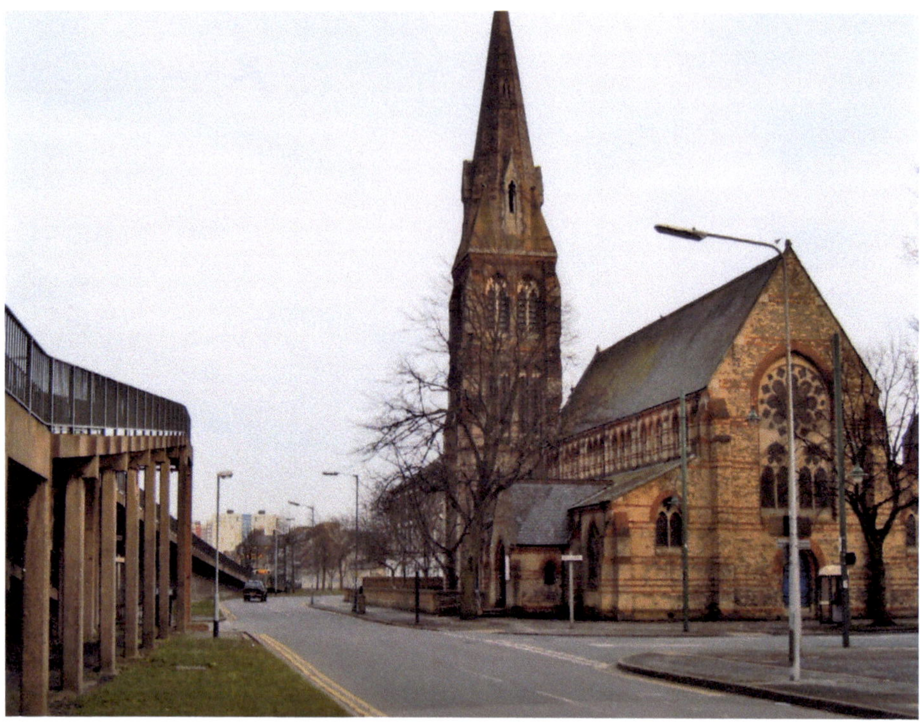

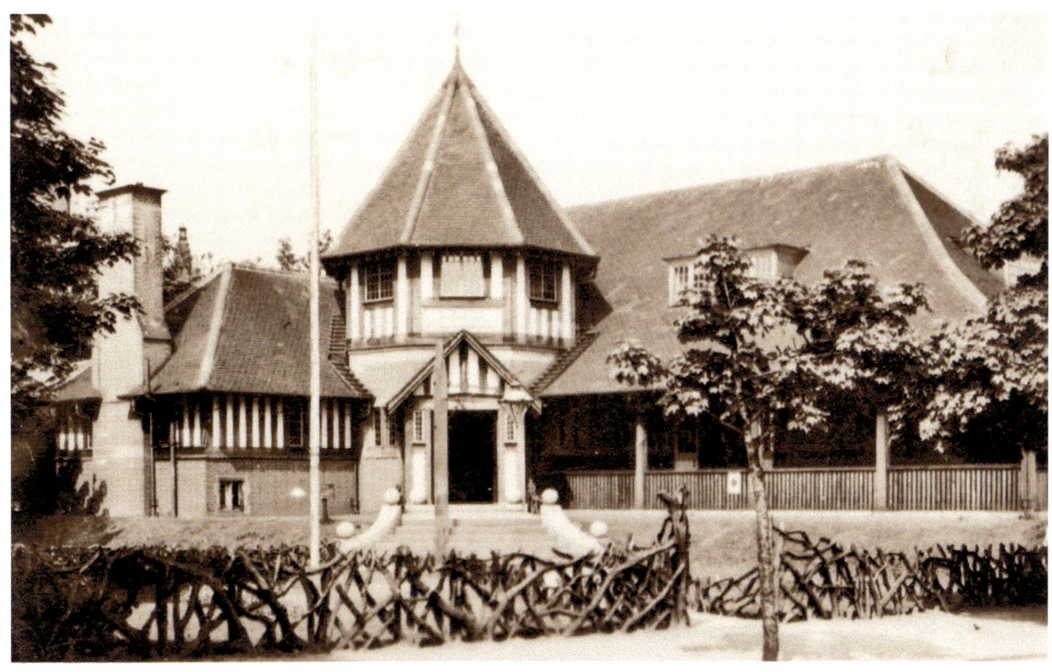

West Park Library

The beautiful Carnegie library is at the entrance of West Park on Anlaby Road and dates back to the early 1900s. An unusual feature is the half-timbered two-storey building shaped in an octagon design. The building is now over 100 years old and has changed very little. It is now the Carnegie Heritage Centre.

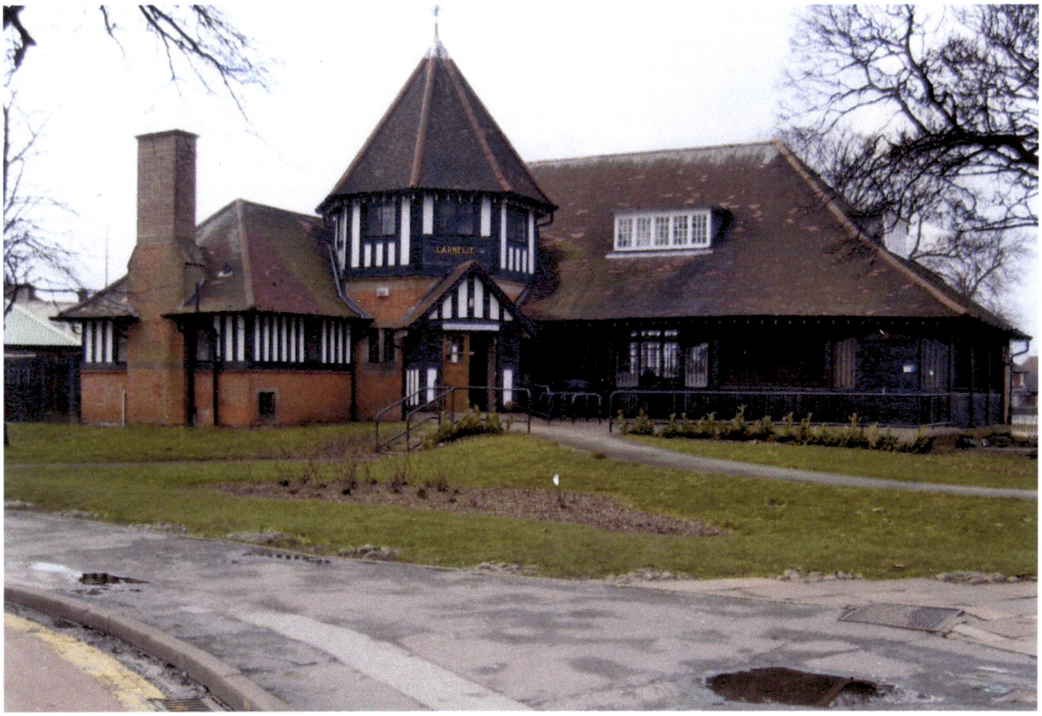

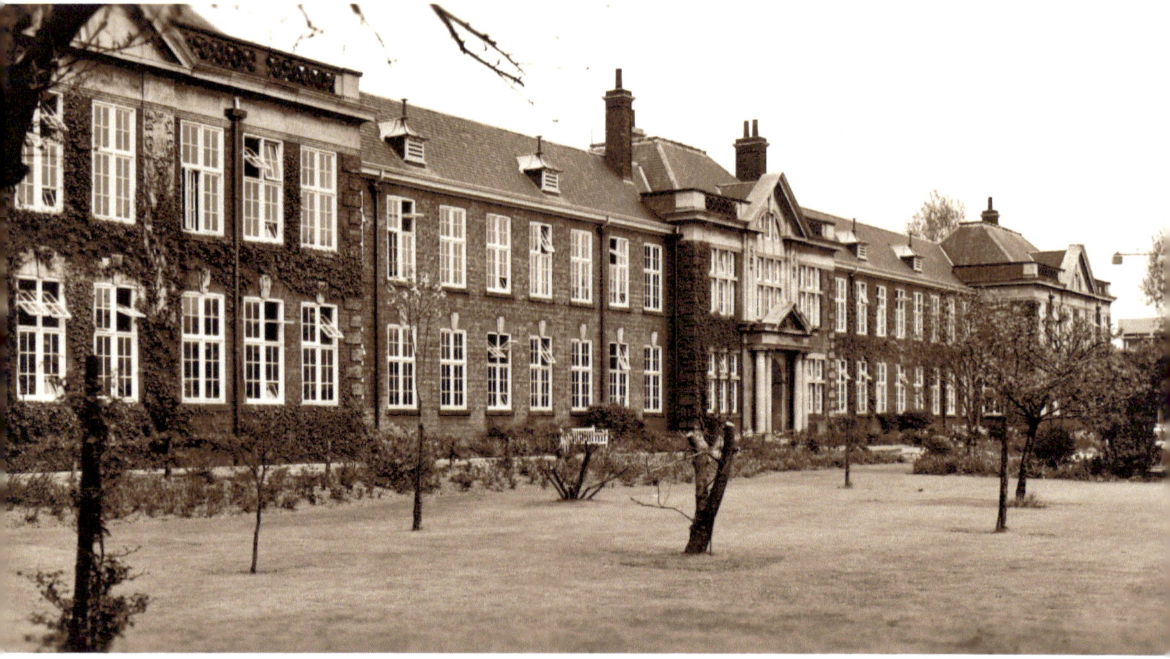

Newland School for Girls

The foundation stone for the new Newland School for girls on Cottingham Road was laid on 26 June 1914, by H.M. Queen Mary. This photograph shows the impressive frontage of the school. Except for the growth of the trees, the school has changed very little in over a hundred years.

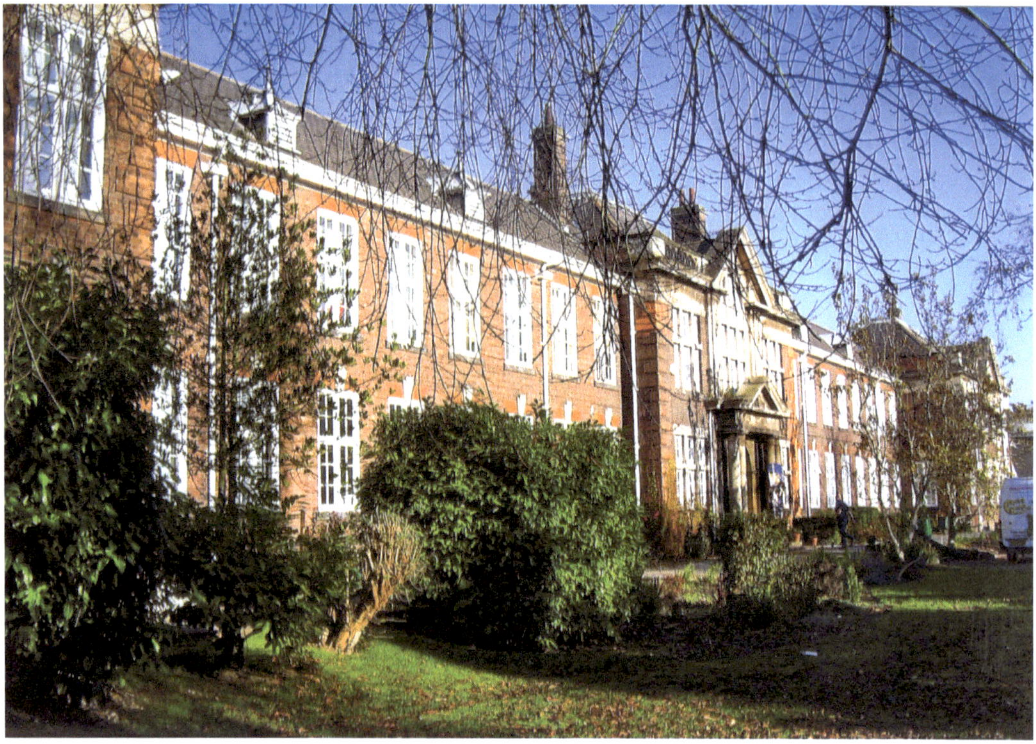

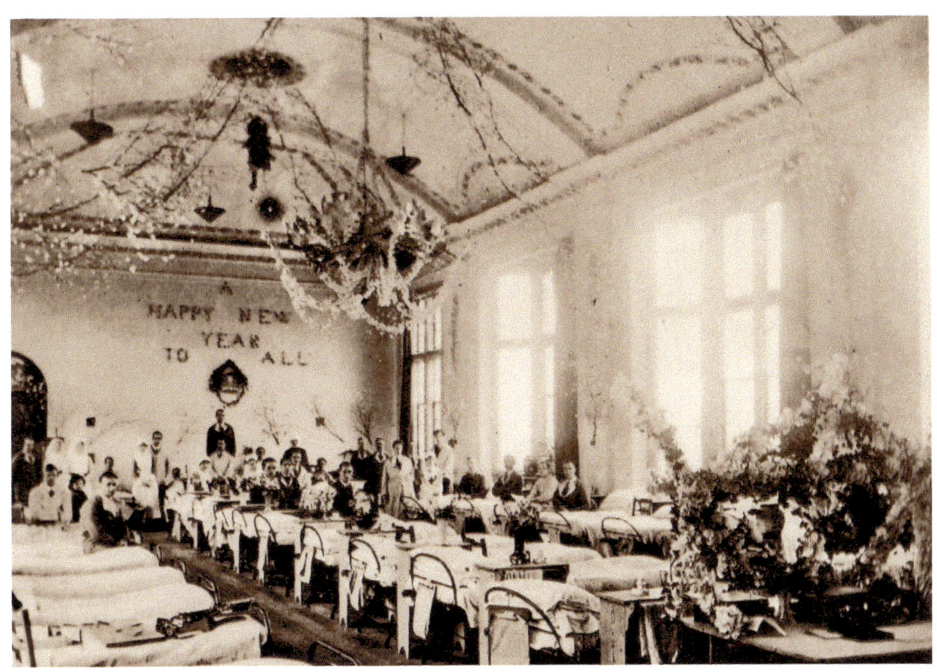

Newland School for Girls (II)

In 1914, England was at war with Germany and the school was commandeered for use as a military hospital. The headmistress Miss Rowland, members of the staff and the girls were voluntary helpers at the hospital. The hospital was visited by King George V and Queen Mary in 1917. This view of one of the wards was taken in December 1918, just after the armistice. The new photograph shows the same ward now used as a library.

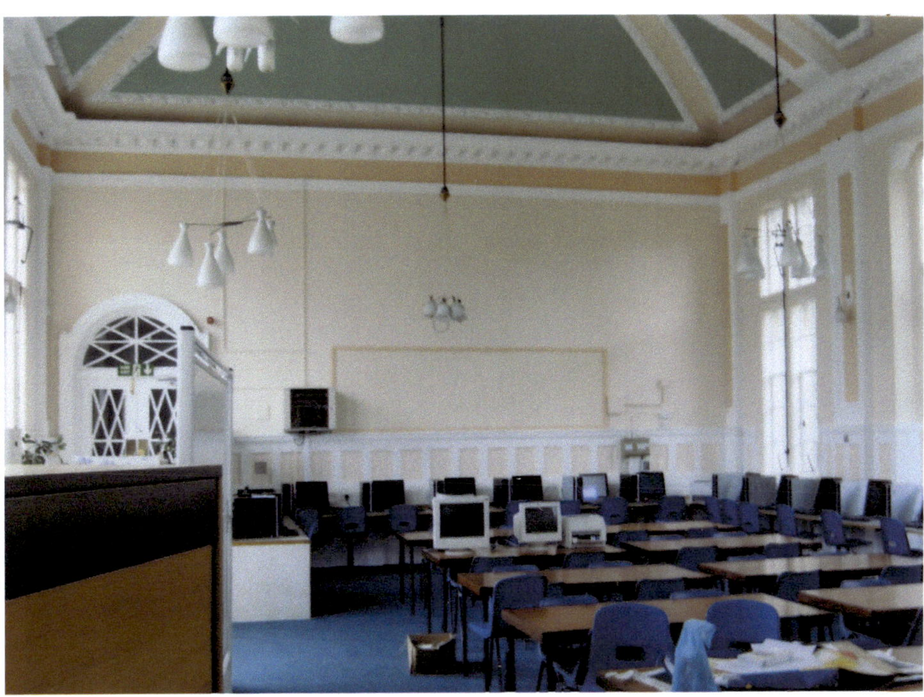

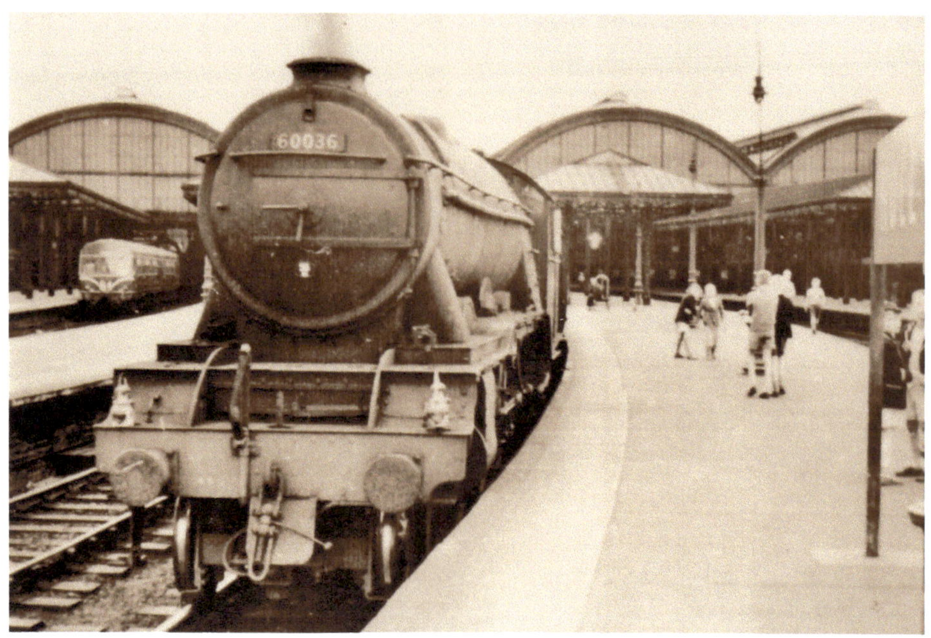

Glory Days of Steam

A class A3 4-6-2 engine, *COLUMBO,* Number 60036, awaits departure time from the impressive Hull Paragon railway station. In this early 1960s view, steam trains were still used on long distance journeys. The future of trains can be seen on the far left. A DMU (diesel multiple unit) on a local service can be seen. Paragon Station was opened on 8 May 1848, designed by G. T. Andrews. During the turn of the twentieth century, alterations were made and additional platforms were added as well as a new roof. The new photograph shows a DMU class 158 leaving for Doncaster, while a First Hull train class 180 has just arrived from London.

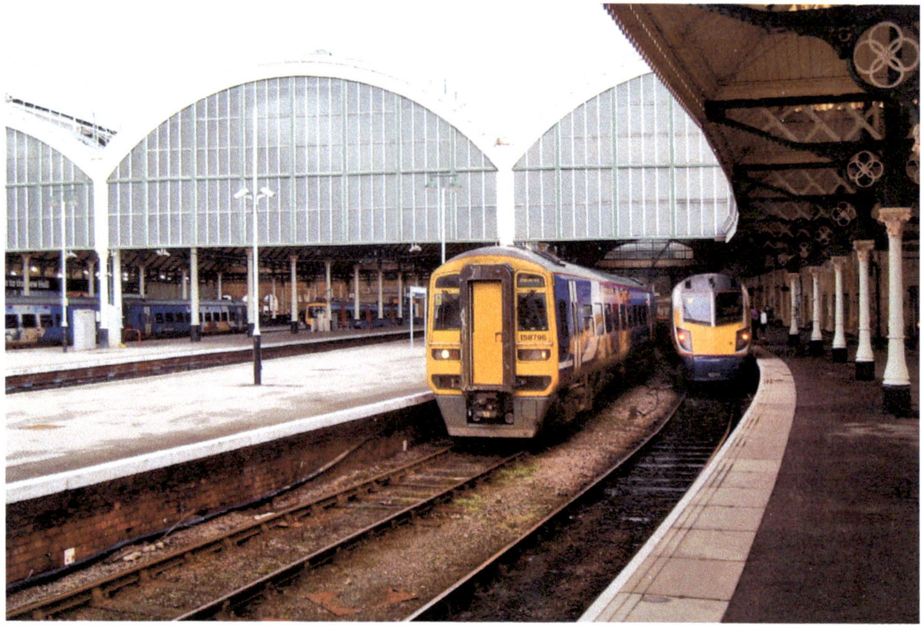

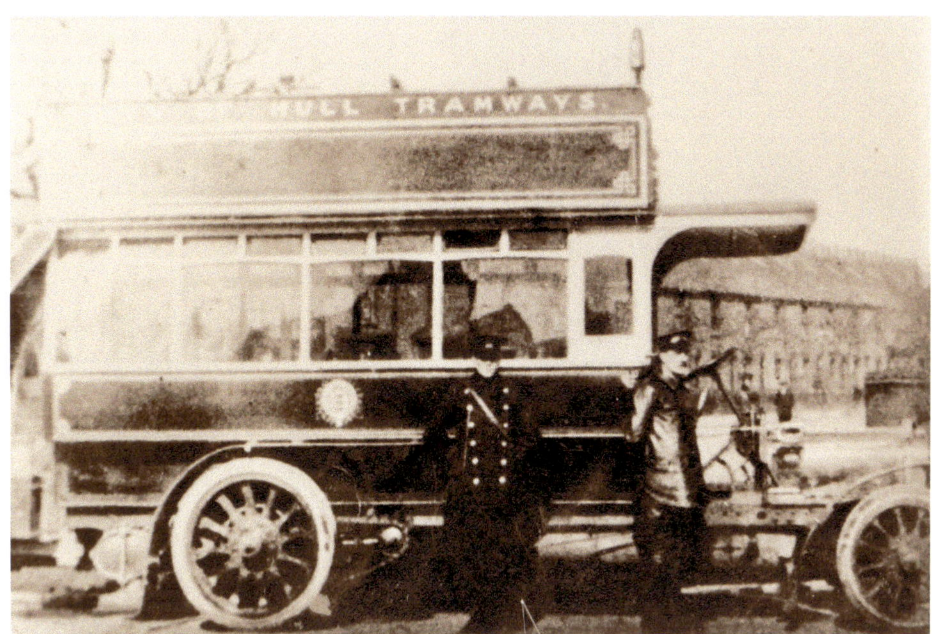

On the Buses

Buses in the very early 1900s were very basic indeed. The bus services were operated by City of Hull tramways. As can be seen in this photograph of a Saurer 34-seat double-decker bus, they had no roof and had solid tyres. This bus was new in 1905 and is seen operating on the Stoneferry service. It would be a number of years before passengers had the comfort of an enclosed bus. The driver and conductor pose with their bus at Stoneferry Green. Today, the majority of bus services in Hull are operated by Stagecoach in Hull, using modern, easy access low floor buses, as can be seen by this bus on the 14 Orchard Park service photographed at the new interchange.

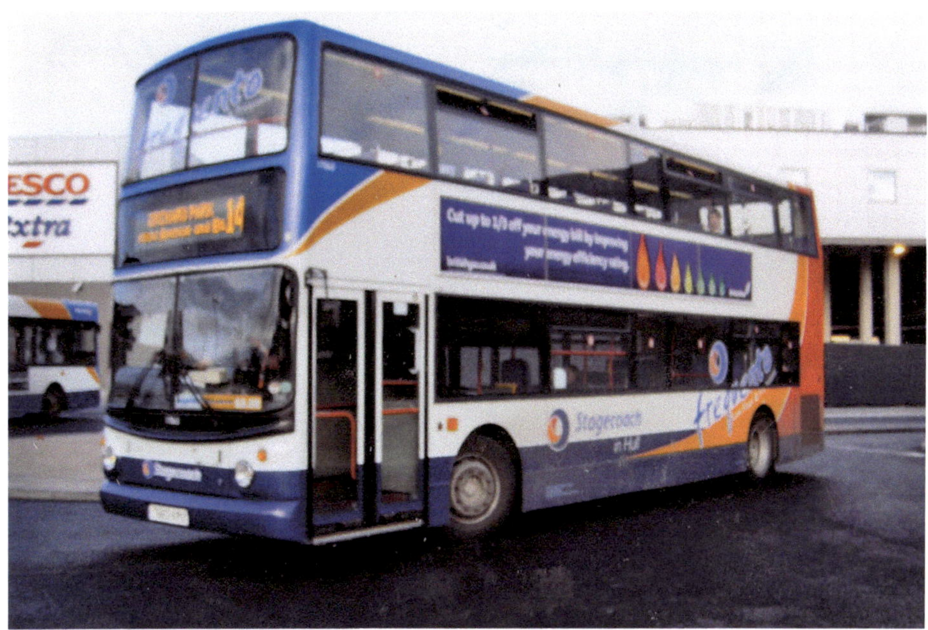

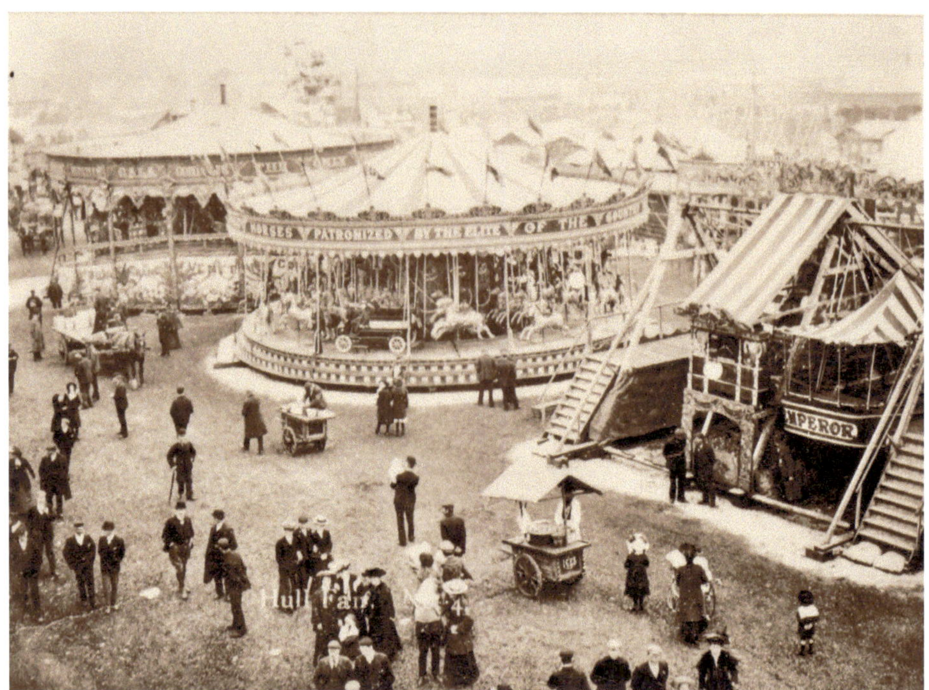

Hull Fair

All the fun of the fair! Hull fair is Europe's largest travelling fair. All the travelling fairs always meet up in Hull. In 1993, the fair celebrated its 700th anniversary. The fair moved to its present site in 1888. All the traditional stalls, with hook a duck, darts and the rifle range, along with traditional rides such as the waltzes and the big wheel, still form part of the fun; as well as the many stalls selling chestnuts, brandy snaps and, of course, coconuts. Thousands of people still visit the fair either to go on the rides or just enjoy the atmosphere.

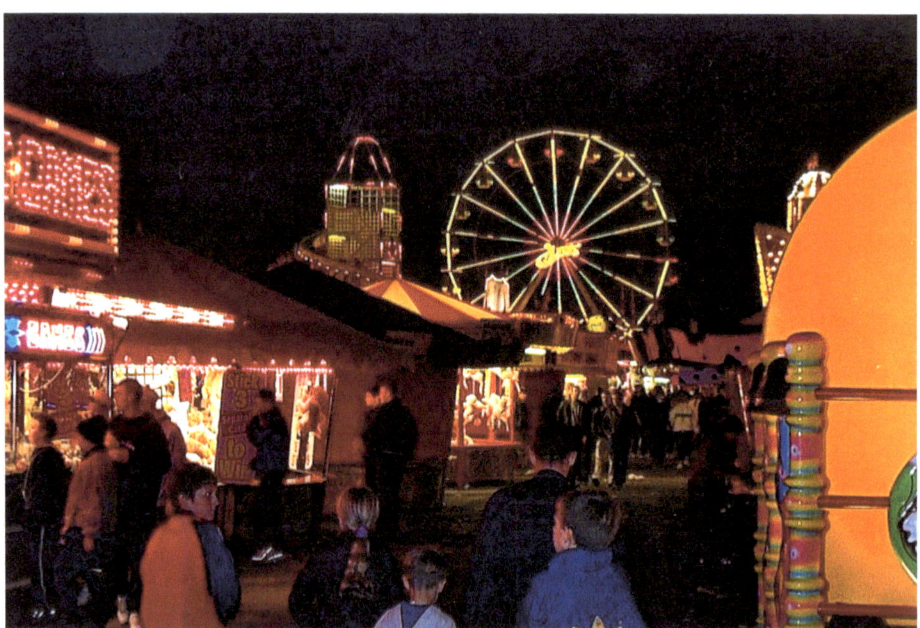

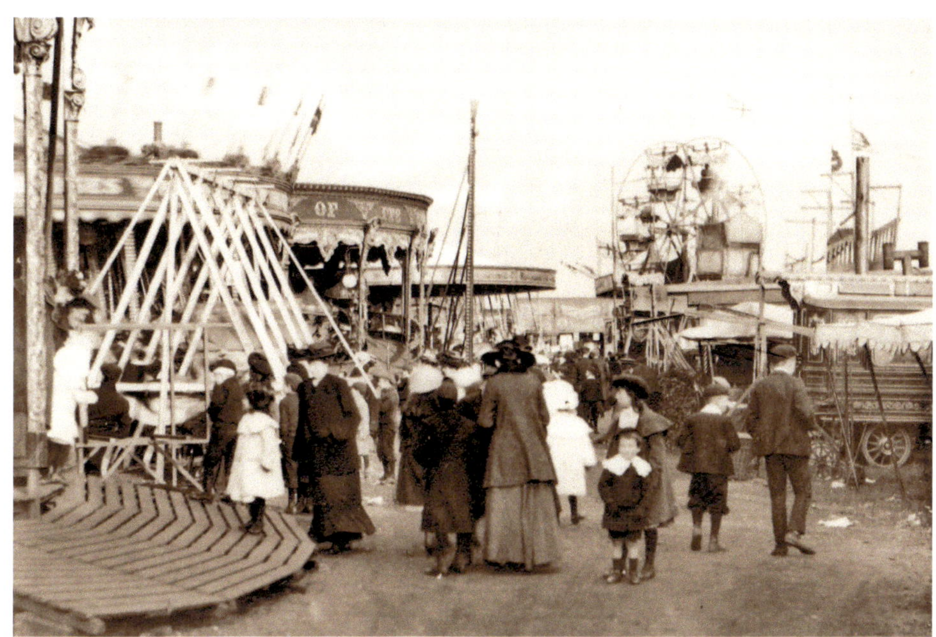

Hull Fair (II)

The top photograph shows the crowds which attend the Hull Fair. Visible is the big wheel and the swing chairs, photographed when the swing chairs was possibly the fastest ride at that time. Despite the very modern and very fast rides of today, many of the older traditional rides still remain. During the afternoon, the fair is quiet; a scene which changes during the evening.

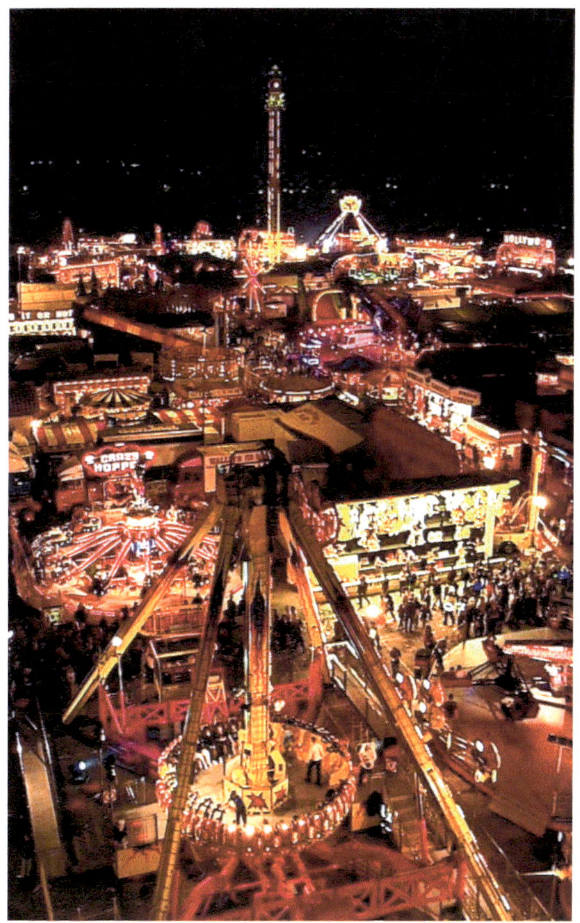

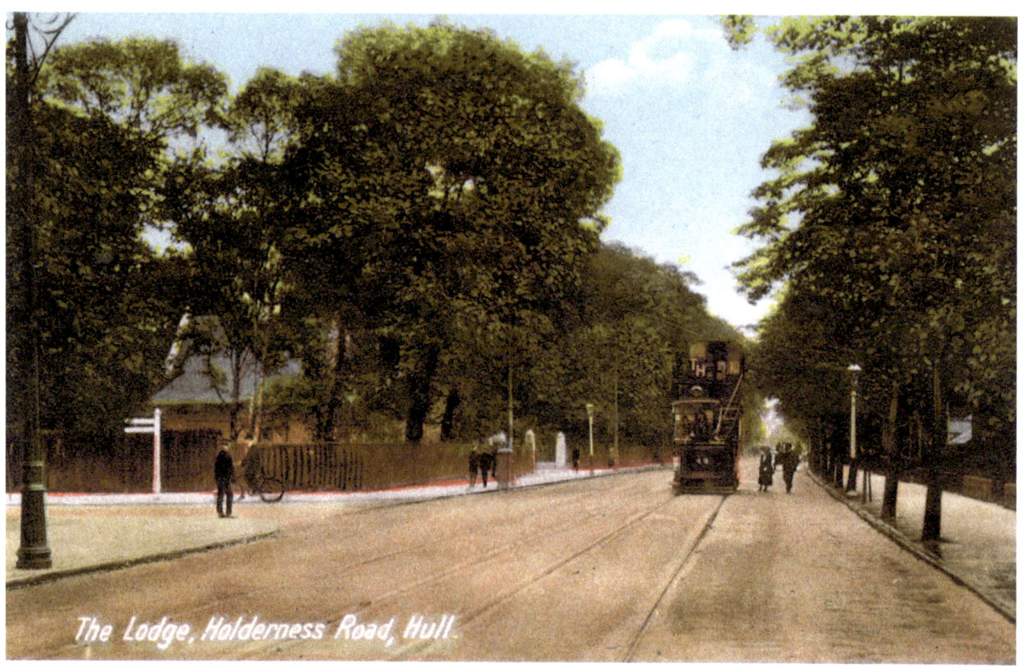

Holderness Road

An electric tram on the 'H' service is seen passing the Lodge on Holderness Road. Besides the tram no other road vehicles can be seen.

Acknowledgements

I would like to thank the following people who allowed me to use their photographs. Royal Mail, the *Hull Daily Mail*, Mr and Mrs Stephenson, Newland School for Girls, Geoff Newmann, Peter E. Rinter and my special thanks to Steve Goodaire who supplied me with a number of postcards.

I would also like to thank the many photographers who took photographs of Hull in the 1900s; without them taking these early photographs this book would not have been possible.

I would also like to thank my brother, Brian, who helped me in taking the modern-day photographs.